AN UNLADYLIKE PROFESSION

AN UNLADYLIKE PROFESSION

American Women War Correspondents in World War I

CHRIS DUBBS

Foreword by Judy Woodruff

Potomac Books

AN IMPRINT OF THE UNIVERSITY OF NEBRASKA PRESS

Portions of chapter 8 are reproduced from *American Journalists in the
Great War: Rewriting the Rules of Reporting* by Chris Dubbs and are used
by permission of the University of Nebraska Press. Copyright 2017 by
the Board of Regents of the University of Nebraska.

Library of Congress Cataloging-in-Publication Data
Names: Dubbs, Chris (Military historian) author. |
Woodruff, Judy, author.
Title: An unladylike profession: American women war correspondents
in World War I / Chris Dubbs; foreword by Judy Woodruff.
Description: Lincoln: Potomac Books, and imprint of the
University of Nebraska Press, 2020.
Includes bibliographical references and index.
Identifiers: LCCN 2019053513
ISBN 9781640123069 (hardback)
ISBN 9781640123175 (epub)
ISBN 9781640123182 (mobi)
ISBN 9781640123199 (pdf)
Subjects: LCSH: World War, 1914–1918—Press coverage—
United States. | Women war correspondents—United States—
Biography. | Women journalists—United States—Biography.
Classification: LCC D632 .D83 2020 | DDC 070.4/499403092520973—dc23
LC record available at https://lccn.loc.gov/2019053513

Set in Questa by Mikala R. Kolander.

CONTENTS

ILLUSTRATIONS

FOREWORD

JUDY WOODRUFF

In the early decades of the twenty-first century, Americans don't think there's anything unusual about women putting themselves at risk to report the news, from war zones and post-conflict arenas to countries where any truth-seeking press is considered a threat. On the PBS *NewsHour*, where I work, correspondent Marcia Biggs has been on the scene repeatedly in recent years as bullets flew and bombs exploded in Syria, Yemen, and Iraq, while Jane Ferguson built a career reporting from hot spots in Afghanistan, Yemen, and Somalia. Both, along with CNN's Christiane Amanpour and many other women, have been among the first reporters on the front lines when conflict breaks out—not to mention in places where there's profound political instability, making it unsafe for journalists to go poking around, asking questions.

Of course it hasn't always been this way. Today's intrepid female reporters stand on the shoulders of women who pioneered in the role. Women had to fight for a place in the ranks of the press covering World War II and even decades later in Vietnam. But it was during the "Great War," World War I, that women began showing up, against all odds, laying the groundwork for women who would, much later, follow their example. Whether they wrote for news services and newspapers or women's magazines such as *Good Housekeeping*, a more common outlet then for female reporters, they had to persuade editors, colleagues, sources, and a skeptical public that they had what it took to report on some of the most dangerous places on earth at the time.

Despite the doubters and the lack of precedent, more than three dozen women—journalists and writers—traveled overseas to be eyewitnesses. From 1914 until 1917, while the United States was neutral, and then, on different terms after the United States entered the war and became a participant, for the final year and a half, they made their way to the western front and all the belligerent countries and wrote dispatches that often told the "backstory" of the war, the hospitals, and even the homes where they found not only wounded soldiers but the lives of women and children turned upside down by conflict. Since the combined World War I death toll of military and civilians ran over sixteen million, there were countless stories to tell. These women reporters helped bring those stories to American audiences, shaping the narrative of this brutal conflict that ranks among the deadliest in human history.

They were not given the access to the front lines or the freedom to write about everything they knew: governments were determined to control what the public learned. But these women broke down barriers regardless: they showed up against all odds. They made it harder for news editors and publishers to turn women down two decades later, when World War II broke out. And they served as role models for women in years to come, giving them confidence to take on assignments that had been male dominated, from politics to business, from war zones to smoke-filled rooms. Every wave of women set the stage for the next wave. As women journalists today look back, we are grateful.

In *An Unladylike Profession: American Women War Correspondents in World War I* Chris Dubbs rediscovers the American women who reported World War I. His dramatic retelling of their stories captures their distinctive voices, their persistence against official obstacles, and their unique "women's angle" on the war. The veteran newspaperwomen, freelancers, novelists taking a turn at war corresponding, suffragist and pacifist reporters, the German American correspondent who thought Germany was being unfairly maligned, the mother reporting the war for other mothers, and the fearless Eleanor Franklin Egan intent on reporting the Armenian genocide—after a century they make another appearance on the stage, and we see just how rich was their contribution to the history of the Great War.

ACKNOWLEDGMENTS

During the several years it took to research and write this book, I relied upon the encouragement and expertise of many generous friends and professionals. Archivists at universities and historical societies helped me sort through dusty tomes and obscure electronic files. People I met online warmed to the project and lent a hand. David Miller sleuthed out Nellie Bly photographs. Lucy London drew on her exceptional knowledge of women in World War I to answer many questions. Mark Fastoso connected me to people. Pamela Moore ventured into the National Archives to retrieve a photograph that hadn't seen the light of day for over a century.

The staff at the Gannon University library chased after dozens of interlibrary loans. Bridget Barry, my editor at the University of Nebraska Press, patiently answered questions and steered me through the process. Tracy Simmons Bitonti and John Coleman took sharp editorial pens to the final manuscript. For their considerable assistance, I am exceedingly grateful to all of these people. I see them as fellow travelers on this journey, sharing my fascination and excitement as these extraordinary women emerged from the fog of history.

Here, too, I must acknowledge—and offer apology—to the women journalists who covered World War I. Their professionalism, pluck, and determination inspired me to write this book. The apology is for not telling their stories when I wrote my 2017 book, *American Journalists in the Great War: Rewriting the Rules of Reporting.* Women correspondents made a small appearance in that book, particularly in their coverage of the Russian Revolution. However, that book did not give a fair assessment of the significant role that women journalists played in shaping public opinion about the war, defining the issues surrounding it, and illuminating the role of women in the warring countries.

In hindsight I realized that I was just as guilty as many other historians who have tended to overlook or diminish the unique role played by these women, a common fate for women in history. This book attempts to make amends by placing their stories back into the history of the war, where they so justly deserve to be.

INTRODUCTION

For be it known unto you that the gods who preside over the
destinies of Women and War have decided that these two
shall not meet . . . great generals brushed me away as
though I were an impertinent fly.

—KATHLEEN BLAKE COLEMAN,
Toronto Mail and Empire, June 20, 1898

In the opening days of World War I, London-based journalist
Mary Boyle O'Reilly hurried to Belgium and delivered some of
the earliest reporting on the German invasion. The *Saturday Evening
Post*, the largest-circulation magazine in the United States,
rushed two women, Corra Harris and Mary Roberts Rinehart,
to the war zone. Harris highlighted the surprisingly large role
women played in the war, and Rinehart became the first journalist
to visit the frontline trenches. Throughout the four years
of the conflict, dozens of other American women followed in
their footsteps. They battled official restrictions and entrenched
prejudice to gain access to the news and in the process helped to
redefine how wars were reported.

The very idea of a female war correspondent required a mental
adjustment to the way one thought about war reporting, women
journalists, and indeed women. Reporting war had traditionally
been the province of only the most adventurous of male correspondents.
Women were still novelties on most American newspapers,
often relegated to writing about society, fashion, and

domestic topics for the Women's Page. In the decades straddling the start of the twentieth century, they had begun to report on the broader topics of suffrage, crime, and social ills, sometimes as undercover "stunt girls" or muckrakers.

When a few newspapers and magazines thought that it would be a good idea to send women to cover the war in Europe, it was with the notion that they would provide a woman's perspective on things. They would not cover the fighting war or such serious topics as politics or economics but rather would give their impressions of life on the home front. They would capture the "little stories," the human interest element.

More so than their male counterparts, women war correspondents defined the Great War in terms of its impact on individual lives. But they also covered the war in the more traditional, war correspondent role. Women reported from all the belligerent countries, from the trenches and frontline hospitals. They traveled on official war tours, took assignments in the most difficult and dangerous locales, repeatedly crossed the U-boat-infested Atlantic, mingled with revolutionary fighters in Russia, interviewed generals, and smuggled forbidden writings out of warring countries. They came under aerial bombing attacks, sniper fire, and artillery shelling; were wounded and held prisoner; got lice infestations; suffered from influenza and pneumonia; and were arrested as spies. In other words, they embraced the role and endured everything it was the misfortune of war correspondents to suffer.

Their assignment to cover the "woman's angle" proved to be one of the most impactful stories of the war. In the early months of the conflict, the *Saturday Evening Post*'s Corra Harris redefined the image of women in the war, from passive victims to fully engaged participants, with their own burdens and heroic sacrifice. In a time so focused on women's suffrage and the expanding public role for women, American publications, especially women's magazines, found inspiration in the experience of women in the warring countries.

By the time Mabel Potter Daggett traveled to warring Europe in

1916, for the women's magazine *Pictorial Review*, she discovered a revolution in women's empowerment. Before the war women had been forced to push their way into virtually every business, industry, and profession; now they were actively invited in, to replace the men sent to fight. An army of women worked in the munitions factories, on the farms, and in war charities. For the first time many universities graduated women in the sciences and engineering. Professional societies and trade unions accepted their first women members. In the war zone women drove ambulances and staffed hospitals as nurses, orderlies, and physicians.

If readers failed to grasp the seismic implications of women's role in the war, Daggett spelled it out: "Nothing that anybody ever said about women before August, 1914 . . . goes to-day. . . . Everything they said she wasn't and she couldn't and she didn't, she now is and she can and she does." Daggett and other women journalists from the neutral United States brought these profound changes to public attention.

The focus of war reporting took a major shift when the United States entered the war in April 1917. American readers wanted most to know everything about their boys. How did they get on with their allies? What was their life like in the training camps? How did they fare in combat? The American Expeditionary Forces (AEF) credentialed a very limited number of journalists to be attached to the army. Mostly from the large urban newspapers and the syndicated news organizations, they donned the uniform of officers and got privileged access to AEF activities. None of them were women. Likewise, civil and military authorities in England and France were often reluctant to assist women correspondents, especially those from smaller-circulation newspapers and women's magazines. Did the French military really need to waste time escorting to the front lines a writer from *Good Housekeeping* magazine?

In the face of such roadblocks, women journalists adopted a strategy that gained them access to the troops and to frontline locations rich in news stories—they volunteered with aid organizations. Charitable organizations such as the Red Cross, YMCA, and Salvation Army conducted extensive activities to support U.S. troops. Working as a volunteer Red Cross nurse gave journalist Elizabeth Frazer access to hospitals near the front. When military police stopped even the AEF-credentialed reporters from reaching the battle line, they waved through the YMCA canteen unit, with reporter Elizabeth Radford Warren, taking food to men in the trenches. The stratagem proved so effective that the majority of women war correspondents employed it at some point.

At this stage of the war, women journalists offered a distinctive tone in their reporting, in part because soldiers responded differently to women reporters, more readily sharing their thoughts and emotions. Then, too, women often placed themselves in supportive, nurturing positions that were more conducive to personal disclosures. They translated menus for doughboys in Paris cafés. They rode with them in ambulances and nursed them in hospitals. They helped wounded soldiers write letters to mothers and sweethearts. They served hot chocolate in the trenches. Reporter Rheta Childe Dorr had a son serving in the AEF. In a series of syndicated newspaper articles titled "A Soldier's Mother in France," she offered herself as a mother reporting for other mothers about the things that most concerned them. This intimate connection with the experience of the soldiers is a vein of reporting largely missing from the work of male correspondents.

From the opening days of the Great War through the post-armistice chaos, women journalists carved out a distinctive role for themselves. By insisting on adding their voices to the story of the war, they put a feminine stamp on what had always been seen as the masculine pursuit of war correspondence. This book collects the stories of these courageous and determined women to preserve their important contribution to our record of World War I and their role in challenging the restrictions against women in journalism. It is dedicated to their memory.

AN UNLADYLIKE PROFESSION

Mary Boyle O'Reilly, First on the Scene

I am just back from a pilgrimage to that part of Belgium around
which the German war machine has ringed its belt of iron.

—MARY BOYLE O'REILLY, "Woman Writer Sees Horrors of Battle,"
Seattle Star, September 23, 1914

In the opening weeks of the World War I, it was still possible to
find Belgians guardedly optimistic about their country's chance
of survival. They greeted each other on the street with "The
fort still holds," a reference to the fortified border city of Liège,
holding off the German invasion. The success of those defenders came as a surprising David-and-Goliath turn of events that
just might delay the invaders long enough for Belgium's French
and British allies to come to the rescue.

In Brussels, Brand Whitlock, minister of the American legation, cast Belgium's gallant stand in epic but more realistic terms
as the holding of the "Thermopylean pass for democracy." Liège
would eventually fall, and the German army would push into Belgium and collide with two other great armies. As Whitlock noted
in his postwar memoir, *Belgium: A Personal Narrative* (1918): "In
the universal and naïve ignorance, every one was expecting a
great battle somewhere there on that historic battle-ground of
Europe which it had ever been Belgium's fate to be; every one
spoke of it, waited for it!"

Whitlock's account of those momentous days captures a picture of tiny Belgium caught in the crosshairs at the start of the

Great War, when Whitlock himself played such a key role. On those pages his activities flash a montage of frenzied diplomatic meetings, cables to Washington, and telegrams from Berlin. When embassies in the city closed, Whitlock assumed their duties and responsibility for the welfare of their citizens. When war mobilization shut down Europe's banking system and hotels and interrupted travel, distraught travelers from many nations lined up at the U.S. legation, seeking assistance. A colleague quipped that Whitlock had become the most powerful diplomat in the world, as he now represented the United States and all of Europe.

On August 14, 1914, amid this chaos, Whitlock received word that some two hundred American journalists, waiting in London, were about to descend on Brussels. A separate telegram arrived from the legendary Richard Harding Davis, alerting Whitlock to his pending arrival.

Famous as a journalist, fiction writer, and dramatist, Davis also stood at the pinnacle of that rough brotherhood of men who reported on wars. When fighting erupted anywhere on the globe, newspapers and magazines paid Davis lavish sums to capture the action for their readers. The Spanish-American War, Boer War, Philippine Insurrection, Russo-Japanese War, Greco-Turkish War, and the recent U.S. military adventure in Mexico—Davis chronicled the conflicts through his exuberant personality and prose. Now Davis and his brethren were rushing to Belgium to find their next war. Whitlock had no time to waste on newsmen, but he knew they would impose themselves nonetheless. He immediately alerted the Belgian Foreign Office, requesting its cooperation. But before those war correspondents arrived in Brussels, Whitlock was already contending with the rather insistent reporter for the American news syndicate the Newspaper Enterprise Association (NEA)—Mary Boyle O'Reilly. The news services—NEA, United Press (UP), and Associated Press (AP)—were typically first on the scene and had a voracious appetite for news. Stationed in London, O'Reilly arrived on the Continent in advance of the journalists hurrying from the United States.

O'Reilly had been hounding Whitlock to arrange an interview

for her with Queen Elizabeth, the German-born queen of Belgium. Having the queen give voice to the anguish caused by her country of birth attacking her adopted country might make for a poignant article. Whitlock felt embarrassed imposing on the queen at so inopportune a moment, but he wanted to buffer her from the "imperiousness of American journalism, which goes where it will, and when it will."

The visit came off on August 16, the very day that the last of the forts at Liège surrendered. It did not go as O'Reilly expected. The queen had a few gracious words for the American newspaperwoman, but no interview occurred. In this curious interlude in the life of Belgium—between being invaded and being occupied—the queen was clearly not in a reflective mood. She showed O'Reilly a wing of the palace, previously the setting for lavish state balls, now lined with hospital cots, awaiting the wave of wounded from the fighting at Liège. The record of this abortive early attempt at news gathering in the Great War exists now only in Whitlock's memoir.

In 1914, at a time when women were still novelties in American newsrooms, forty-one-year-old Mary Boyle O'Reilly served as London bureau chief for the NEA. In the vernacular of the trade, she was a "foreign correspondent." She had been reporting from Europe for more than a year, crisscrossing the Continent for the type of feature stories that were the NEA's bread and butter. Unlike its much larger rivals, Associated Press and United Press, the NEA dealt mainly in features rather than spot news. The NEA supplied its member newspapers with editorials, cartoons, news analyses, human interest stories, Women's Page features, and photographs.

During her first year on the job, 1913–14, O'Reilly had reported on rumors of rebellion in Ireland, the flood of Mediterranean immigrants heading to the United States, the British suffrage movement, and a mummy curse at the British Museum. Interviews with the aristocracy were standard fare, as were sensational trials, which often offered lurid accounts of murder and

1. A 1913 photograph of Mary Boyle O'Reilly, London bureau chief for the Newspaper Enterprise Association. Harris & Ewing Collection, Prints & Photographs Division, Library of Congress, LC-DIG-hec-01937.

illicit romance. The previous fall O'Reilly had reported from Russia on the trial of a Jew accused of murdering a Christian boy to use his blood for a secret ritual. The resulting story, "Mary Boyle O'Reilly, in Russia, Investigates 'Ritual' Murder," uncovered Russia's institutionalized anti-Semitism.

Criminal trials with a special women's interest also proved popular: a divorce trial in Turkey, a wife murderer in Italy, and the highly publicized Caillaux trail in Paris. Henriette Caillaux had murdered the editor of *Le Figaro* newspaper, suspecting that he planned to publish compromising letters about her and her husband. O'Reilly landed a spectacular scoop with personal interviews with Henriette Caillaux and her husband. Caillaux's attorney convinced the jury that the murder had resulted from uncontrollable female emotions. Her acquittal came on July 28, 1914, the very day Austria-Hungary declared war on Serbia, triggering the world war.

O'Reilly was in London at the start of August, when dozens of dramatic war developments captured front-page headlines. She gave her initial assessment of the conflict on August 3, the day before Britain entered the war: "The cause of it is so involved the soldiers don't know what they are fighting about. While the able-bodied men are all at the front the burden of the war will fall cruelly on the women and children at home." That distinction between the fighting war and its impact on civilian lives would continue to be a focus for O'Reilly's war reporting and for that of many other women journalists who covered the war.

Within days the conflict exploded to involve all the major powers of Europe. The NEA, and every other news service, realized that it was now dealing with the largest war in history, perhaps the biggest news story ever. On August 4 the NEA sent a memo to its subscriber newspapers suggesting that they devote 75 percent of their news space to war coverage.

The NEA needed war news, and lots of it, from its London bureau chief. Unfortunately, Britain seemed to be doing everything it could to restrict war news. It moved quickly to cut Germany's undersea cable, eliminating news from Berlin and leaving its own heavily censored cable as the sole conduit for war dispatches to America. Britain's hastily approved Defence of the Realm Act imposed stifling press censorship that made it a crime to "spread reports likely to cause disaffection or alarm among any of His Majesty's forces or among the civilian population." The British and French refused to accredit reporters with their armies and forbade reporters from entering the war zone. To keep their readers abreast of developments in the war, London newspapers relied on official bulletins from the British and French War Offices that were masterpieces of brevity and obfuscation.

In London, O'Reilly hurried out an article on the shadowy monk behind the throne of Russia, Grigori Rasputin, claiming he was behind Russia's decision to enter the war. Then came a story on stranded Americans. "Conditions on the continent are appalling," she reported. Foreign automobiles were being confiscated, excursions and sailings canceled. "Thousands of Americans are stranded without means or opportunity to reach a place of safety."

But the NEA had already concluded that its correspondent was in the wrong location to gather war news. "Is there any possibility of you getting into Brussels? Take no risk," read the cable from O'Reilly's editor, who wanted her closer to the action. Germany's invasion of neutral Belgium had triggered Britain's entrance into the war on August 4, and the German army was currently attacking Liège. The big war stories over the next few weeks would be found in Belgium, as the gritty little country tried to hold back the German tidal wave. Despite military restrictions, individuals could still travel to Belgium.

Within two hours of receiving the NEA telegram, O'Reilly packed a satchel with a change of clothes, compressed food for emergencies, and $500 in gold, bought at a 10 percent premium. "War-time travelers must fend for themselves," she explained in an article about the adventure of getting to the war zone.

The harrowing experience of crossing from England to the Continent in wartime earned a cameo in many news stories and memoirs. Being thrown together with an eclectic mix of travelers on an assortment of wartime missions, sailing on perilous waters, and passing from the civilian home front to the active war zone filled the journey with the titillating sense of danger. O'Reilly crossed with nineteen other passengers and a shipment of British gold heading for Brussels. Rigid security in England and again in Ostend, where she landed, sorted out several people suspected of being German spies. "A hundred such 'agents' were shot yesterday in Belgium," O'Reilly noted in one early story.

Despite rumors that German cavalry operated in the area and might cut the rail line at any moment, O'Reilly's group pushed on to Brussels. They arrived at a rail station guarded by armed citizens. A large crowd stood silently outside the station, waiting to "welcome the litters that bring home the defenders of Belgium."

O'Reilly was quickly learning the ropes of war reporting— namely, that a journalist's personal adventure in pursuit of a war story *was* a war story. Her article about traveling to Brussels delivered all the necessary elements: gaining access to the war zone, the presence of danger, conditions in warring countries, and the pluck of the correspondent persevering against all obstacles. Everything she experienced, every detail she shared, illustrated the dramatic changes wrought by war.

For her first story datelined from Brussels, O'Reilly interviewed an Amsterdam merchant just arrived from Liège. The merchant had visited the battlefield in the immediate aftermath of some of the fighting and told the reporter: "Here a man's whole body turned over. Another was jerking spasmodically in the death grip. There a bloody arm was raised, and further on a hand beckoned in appeal." He continued to paint the grisly scene for O'Reilly: "Bleeding forms were painfully crawling over the shambles as aimlessly, it seemed, as singed insects. Red Cross surgeons and ambulances were working their way methodically across the field, which under the gloomy drizzle of rain had grown sodden. Its mire and mud puddles were stained red. . . . I have been into hell—not of fire, but of macerated flesh and gore, of lingering agony and ghastly death."

O'Reilly's article was datelined August 11, one week into the war. No one had yet offered such graphic reporting. And given how carefully controlled the press would be, such reporting would not soon be repeated.

A Harrowing Few Days in Brussels

By the time Richard Harding Davis and a handful of other American war correspondents arrived in Brussels, on August 17, the last Belgian fort had fallen at Liège, a mere sixty miles away. Brussels's days were numbered. Ditches and barricades went up around the city as makeshift defenses. The reporters received no credentials from the army, but the Foreign Office provided passes that, along with their U.S. passports, allowed for limited travel around the war zone.

The gold standard of war reporting as practiced by Davis was to be at the scene of the fighting, to see guns flash and men fall, to smell powder and hear the whine of bullets. Visceral, eyewitness accounts sold newspapers and magazines and built reputations. Every day, in taxis or hired cars, Davis and several other war reporters ventured from Brussels in search of the war, passing through the city barricades and through the wave of refugees fleeing the German advance.

Journalists were routinely arrested as spies by makeshift village police forces made up of youngsters and the elderly. "The most dangerous part of the game," one journalist complained, "is that the average peasant, armed with a rusty blunderbuss, who harries one along the roads in the country, cannot even read, and official papers mean nothing to him." Such ragtag militias dragged journalists to the nearest army headquarters while being pursued by an irate mob whose members suspected them of being spies and wanted their blood.

When another small group of American correspondents arrived in Brussels the following day, they, too, wanted to find the war. Whitlock informed them that the last fort at Liège had just fallen and that if they simply waited a few hours in Brussels, the war would come to them. But they impatiently set off to see the fighting. Irvin Cobb (*Saturday Evening Post*), Arno Dosch-Fleurot (*New York World*), Will Irwin (*New York Tribune*), and John McCutcheon (*Chicago Tribune*) taxied to the picturesque university town of Louvain (Leuven) and there collided with the German army as it marched through. They scooped their colleagues with the first eyewitness stories about the invading army.

Mary O'Reilly chose to remain in Brussels during this period. As the doomed city braced for the inevitable, one disheartening scene after another unfolded before her. She glimpsed Belgian king Albert departing his capital in an automobile and later the queen driving away with her children. After dinner at the American legation, O'Reilly stood with Brand Whitlock on a deserted street of shuttered houses when a company of cyclist soldiers pedaled by, rifles strapped to their backs. In their midst drove three trucks loaded with state papers from the palace of government. "They plan to abandon Brussels to the German army," Whitlock offered sadly.

That night, August 19, O'Reilly captured the somber mood in Brussels when she joined thousands of citizens gathered in the great city square. "They were curiously calm; only their tense white faces told of calamity," O'Reilly reported. "The sun set; the arc light flashed; and the evening breeze showered down blackened flakes of the harvest and neighboring villages burned by the advancing Prussians. In the silence Brussels could hear thunderous growlings beneath the horizon. The threat roused the Flemish spirit. Steadily, fearlessly, facing the fate of tomorrow, they began to sing."

O'Reilly's editorial note accompanying her story "The Death Song of Brussels" explained: "This note goes to you by a friend, who will post it in France. There are no longer any mails. The Prussians are closing in. Today all the journalists left except for a few Americans and the staff of the London *Times*."

The next day, when German forces marched unopposed into the city, Richard Harding Davis penned one of the most memorable word pictures of the war. For three days he watched the invading army parade through Brussels, describing it in apocalyptic terms as a killing machine creation of the modern age: "This [the German army] was a machine, endless, tireless, with the delicate organization of a watch and the brute power of a steam roller. And for three days and three nights through Brussels it roared and rumbled, a cataract of molten lead . . . like a river of steel . . . a monstrous engine." His story had to be smuggled to England by courier.

For the moment Mary Boyle O'Reilly stood in interesting contrast to the male journalists attempting to report the start of the Great War. Her reporting focused behind the scenes to show the impact of war on the civilian population, which was generally conceded as the woman's perspective, whereas the male reporters equated war with armies and fighting and single-mindedly sought them out. But as the capture of Brussels demonstrated, the fighting war and the civilian population had begun to collide.

F. Tennyson Jesse and the Fighting War

As the line between the battlefield and the home front began to merge, the concept of a "woman's perspective" on the war gained currency among newspaper and magazine editors. Reasoning held that because of their innate qualities of compassion, empathy, and sensitivity, women would excel at reporting how war affected the individual, the family, and the community.

That did not alter the well-entrenched belief that women were out of their element in trying to report on something as thoroughly masculine as armies or as dangerous as combat. Their naïveté would cause them to misrepresent the military experience. They were at best a nuisance, at worst a danger to themselves and others. Acting on this assumption, military officers, civil authorities, male war correspondents—and men in general— threw obstacles in the path of women who sought to cover the fighting war. Women were discouraged from getting too close to the action, rules restricted their access, and their efforts at battlefield reporting were sometimes belittled.

The challenge was formidable for any woman thrown into the turmoil, especially in the uncertain early weeks of the conflict. And yet that is exactly what the *London Daily Mail* chose to do with Fryniwyd Tennyson Jesse in August 1914, when it sent her to Belgium to capture a woman's view of the war. Jesse was the grand-niece of the poet Alfred Tennyson and an accomplished playwright and novelist in her own right. She had been in the United States when the war began but hurried back to her native England intent on covering the war. In her brief career as a war correspondent, she wrote for both British and U.S. publications.

Having previously written for the *Daily Mail*, Jesse offered her services as a war correspondent to that newspaper. Editor Thomas Marlowe promptly nixed the idea. If he sent a woman into danger and anything happened to her, he explained, he would be soundly criticized for sensationalizing. Jesse insisted that she planned to go with or without his backing but would be safer with the support of the newspaper. She prevailed and headed for Belgium in mid-August.

Using Ostend as her base of operations, Jesse made forays to other towns and sent numerous stories to the *Daily Mail*. The frankness and colorful description of the articles made such an impression on readers that the newspaper was soon touting Jesse as its very own star war correspondent. American readers got to sample her reporting in a November 1914 issue of *Collier's* magazine. Titled "A Woman in Battle," the article told about the fall of Antwerp and Jesse's efforts to cover the fluid scene of military encounters in late September and early October.

For readers to fully appreciate that story, Jesse first had to explain the difficulties faced by correspondents. "The Germans have orders to shoot any they may catch as spies, the Belgians object to them for fear the enemy might force information out of them when caught, and the English authorities are consistently uncivil and ungracious," she informed her readers.

As a female journalist, Jesse faced additional challenges. "For a girl the difficulties are multiplied, as all sides consider one a spy, and, when it comes to getting out with the other journalists, the nice men do not want one because of the danger to oneself, and the others because it so increases the danger to them." Additionally, correspondents could not get anywhere without an automobile, and "women were not allowed in motor cars in Belgium, and the chief of staff himself could not take his own wife in one."

Jesse overcame those obstacles by using the "personal equation." She did not elaborate on what that was other than to credit the "sympathy and courtesy of certain Belgian officers." She also mentioned three American journalists in the city who had managed to acquire the necessary permits to travel in the countryside: E. Alexander Powell (*New York World*), Joseph Patterson (*Chicago Tribune*), and the photographer Donald Thompson (*Leslie's Illustrated Weekly*). Apparently, the personal equation also convinced them to take her on one of their news-gathering excursions.

Using dated, diary-like entries, the *Collier's* article captures a jumble of Jesse's experiences in September and October, such as her breathless encounter with that mysterious new weapon, the Zeppelin: "Finally got into Ghent at midnight, and there, as we were crossing a bridge, we saw a Zeppelin right above us, so high she was soundless, making her way westward. . . . Gray and ghostly, blotting successive stars, like a mouse along the sky, and the menace of her somehow only added to the wonder and the beauty of her, so tiny at that height and yet so deadly. I found I was shaking all over with a mad excitement—the first time in all the weeks I have been at this wretched war when I got a pure thrill of emotion."

Unlike the journalists in Brussels, Jesse got to witness the fighting and then became part of it during the siege of Antwerp. She was living with a Belgian couple in Antwerp when the Germans began lobbing shells into the city from their giant siege cannons. "Now and then, as the shell's wail swung over its long parabola, there came with the detonation, across the roofs, the rumble of falling masonry," she reported. "Once, I passed a house quietly burning, and on the pavement were lopped-off trees. The impartiality with which these far-off gunners distributed their attentions was disconcerting."

Jesse's *Collier's* article describes the occasion when she accompanied the American reporters into the field, as they followed a Belgian cavalry unit. The difficulty of being a female war reporter was quickly impressed upon her. At one checkpoint a "very polite colonel" regretted to inform her that because she was a woman, he could not let her pass. While the male correspondents continued, Jesse was left to stroll around a village. However, she managed to sneak past a sentry and then walked several kilometers toward the sound of gunfire.

Surprisingly, she came upon the Americans stopped at the scene of a skirmish. She was looking at two dead Germans soldiers when bullets began zipping by her. Suddenly, the scene "took on a hustling, confused quality—the Americans and one or two officers coming up and saying we were all in the direct line of fire." With bullets clipping leaves off the trees and kicking up puffs of dirt at her feet, it "gave the odd feeling of being in a dream."

"I was put into a doorway," she explained, while "others took cover behind trees or in the ditch; then the order to retreat was given and I was hustled into the car and told to lie as flat as possible." Such a brush with danger—by a woman—made a great story.

Alexander Powell, one of the American reporters with Jesse on that occasion, painted a vastly different picture of that event in his postwar memoir, *Slanting Lines of Steel* (1933). Powell occupied a unique position among journalists in Belgium in those early months. Belgium had no policy in place for handling the many war correspondents who appeared on the scene. Because Powell wrote for the *New York World* and *Scribner's Magazine* and his articles were syndicated in many U.S. and British newspapers, he was selected as the sole American reporter permitted to travel with the Belgian army. Apparently, his permit also extended to those who traveled with him.

Powell made clear his low opinion of the swarm of "journalistic free-lances" who had descended on Belgium in its hour of crisis, demanding to be taken to the front. One hapless correspondent for the *Ladies' Home Journal* was arrested while bicycling to the firing line, he claimed. Another carried a vague letter of interest in an article from a periodical devoted to society and women's fashion. Then there was the clergyman from Cleveland gathering material for a series of sermons on the horrors of war and the young Boston lawyer who had come over just to "have a look at the show." To a veteran journalist like Powell, these individuals were a dangerous nuisance.

In his memoir Powell singled out only one of these wannabe war reporters—"By far the most attractive figure in the war zone during those early days of the great conflict was a slim young English girl named Frynwyd [sic] Tennyson Jesse." Powell met Jesse at the American consulate in Ghent, where she was being informed by a consular official that the war zone was no place for a pretty young woman like her. Jesse made an instant impression on Powell: "She had bobbed brown curls with a hint of chestnut in them and steady gray eyes and a peaches-and-cream complexion. Altogether a very lovely person." On learning that Powell had permission to travel with the army, Jesse turned her persuasiveness on him. "That girl was as insistent on seeing a battle as a child is on seeing a circus," he wrote. Powell reluctantly agreed to take her along on his next excursion.

That opportunity came in late September. While they drove behind a Belgian cavalry unit through a peaceful landscape near the town of Alost, "without the slightest warning, hell broke loose." The unit got ambushed by German machine guns. "Bullets sang overhead or on the road kicked up spurts of yellow dust and shells burst nearby. Riders fell from their saddles and riderless horses galloped from the field," Powell reported. "We were caught in the midst of a very hot engagement, with no way to escape and a pretty girl on our hands."

Powell took up the story from there: "While peering cautiously around the corner of the building to see what was going on, I addressed Miss War Correspondent over my shoulder. 'Well,' I said sourly, 'Here's your battle, I hope you're satisfied.'" Jesse was nowhere to be found, until Powell spotted her rummaging in their car, where the bullets were flying thickest. "I sprinted out, caught her up in my arms, and dashed back to deposit her in the shelter of the building," he recounted.

2. British reporter Fryniwyd Tennyson Jesse reported from Belgium in the opening months of the war. Author's collection.

"What the hell did you do that for?" I demanded angrily. "Are you crazy? Do you *want* to be killed? I've half a mind to give you a damn good spanking."

She regarded me reprovingly with her disconcerting candid gray eyes.

"I left my vanity case in the car," she said. "I felt quite certain you wouldn't get it for me and I really had to have it. You see, my nose needs powdering."

Powell's memoir appeared nearly two decades after this event, leading one to suspect the accuracy of his account. Or to wonder whether he embellished the story to support his criticism of wannabe war reporters, a group into which he clearly placed Jesse. However, Powell did conclude his Jesse anecdote by praising her story about the fall of Antwerp as "one of the most graphic and moving stories written during the war."

When the surrender of Antwerp became inevitable, citizens began to bury their money, jewels, and family silver, Powell explained. Jesse had been lodging in the home of a dressmaker in that city. In her story Jesse described the dressmaker digging a hole in her garden at night by lantern light to bury her valuables—a few yards of cloth and small packets of embroidery and lace. "It was the sort of story that brought a lump into the reader's throat," Powell acknowledged with perhaps a twinge of professional admiration.

Journalism scholar Joe Saltzman has summed up the dilemma facing early female journalists in general, but his remarks apply as well to their coverage of war. How could a woman balance the masculine requirements for success in journalism—"being aggressive, self-reliant, curious, tough, ambitious, cynical, cocky, unsympathetic—while still being the woman society would like her to be—compassionate, caring, loving, maternal, sympathetic?" Those competing expectations impacted how women journalists reported the Great War.

"It Was the Very Crater of War!"

After Brussels fell, on August 20, Mary Boyle O'Reilly took up temporary residence in Antwerp but returned to occupied Brussels when German authorities seemed mildly tolerant of neutral reporters. Exactly how to cover this war remained a dilemma. Still intent on catching the climactic battle that might end the conflict, Richard Harding Davis left Brussels to travel in the rear of the German invading force as it pushed toward France. He was arrested and came close to being shot as a spy, before being sent back to Brussels. Other reporters took a similar approach, venturing off on their own, traveling in the wake of the advancing German army, often seeing destroyed villages and the aftermath of skirmishes but never an actual battle. For three days Irvin Cobb and several other reporters followed the "distant voice of the cannon" in the general direction of the French border.

Cobb, who had never before covered a war, joined O'Reilly in becoming one of the first correspondents to appreciate that the toll on the civilian population was as much of a war story as the clash of arms. The German army eventually rounded up Cobb and his traveling companions and shipped them out of the country. Cobb would write a moving article about the impact of the war on one small French village, after its brush with the invasion force. However, by the time it appeared in an October issue of the *Saturday Evening Post*, an extraordinary event had occurred. Reporting on that event by Richard Harding Davis and Mary Boyle O'Reilly shocked the world and changed the perception of Germany.

For O'Reilly confrontations between the German occupiers of Brussels and the residents felt much like a battleground. "Life in Brussels is intolerable," she reported. "Stern, often galling orders fan the smoldering rage of the citizens." In an undated story she reported an incident in which she stepped outside her role as reporter of the news to participate in an event that made news. A French Red Cross nurse alerted O'Reilly to the German prohibition on peasant milk carts entering the city. The lack of milk deprived babies of the food they needed. O'Reilly agreed to join a delegation of four women to appeal to the German army governor of the city, and her article captured their meeting. They requested, they pleaded, they argued, they demanded that milk be allowed into the city for the starving babies. The commander was not moved. "You ask the absurd—the impossible. We Prussians recognize no distinction of persons. Men, women, children, ALL are enemies of the Fatherland when Germany makes war!"

The *Seattle Star* ran O'Reilly's story on page 1, *above* the name of the newspaper. It featured a stock photo of O'Reilly in a large flowery hat. That front page also featured an article by United

17

Press reporter William Shepherd about a Zeppelin raid on Antwerp, the first aerial bombing of a city in history. "Up against the stars, perhaps a mile high, I saw the Zeppelin. There's a sick feeling of utter helplessness which goes with such a sight, and with it a kind of fascination at the thought that the thing is not superhuman—that up there in the sky, men, human beings, are working, carrying out orders, watching maps, tracing streets, pulling levers, adjusting greasy machinery, twisting steering wheels, and lighting fuses of bombs intended to kill men, women, and children."

The character of the German army and its brand of warfare was emerging as a distinct story line in the Allied press and in the neutral United States. It held that German soldiers were barbaric, worthy descendants of the rapacious Huns who had despoiled Europe between the fourth and sixth centuries. They fought not only against an enemy army but against civilians, norms of decency, and civilization itself. Denying milk to babies and bombing cities fit neatly with the more egregious charges of British propaganda that Germans raped nuns, cut the hands off of boys so they could never use a weapon, and crucified captured soldiers.

Editors in the United States began to hear complaints from readers about biased reporting: that their newspapers never reported on the war from the German point of view and swallowed uncritically the wildest fabrications of British propaganda. A more balanced coverage would be in line with American neutrality and the sympathies of the 8 percent of German Americans in the U.S. population. The NEA sent regular cautionary notes to its member newspapers not to give any appearance of "taking sides."

By late August, American reporters were no longer welcomed in occupied Brussels, nor could they function there. They could not travel out of the city to gather news and could not mail or cable stories to their publications. On August 27 the five American journalists remaining in the city boarded a train, along with British prisoners and German wounded, heading to Aachen, just across the German border. In times of peace it was a three-hour journey. On this occasion it would take twenty-six hours. Circumstances were about to thrust O'Reilly and Davis into a shared confrontation with a shocking element of the fighting war that neither of them had ever imagined.

That train, carrying Mary Boyle O'Reilly, Richard Harding Davis, Arno Dosch-Fleurot (*New York World*), Will Irwin (*New York Tribune*), and Gerald Morgan (*London Daily Telegraph*) stopped for an unexpected two-hour layover at the station in the university town of Louvain, at the very time the town was being destroyed by the German army. Most of the American reporters had visited Louvain prior to or during its German occupation. They had wandered its narrow, twisting streets lined with attractive shops and cafés and been charmed by its white-walled houses with red roofs and gardens. Its church of Saint Pierre and its university dated from the fifteenth century. Its five-hundred-year-old town hall was the most famous in Belgium.

The correspondents were forbidden from leaving the train, but what they saw from its windows transformed their views of the war. The entire heart of the city lay in ruins. Flames rose from the university, including its library, which housed a collection of irreplaceable medieval manuscripts. Davis had heard in Brussels that some citizens in Louvain had fired at German soldiers and therefore the town had been marked for retribution—even though The Hague Convention of 1899 expressly forbade such collective punishment.

Amid explosions and gunshots, German soldiers moved street-to-street setting houses ablaze. The spreading flames worked their way toward the train station, sweeping before them a stream of terrified residents carrying children and bundles of their possessions. From the group soldiers selected a dozen men for reprisal execution. A firing squad led them away, and moments later came the shots. One soldier thrust his head through the open train window, yelling and drunk with the violence. To the sound of distant explosions, he pantomimed shooting, cutting, and thrusting with a bayonet. While the correspondents stared transfixed through the train windows, the biggest story of the war thus far unfolded before them like a horrific moving picture show.

When the train eventually reached Aachen, the correspondents traveled on to Maastricht, in neutral Holland. From there Davis rushed out a scoop on the destruction of Louvain. The most experienced war reporter had finally caught sight of this war, and it had shocked him to his core. He abandoned any pretense of objectivity and struck a strident anti-German tone: "At Louvain it was war upon the defenceless, war upon churches, colleges, shops of milliners and lace-makers; war brought to the bedside and the fireside; against women harvesting in the fields, against children in wooden shoes at play in the streets." Arno Dosch-Fleurot's account stressed the reporters' frustration and helplessness: "We wanted to interfere in behalf of these citizens of Louvain whose personal innocence we felt in our hearts, but there was a tensity, an hysteria, a madness produced of fire and blood, in the air that made us realize our helplessness."

It is worth noting that in their Louvain stories both Davis and Dosch-Fleurot mentioned the other male reporters with them on the train but did not mention Mary Boyle O'Reilly. It hardly seems an accidental oversight. Other war correspondents would later show a similar reluctance to note the presence of female reporters. The most logical explanation for such a tactic was that dangerous news-gathering adventures experienced by war correspondents lost some of their aura of martial daring if middle-aged women in flowery hats had the same adventure.

When all the other reporters on the Louvain train hurried off to London to file their stories, only Mary Boyle O'Reilly returned to the scene to get the rest of the Louvain story. O'Reilly was not a total novice in the business of war reporting. In 1913 she had roamed the dangerous United States–Mexican borderlands during the Mexican Revolution, talking to soldiers and civilians on every side of the conflict.

Still, going in pursuit of the fighting and placing herself in danger were departures for her. But she realized the importance of this story. The war still hid from the public in a perva-

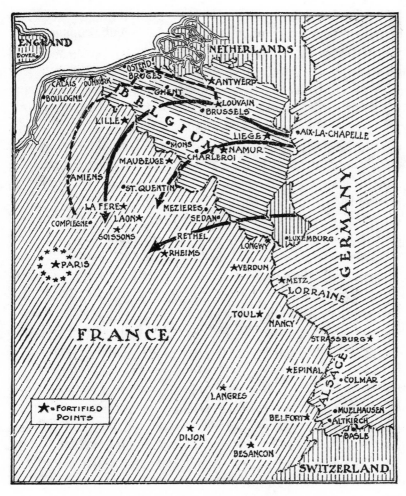

3. Arrows mark the path of the German invasion through Belgium in August 1914. Abbot, *Nations at War*.

sive fog. Reporters continued to be systematically excluded from the war zone by all armies. The public in England knew only that the German army was marauding through Belgium and that Britain had sent an army to aid its French and Belgian allies in stopping the Germans. Wild fabricated stories filled the newspapers in the United States, Britain, and France. But here was a real story about the true character of this invasion.

Louvain has been described as "the city that turned Germans into Huns" because it confirmed all that the British propagandists wanted the world to believe: that the German army in Belgium was a barbaric fighting machine, without civilized constraint. The correspondents on the train who observed the night of destruction became eyewitnesses to atrocity. No rumor, no fabrication. They saw civilians executed, homes burned, priceless artifacts of civilization intentionally destroyed. War had taken on an ugly new dimension when innocents were as much direct participants in it as combatants. Mary O'Reilly was about to uncover their story and, in the process, find her war voice.

In Maastricht, O'Reilly was arrested as a spy but cleared after a hearing. She persuaded the German consul to allow her to return to Brussels to retrieve some valuables she had left behind. It was a subterfuge, but the pass he granted permitted her to return to Belgium, thanks to the assistance of a daring Dutch automobile owner willing to drive her. She first headed down the River Meuse to Liège, where she found a train on a siding packed with women and children from Louvain. Several Red Cross workers distributed water to the captives who were locked in the train. With a bucket of water and a cup, O'Reilly assisted and in the process heard stories from the captive women. In O'Reilly's account of this experience, the captives became the "Lost Women of Louvain," ten thousand of them, taken from their homes and families, sent to an unknown fate no one knew where. One terrified woman told how the men of the town had been marched away, taken to work the mines in Germany. She still did not know what was planned for the women and children.

On August 29 O'Reilly arrived back in Louvain, where the terror continued. She found thirty bodies laid in a row along one street, all shot or bayoneted, among them gray-haired women. A body chained to a post had been burned. German scouting parties roamed those parts of the city still standing, marking homes destined for destruction. Destruction squads followed them to spill gasoline and plant bombs. Methodically, they worked through whole neighborhoods. "Thus proceeded, street after street, this great war crime," wrote O'Reilly.

A local priest confirmed what O'Reilly had heard earlier, that the German army justified its destruction of the town by claiming civilians had shot at soldiers. But the priest insisted that the shooting had really been friendly fire between German units during the confusion. In retribution they executed ten citizens for every German soldier shot. The mayor, police chief, and administrators and professors from the university were publicly executed. Three hundred citizens were corralled and slaughtered.

When O'Reilly's Louvain story ran on the front page of the *Seattle Star*, it carried the editorial note: "Read this accompanying GRAPHIC PICTURE OF THE WAR BY A WOMAN." Using all caps gave stress to the two key points: the eyewitness article was more detailed and explicit than other reporting of the time, and it was unique in coming from a female reporter. "On August 26, 27, 28 and 29 the growl of battering gun fire and the roar of flames was incessant in Louvain," O'Reilly reported, "and I, an American woman, armed only with a German vice consul's pass, innocently obtained in Holland, sat in a motor car WATCHING WAR, AS 20TH CENTURY CIVILIZATION APPLIES IT!" O'Reilly herself had a penchant for using all capitals when sufficiently provoked.

Distributed through the NEA, her story received banner, front-page headlines in hundreds of American newspapers. Along with the accounts of Richard Harding Davis and others, these stories lent credence to the "Rape of Belgium" theme emerging in the Allied press.

The residents of Louvain may have disappeared, but thousands of other refugees flooded this ravaged corner of Belgium. "Rich and poor, gentle and simple," they collected on the road from the destroyed towns. O'Reilly's return to Louvain had been an audacious move, but she went that one better by abandoning her car and joining the column of refugee. The move exposed her to considerable hardship and danger, but along with her experiences in Liège and Louvain, it delivered several headline-grabbing stories that lifted O'Reilly to prominence in the opening weeks of the war.

"Out of this smoke-shadowed district came such stories of sacked villages and slaughtered non-combatants as to horrify mankind. To prove these stories untrue, I became a refugee inside the Prussian lines," she explained to her readers. In front-page stories with such headlines as "Ten Thousand Women Lost!" and "Woman Writer Sees Horrors of Battle," O'Reilly recounted her five-day pilgrimage with the war refugees of Belgium. Through the region bounded by Liège and Brussels, Louvain and Vise, the column of refugees wandered a meandering course toward sanctuary in neutral Holland. All along the route, the destitute swelled their ranks.

O'Reilly painted a picture of her fellow wanderers: "Hundreds of wan-faced women, children whimpering at their skirts; scores of aging men in self-respecting homespun; a little boy carrying his pet kid; a girl clasping her bolt of wedding linen . . . strong old women staggering under huge jars; dogs tugging at over-laden trucks; a cart with a white flag; a dying child in its father's arms; a paralytic, a blind man—all, all of them homeless, penniless, heart-broken."

Every destroyed town they passed offered its own catalog of horrors: peasants lying dead in the doorways of their homes, churches and fine homes ruined and plundered. Every additional refugee to join the group brought stories of tragedy and suffering. The brother of the delirious old woman being transported in a wheelbarrow had been buried alive, upside down in a hole, because he was an army scout. Only an old curate remained in one village to conduct O'Reilly on a tour of a destroyed chateau. In another village O'Reilly learned that five priests had been executed in reprisal killings because some in the town had taken up arms to resist the invasion.

O'Reilly jotted notes of her experience on the white silk lining of her blouse—recording, for instance, how the refugees spoke in whispers as they approached the destroyed town of Bander-sea. From a distance they could see two old men hanging from trees along the road, hostages whose lives were taken by the

Germans. "I passed that tree, but never as long as I live will I be able to erase from memory the dead faces of those two old men."

Finally, O'Reilly noted how the weary group staggered over the last mile, approaching safety in neutral Holland: "Slowly, so slowly that the last sink down exhausted, our sad little company crosses the frontier."

By September 5 O'Reilly was safely in The Hague, writing her biggest story of the war: first the night on the train with the other journalists witnessing the destruction of Louvain, then the "lost women" on the train, the return to Louvain, and the extraordinary journey with the refugees. As separate stories, they went by mail to the United States and then out to newspapers via the Newspaper Enterprise Association.

It's ironic that on the very day that O'Reilly witnessed the destruction of Louvain from that train, the NEA warned its readers to be wary of atrocity stories. "Be slow to believe a tenth part of the charges and countercharges that have been and will be made of atrocities in the war's wake," the news service cautioned. However, O'Reilly's dramatic eyewitness account of the destruction of Louvain and her harrowing adventure with the refugees behind the German lines was simply too good a story to quash because of suspicions about bogus atrocity stories. One month into the conflict, O'Reilly had already demonstrated with her courage and initiative that a woman could face the dangers of war reporting as well as a man.

2

Among the First Reporters

MITROWITZ, SLAVONIA—I leave tomorrow at 7 a.m. in a
wagon for a two days' trip to the firing line of the
present Austrian-Hungarian-Servian war.

—NELLIE BLY, "Nellie Bly Describes Slavonian Town Demolished by
Austrians in Invasion," *Richmond Palladium*, February 1, 1915

When legendary American journalist Nellie Bly (Elizabeth Jane Cochran Seaman) departed for Vienna on August 1, 1914, four days after the outbreak of the Great War, it was with no special apprehension. American newspapers already carried articles about the tens of thousands of travelers stranded in Europe by war mobilization that had closed hotels and banks and shut down transportation. But Bly, who had built her reputation in the last two decades of the nineteenth century on risky investigative reporting and hair-raising adventures, did not scare easily. By her own calculation she was traveling to Vienna to escape trouble, not to find it. She expected to be back home in three weeks.

Bly headed into the maelstrom confident that she could navigate any difficulty. "There is no telling where we shall land or if I shall ever reach Vienna," she wrote to her mother during the voyage. And displaying her typical equanimity, she added, "So, I have as plans—I shall simply do what the moment calls for." At this point Bly had no thought that she would become a war correspondent and be the first woman and one of the first American reporters to cover fighting on the eastern front.

More than two decades had passed since Nellie Bly's byline last graced the front page of a newspaper. While her career burned brightest, from 1887 to 1895, she became an international celebrity and the personification of the type of reporting known as "stunt" journalism. Bly made her reputation writing for Joseph Pulitzer's flamboyant *New York World*, particularly through a series of much-publicized articles based on daring exploits. She launched her *World* career by masquerading as a lunatic. Bly had herself committed to the infamous asylum on Blackwell's Island in New York to expose its abusive treatment of mental patients. The resulting articles led to improvements at the facility and changes in the treatment of the mentally ill. Other undercover assignments exposed corrupt employment agencies and the market for the sale of unwanted babies.

The stunt for which she became best known involved her attempt to better the record for around-the-world travel set by the main character in Jules Verne's novel *Around the World in Eighty Days* (1873). When she proposed the idea to her editor, he said it was impossible—she was a woman and would need a protector. But she prevailed, and on November 14, 1889, she set off on her solo, twenty-five-thousand-mile adventure.

Involving travel by steamboat and train—through England, France, Italy, the Suez Canal, Ceylon, Singapore, Hong Kong, Japan, and the United States—the venture became a test of endurance and logistical calculation. Did her schedule permit her to accept the invitation to meet with Jules Verne in Amiens, France? Would she save time by sailing through Florence or Milan?

Bly sent brief cable stories about her progress back to the *World*, populating her accounts with the peculiar people she met and her odd experiences. Longer articles went by mail. The newspaper promoted Bly's months-long journey with continuous coverage, games for readers, breathtaking accounts of her scramble to make train or boat connections, and reaction stories from the foreign press. By the time Bly returned to her starting point, in a record-setting seventy-two days, she had become an international celebrity.

Thanks in large part to Nellie Bly, stunt journalism enjoyed a brief period of popularity, providing women journalists with the opportunity for public and professional notoriety. Annie Laurie fainted on the street so she could report for the *San Francisco Examiner* on the poor care provided in a public hospital. Eva Gay gained fame at the *St. Paul Globe* with a series of undercover stories that exposed the low wages, unhealthy working conditions, and long hours for domestic workers, factory workers, and store clerks. However, in the decades that followed, female reporters who employed such tactics would be labeled with the derogatory term *stunt girls*. It rivaled the derisive term *sob sisters*, coined to criticize a brand of reporting that sentimentalized a topic.

Bly's journalistic fame peaked in the heady days of "yellow" journalism, when New York's competing dailies battled to build circulation. For Joseph Pulitzer's *New York World*, Bly's employer, and William Randolph Hearst's *Journal American*, no stunt, no glaring exposé, no sensationalized story, proved too much if it grabbed readers' attention. When Cuban nationals rebelled against Spain, the *World* ran a three-quarter-page story headlined "Nellie Bly Proposes to Fight for Cuba." Readers learned of Bly's secret plan to create a "new terror of war." The story was supposedly uncovered by a persistent reporter who accompanied Bly as she went about recruiting her own regiment of soldiers. She had already designed a handsome uniform, it was revealed, and visited prestigious men's clubs to enlist support and financial backing. "At first thought you would say that it would be impossible for a slender, comparatively frail young woman to do such a fearsome thing. But that is because you are not thoroughly acquainted with Nellie Bly."

The truly revolutionary key to the success of her plan, the reporter explained, was to recruit the best officers: "brave, capable of endurance, faithful, sober, intelligent, full of personal magnetism that will inspire the soldiers to do and dare." In other words—women. Women embodied those qualities better than men, according to Bly. No soldier would ever run away if led by a woman. Every battle would be fought to the bitter end. Wars would be briefer, more decisive, and less destructive, she contended: "The wars of the future must and will be planned and led by women. There is no mistaking the way the hands on the signboards point." That was the last *World* readers heard about the plan. If it ever existed, nothing came of it.

Bly largely disappeared from public view when she left her journalism career in 1895 to marry wealthy New York industrialist Robert Seaman, forty-two years her senior and in failing health. Bly involved herself in the management of his company, Iron Clad Manufacturing, and after Seaman's death in 1904, she ran the company. Despite some success, she was dogged by numerous and expensive lawsuits. By 1914 she faced financial ruin and sought relief through a wealthy friend living in Vienna.

In later years Bly would claim that she had traveled to Austria to cover the war, but that was not the case. She went to seek assistance from a friend for her legal and financial problems. However, within weeks of her arrival in the warring country, visiting the fighting line became her main interest. For American newspaper readers the eastern front was terra incognita. In the opening weeks of the war, Russia pushed into German Prussia and Austria's northern province of Galicia. In response Germany urgently drew vitally needed troops from the western front to force back the Russian advance in the Battles of Tannenberg and Masurian Lakes. Fighting on the eastern front may well have saved Paris, and yet the titanic battles fought there received scant coverage in the American press.

There had been virtually no coverage from any front line in this war. No woman had yet reported from any front. Bly must have heard the siren call of her glory days of grabbing front-page headlines and the chance for a thrilling distraction from her legal troubles. She had built a career by going places where she shouldn't, defying expectations, and pushing against the restrictions imposed on women reporters. She was now fifty

4. Nellie Bly's 1914 passport photo. Arguably the most famous woman journalist in the world in the nineteenth century, Bly returned to journalism to report on fighting on the eastern front. Certificate no. 1250, U.S. Passport Certificates 1101–1500, June 22–24, 1915, National Archives Record Group 59, Archives II, College Park, MD.

years old. Another opportunity like this might never again present itself.

Bly began cultivating contacts among the aristocracy, politicians, and military officers, expressing her desire to visit the front.

This effort proved vital in establishing her credibility. However, her quest was aided by the fact that Austria-Hungary was unique among the warring nations in actually having in place a plan for how to handle war news. On July 28, the day Austria-Hungary declared war against Serbia, it created the Imperial War Press Bureau, the Kriegspressequartier (KPQ). Austro-Hungarian and German journalists and artists could join the KPQ in lieu of military service. Foreign correspondents from neutral countries could join as well. KPQ correspondents took up residence at the bureau's headquarters in the town of Neu Sandez, some ninety miles behind the front lines. From there guided tours took them to various military locations and to the front lines. Their dispatches had to pass military censors. Although not as formally organized as the KPQ, Germany had also begun offering tours for neutral journalists.

At this point in the war, an escorted tour was about the best a correspondent could hope for. On the western front the English and French still restricted journalists from the war zone. In Austria and Germany they had become welcomed guests, as those nations sought to gain the upper hand in the propaganda war. After arranging to write for the *New York Evening Journal*, Bly joined the first group of Americans on a KPQ tour in late October 1914. Her companions included Robert Dunn (*New York Evening Post*), and George Schreiner (Associated Press), and William G. Shepherd (United Press).

Out-Scooped on an Austro-Hungarian Exclusive

At the end of October, just as the KPQ escorted its first American correspondents to the front lines of its war with Russia, another American reporter scooped them with the first reports from the dual empire. The previous month Alice Rohe had been appointed manager of the United Press office in Rome. Rohe would be in place to monitor the development of war sentiment in Italy and its ultimate entry on the side of the Allies. However, one of her first assignments took her to Vienna to gauge the mood in that warring country.

Although only twelve years separated the thirty-eight-year-old Rohe from Nellie Bly, they represented two distinct generations of newspaperwomen. In the 1880s Bly was among the first women to venture into newspaper work. With no formal training or professional experience, she stumbled into the work after writing a letter to the editor to the *Pittsburgh Dispatch*. The paper wanted her to take on the traditional newspaper job for women of editing its Women's Page, which dealt with society, fashion, and domestic issues, but Bly pushed for a larger role. Only when she later moved to the *New York World* did she undertake the many stunt articles that brought her fame.

Rohe represented the new generation of newswomen, college graduates, who were intent on pursuing careers in journalism, not just freelancing on women's topics or writing from a "woman's angle." After graduating from Kansas State University, in 1896, Rohe worked for several Kansas newspapers before moving to New York for a decade of work with the *Evening World*, another Pulitzer newspaper.

With the start of a new century, journalism began a period of transition, with formal education and professional standards emerging in response to the yellow journalism of previous decades. The University of Missouri opened the first formal school of journalism in the United States in 1908. When the first American professional society for women journalists, Theta Sigma Phi, began in 1909, Rohe became one of its founding members.

After eighteen years in the profession, Rohe got her break with the United Press through the help of her brother-in-law Jack Howard, heir to the Scripps-Howard newspaper empire. Her assignment: foreign correspondent in Rome. When the United Press promoted its stable of war correspondents in newspaper advertisements, it identified Rohe as "one of the first of the modern women reporters—not just feature writers, but general assignment reporters."

Both her gender and her professional approach to news gathering unsettled the patriarchal Italians. While most foreign correspondents in Italy waited for the Italian newspapers to appear,

5. Alice Rohe became the Rome bureau chief for the United Press in September 1914 and covered Italy's descent into war. Prints & Photographs Division, Library of Congress, LC-DIG-ppmsca-32096.

from which they summarized the news for their own papers, Rohe actually went in pursuit of the news. It shocked Italians to see a woman reporter visiting a region devastated by an earthquake or digging for the sordid details about the sensational trial of an American bank clerk who had killed his wife and dumped her body in Lake Como. Although Italy had not yet entered the war, Rohe kept her finger on the pulse of simmering war sentiment. That made a visit to Italy's warring neighbor Austria an early priority.

As representatives of the press of the largest neutral country, American reporters could freely enter any of the warring countries. Rohe arrived in Vienna around the first week of October and set about capturing the war mood in the city. United Press billed her as the first "American-trained newspaper woman who has had the opportunity to see things as they are in Austria."

Not planning to visit the front lines, she did not require the services of the KPQ. She only had to contend with strict censorship and the legion of spies who reported any instance of citizens expressing a negative attitude toward the war or speaking too frankly with a foreign reporter. That did not stop Rohe from gathering her impressions. "Vienna is a city of lost hope, of gloom, of grave despair," she reported. "Once the gayest and most beautiful capital of Europe, it is today the saddest, the most distressed."

The city's hospitals, schools, universities, hotels, and churches overflowed with seventy thousand wounded, while newspapers carried only positive war news. Rohe was more forthright: "I have seen trains arriving, everyone crowded to suffocation, with the wounded and dying. I have seen a procession of 4,000 mothers, whose husbands have died in Galicia, carrying in their arms their fatherless babes. They filed past the great cold, cold palace of the ministry of war." From a snatched conversation with a wounded soldier, Rohe caught the murmur of protest: "'They have buried our dead in heaps,' he said, tears coursing down his face. 'They were killed like sheep driven to a slaughter yard. The Russian artillery has done unbelievable things.'"

Rohe's first article from Vienna, datelined October 6, ran in hundreds of American newspapers in the last week of October, just as Bly prepared for her frontline tour. The dateline on Rohe's story explained the delay and how she avoided Austrian censorship: "By Courier to Rome, thence by mail to New York." The somber tone of her article would be far eclipsed by the reporters on the KPQ tour.

Nellie Bly on the Firing Line

In October 1914 Austria's epic struggle with Russia raged around the fortified city of Przemyśl, in Austria's northernmost province of Galicia, near the present-day Polish-Ukrainian border. Russia had captured most of eastern Galicia in the opening weeks of the war, and now only Przemyśl remained in Austrian hands. But Austria had recently pushed back Russian forces in some sectors, and it was this success that the KPQ wanted to show the correspondents. In the last week of October army officers escorted the American correspondents for an up-close look at the fighting in Przemyśl.

During the sixty-mile, two-day journey from KPQ headquarters to the besieged city, Bly fired off a telegram to the *Evening Journal*, alerting the editor that she was on her way to the front and would cable important developments when possible and mail three articles. The front-page potential of such stories must certainly have occurred to the *Journal*. Two months into the war, there had been virtually no reporting from the firing line of an active battle; no reporting had come from the eastern front; and no woman had reported on a battle. Add in the considerable reputation of Nellie Bly, and you had the recipe for front-page stories.

Bly's war tour, which was supposed to last two weeks, instead extended over a month, with visits to Budapest and the fighting in Serbia added on. Both Bly's and William Shepherd's accounts of the tour were syndicated in numerous newspapers during the winter of 1914–15. Although Shepherd's vivid accounts ran in several articles, the *Journal* parceled out Bly's reports into twenty-one short articles that ran every few days over a two-and-a-half-month period. Syndicated by the International News Service, her articles also appeared in hundreds of other newspapers. Nothing like them was appearing in the American press— eyewitness news from a little-known corner of the war—reported by a woman.

In a conflict that had already become infamous for its brutality and slaughter, a visit to Przemyśl was about as raw an exposure to war as any reporter could get. Bly's opening article described her approach to the firing line. Reacting to the sights, sounds, and smells that ushered her away from the civilized world to a place of privation, suffering, and death, Bly became a Dantesque guide on a descent into hell.

Bly's first article led the reader from her comfortable hotel room into the muddy streets of the town, where she assembled with her fellow correspondents. They fell in with the continuous flow of wagons heading to the front, carrying ammunition and supplies. The entire army moved on horses that were worked until they dropped. Bly noted that one horse with a broken leg was still pulling a wagon. Others, too weak to raise their heads, slogged along until they dropped dead in harnesses. Their carcasses littered the roadside.

The wagon carrying the correspondents rolled toward the rumble of the cannon, past a destroyed village recaptured from the Russians and tent camps of soldiers. The filth of the tent camp drew the strongest reaction from Bly. Waste from the horses and the soldiers so thoroughly covered the ground that Bly could scarcely walk. Dilapidated shacks lined one stretch of the road, each labeled with a white card that read "Cholera." Inside, the piteous sufferers lay in muddy, bloody uniforms on wisps of straw, too weak to stir. "Human creatures they were, lying there in a manner our health authorities would prohibit for hogs," she observed. One horror after another confronted her wherever she looked—the wounded, sick and dying, lifeless human forms, piles of discarded bloody bandages, dead horses. "In times like this one does not lose one's pity, but one realizes one's helplessness. Perhaps that is the most terrible part of war."

Shepherd experienced the same shock and revulsion. "I have seen men killed; I've seen men hanged; I've seen men executed at the wall," he reported, "but this sight I happened upon by accident in Galicia is one of the most piteous that the sun could ever shine upon or that a human being could ever behold."

As the group approached the fighting line, the whine and whistle of shells and shrapnel added a sharp note to the cannonading. Bly finally reached a hill that overlooked the trenches, where forty-five thousand men lived. The high banks that straddled a river were lined with dugouts and barbed wire. An artillery shell landed two hundred feet away. Officers hurried the reporters into a trench, but Bly took her time. "I was not afraid," she declared. "I would not run. Yet my mind was busy. I thought another shot would follow. It will doubtless be better aimed. If it does, we will die."

She ended article number 1 by noting the curious sight of an artillery battery, where soldiers fired off shells without knowing whom or what they killed. Throughout the war correspondents would take special note of such anonymous killing, especially by aerial bombing, submarine warfare, and artillery fire. Bly's sarcastic note: "Killing was easier that way."

Bly had gotten her baptism by fire. If her war reporting was meant to prove to the American public—and to herself—that this middle-aged woman still had the stamina, courage, and poise of her youth, it had succeeded. She had placed herself in the most dangerous and unsettling of circumstances and wrung from it a story of shock and adventure. Three months into the war, no other reporter had given the world so graphic a glimpse of the fighting war as had Bly and the reporters on the KPQ tour.

When Nellie Bly ensured fame with her record-breaking, much-publicized round-the-world trip, her newspaper accounts did not put stress on the network of steamships and railroads that circled the globe and made such a trip possible. Instead, they told the curious adventures of a young woman in challenging circumstances, wrestling with the complicated logistics of world travel, thrust among unfamiliar people with odd customs. Bly followed a similar model in her war reporting. Her reports were less about war on the eastern front than they were about Nellie Bly amid war on the eastern front.

Details of her tour and everyday life in the warring country became part of her articles, as did people she met on trains, her lavish treatment in Budapest, and her accommodations, meals, and the inconveniences and hardships of the tour. Her unique status as an American woman often drew unusual responses. When she visited a hospital, the doctor insisted on posing with her for a photograph. A worker implored her to inform her readers that he used to run a barbershop in New York and hoped to return there after the war. One officer asked her to speak by phone with his regimental commander.

> I put the apparatus over my head and picked up the heavy receiver. "Hello! Who is this?" I called to someone.
>
> "Hello! Who is this?" came back in English. The voice showed surprise.
>
> "I am Nellie Bly, a journalist from New York," I said.
>
> "Oh, you are welcome," said the voice.
>
> "Thank you. I wish Austria success. Goodby."

When local officials suspected her of being a British spy, her fame rescued her. A local physician who spoke English interrogated her. On learning her identity, he threw his hands in the air and yelled: "My God! Nellie Bly!" He hugged her and kept repeating: "Nellie Bly! Nellie Bly!" He explained to the officials that she was famous. He rushed from the room and brought others from elsewhere in the building to introduce them. One woman kissed her hand. They would not let her leave until she promised to dine with them.

On the day she was to leave Przemyśl, she spent the morning in a coffee house. There was no heat in her hotel nor any food to be had. Here, at least, a porcelain stove radiated warmth, and one could enjoy a breakfast of eggs, black bread, and coffee. The place overflowed with officers, and Bly's seat provided a perfect window on traffic passing outside. She turned it into a tableau of life just behind the front lines. Inside, soldiers read newspapers and wrote letters, while outside passed the unceasing traffic of war: horses hauling cannons, herds of cattle, soldiers carrying a body, refugees struggling under bundles of their possessions.

At regular intervals a group of soldiers passed by the window leading a suspected spy, usually a Jew, usually with a barefoot woman and children shuffling along beside him. "These are dangerous days. It needs but the lying word of an enemy to send a man to his death," Bly reported. "What matters one or two more? No one has time to listen or care. Friends cannot sympathize. Their own woes claim all their pangs. Even tears cease to fall. Who can weep for one when thousands are dead and thousands dying every hour?"

A train carried the journalists away from Przemyśl to the Hungarian capital of Budapest. A continuous line of trains moved in the opposite direction, carrying to Przemyśl ammunition, supplies, and fresh, young soldiers, singing and wearing flowers in their caps, heading to the front with enthusiasm. They stood in sharp contrast to soldiers on Bly's train: "Their lips have forgotten how to smile. Their bodies bear wounds. They are sore and bear the pains of long days and endless nights in wet, cold, muddy trenches. Besides their frightful wounds, they have cholera, dysentery, typhoid and the hollow coughs which rack them like the last cough of a consumptive."

Budapest offered a more pleasant venue for war reporting. Bly reported being escorted in a limousine to lavish dinners and plays and enjoying her sumptuous accommodations at the Astoria Hotel. However, even cosmopolitan Budapest did not provide a reprieve from the horrors of the battlefield. One night the doctor from the American Red Cross hospital telephoned Bly at her hotel: "I want you to get into a taxi and come here, Miss Bly. I have received just now the worst cases I have ever seen in my entire life. They may interest you." George Schreiner of the Associated Press, always solicitous of Bly's well-being, urged her not to go. Failing in that attempt, he tagged along by her side. She would later wish she had taken his advice.

At the hospital Bly was immediately rushed into the operating room to see the worst case it had ever been the doctor's misfortune to see. "Look at this body," the doctor urged, and Bly shared the invitation: "Come look, reader, with me." The patient was a Russian soldier, barely alive. He had been shot and lain in a trench for eight days before being brought in. Both of his feet had frozen and fallen off in transport.

"My whole soul sank from the sight," Bly wrote. His pallor was gray; bones showed through the skin of his emaciated body. The soldier's sunken eyes locked on Bly's gaze as he whispered some final words. "I stood, heartsick, soul-sad," she recounted. "Those great hollow eyes searched mine. They tried to question me. They spoke soul language to soul. His lips parted, a moan, a groan of more than physical agony. He spoke. I could not understand. His words were a sound my ears shall never forget."

"'What does he say?' I cried, unable to stand it. 'Can no one understand? Can't you find someone to speak to him?'

"A nurse smoothed his forehead. An attendant held fast the pale, pale hands.

"'He is asking for his children,'" the doctor explained.

Overcome with emotion, Bly had to leave the room moments before the soldier died. "This is only one case. Travel the roads from the scene of battle; search the trains; wounded, frozen, starved thousands are dying in agonizing torture—not hundreds, but thousands. And as they die thousands are being rushed into their pest-filled trenches to be slaughtered in the same way."

The *New York Evening Journal* ran Bly's war reports under the banner "Nellie Bly on the Firing Line." Syndicated by the International News Service, they appeared under such headlines as "Nellie Bly in the Trenches," "Nellie Bly Paints Horrors of War," "Nellie Bly Describes Travel Troubles of War Correspondent," and "Nellie Bly's Experiences in Hungary." Sent by mail from Austria-Hungary, her stories took several weeks to clear military censors and reach home. Her first article, about the visit to Przemyśl, carried an October 30 dateline but did not see print until early December. Through syndication Bly's experiences on the eastern front continued to appear into early 1915.

Her articles succeeded at capturing the gruesomeness of the war that was not yet readily found in the press as well as human interest moments in the cities and on the byroads of Austria-

Hungary. The excess of travel writing included in her articles can be partly explained by the unique circumstances of the KPQ war tour format, designed to expose journalists to a broad itinerary of sights and experiences. In early 1915, however, one critic in the *Davenport (IA) Times* found fault with her approach: "Not the least among war's horrors are Nellie Bly's letters in the Hearst papers. Miss Bly misses a big battle now and then, but never fails to record accurately the flavor of the goulash she consumed or the color of the handsome hussar's mustache."

It was an unjust reproach. The wartime travelogue had already taken firm root in the journalism of the Great War. The challenge of getting a story, the privation and danger of travel in the war zone, interaction with civilians and combatants, the mood in a warring country, gave different perspectives on the impact of war.

At the same time, it is hard to overstress just how remarkable was the reporting that resulted from this KPQ tour in October 1914, three months into the war. Because of French and British restrictions on access to the front, there had been precious little coverage of "big battles." Along with Robert Dunn, George Schreiner, and William Shepherd, Bly provided American readers with their first explicit views of the fighting war.

The KPQ had one more war adventure planned for the journalists: an excursion into Serbia, where an Austrian advance had recently met success. On the boat trip down the Danube, Bly suffered from a mysterious ailment. She ran a fever, agonizing pains traveled up both legs, and "inflamed spots" appeared from ankle to knee.

She attributed it to the handling of a poison bullet in the Red Cross hospital in Budapest. A doctor had shown her an illegal, exploding bullet, brought in by a wounded soldier. "Fastened around between the cap and lead was a bit of cloth and a smear of soft substance, pinkish white, said to be poison." The doctor warned her to be careful, but apparently, she had not been. Charges of using prohibited dumdums, or exploding bullets, were leveled against all sides during the war. In fact, the Allied press accused Austria-Hungary of using exploding bullets in Serbia. The use of poisoned bullets was a more novel charge and may or may not have been true.

Regardless of its cause, Bly clearly suffered through three days. But she chose not to reveal it to her hosts for fear she would be pronounced ill and left behind. Besides, "Poisoned Bullet of Servian Soldier in Hospital Wounds Nellie Bly" made a great headline for one of her stories.

Bly's articles from the Serbian trip began to take on a different tone. After the limousine rides, sumptuous dining, and premier hotel accommodations of Budapest, it was hard to adjust to rattling around in a springless wagon in the biting cold of a Serbian winter. "The clothes I have on and my sleeping bag, a towel, soap, tooth brush and comb complete my baggage," she disclosed. "I hope I don't have to walk. If I do someone else will write this story. My mysterious ailment still makes my nights wretched and my days helpless."

She had wearied of the arduous travel, and her initial spark of fascination with the fighting had also ebbed. This five-day excursion was all about dealing with the grueling travel and observing the privation of the few local inhabitants she met. Unlike her reports from Przemyśl, the trip into Serbia was about the travails of being a war correspondent. It tested Bly's physical and emotional endurance: "War reporting had definitely lost its luster. . . . We were to go over to see the demolished town. It was raining muddy and cold. Same old story. I only repeat lest you forget and think it lets up here sometimes. We were to walk. Not I. Couldn't if I wanted to. Wouldn't if I could. I remembered the advice of my best friend, that there is no glory in the death of a non-combatant on a battlefield. It does not earn decorations. So I asked and obtained permission to hire at my expense an ancient Victoria, reminiscent of Paris before the day of the indispensable taxi."

The group traveled through a snowstorm toward the Serbian front but never saw the fighting. Bly visited Serbian prisoners of war who looked more like poor farmers than soldiers and met several Austrian soldiers along the route. After spending a night in a captured Serbian village, the group returned to Budapest to enjoy a few final days in the plush Astoria Hotel. Bly finished her reporting with a description of a visit to a hospital ward, where forty men with "horrible wounds hover between life and death."

Shepherd's final article about his KPQ tour appeared only after he reached London, out from under the control of Austrian censors. In it he explained that his group had made a hasty departure from Serbia because the Austro-Hungarians were in chaotic retreat: "The retirement from Servia was a rout. It was a nightmare of horror. Officers and soldiers went mad. A terrible blizzard was raging part of the time. The army was in wild flight." Furthermore, he pointed out that in Budapest there was alarm because of Cossack raids in the countryside. Bly's reporting never made note of such military observations.

Both Bly and Shepherd came under criticism from the Austro-Hungarian ambassador to the United States, Konstantin Dumba— Bly for describing the military's unsanitary conditions in Galicia and Shepherd for characterizing the army's retreat from Serbia as a rout. Although Bly would remain in Austria for the duration of the war, this would be her only stint of war reporting.

Back in Italy by the end of October, Alice Rohe sifted war news from foreign papers, government and Vatican sources, and the human flotsam that arrived in Rome. Italian citizen Gaetano Fernaro shared with Rohe his experiences at the siege of Przemyśl. He had joined the Austrian army as a dashing youth and returned a miserable wreck, with one leg shot off. A Belgian couple told of their escape from Liège during the German assault. They wandered many miles to reach the safety of neutral Italy and along the way lost their infant daughter to starvation.

The Vatican teased out a few stories about Pope Benedict XV's attempts to broker a peace, but the mood in Italy ran in the opposite direction. Since 1882 Italy had been a member of the Triple Alliance with Germany and Austria-Hungary. However, at the start of the war, it declared its neutrality. Rohe filed numerous stories through the spring of 1915 as sentiment built for Italy's entry into the war, a move that finally occurred on May 23, when it joined the Allied powers.

A Heretofore Ignored Element of the Great War

Spring 1915 marked a turning point in news coverage of the war. Britain and France began to soften restrictions on journalists, realizing they had more to gain by managing the news than restricting it. The very concept of a "war correspondent" continued to evolve, as did the notion of what constituted war news.

If the opening months of this war demonstrated anything, it was that this conflict bore little resemblance to any that went before. Most of the previous wars covered by veteran war reporters such as Richard Harding Davis would barely qualify as a skirmish in the present conflict. The world had discovered "total war," a conflict without limitations, fought not only between armies but between entire societies. Therefore, nearly everything counted as war news, including all developments on the home front vital to sustaining the war effort as well as the role of women.

The fighting in Belgium and northern France demonstrated how women became victims of the fighting. They lost loved ones, became refugees, and came under direct attack from aerial bombardment in Paris and London. But their positive contributions to the war effort also began to draw attention from the press: their mobilization into the workforce, their role as nurses and ambulance drivers, and their participation in war charities.

It came as no surprise that many American newspapers and magazines thought to send female reporters to Europe to uncover this angle on the war. Even women's publications that typically concerned themselves chiefly with domestic issues and fashion began to see how the plight of their sisters in Europe was relevant to American women. Magazines such as *Good Housekeeping* and *Ladies' Home Journal* would eventually send their own correspondents to cover the war. In the winter of 1914–15 the awareness was dawning that in addition to making women victims, the war gave them an inspiring sense of empowerment.

The English writer May Christie sailed for America one month before the outbreak of war and was immediately hired by the *Philadelphia Evening Public Ledger* to edit its Women's Page. Writing under the pen name Ellen Adair, she began a regular column that offered opinions on romance, jobs, social engagements, and personal fulfillment. The rest of the page covered such standard topics as fashion, cooking, society, and parenting.

The war did not intrude onto the *Ledger*'s Women's Page until December 1914. It came in the form of a letter Adair received from an Englishwoman working as a nurse on a ship that evacuated British wounded from the Continent. She described her exhausting, emotionally draining duties with the wounded and dying. Adair observed that the heroism of women during the present war frequently passed unnoticed.

That article struck a discordant note not only by introducing the topic of war onto what had previously been a well-defined journalistic space devoted to women's issues but because of how the nurse concluded her letter: "'My present life is thrilling to the extreme,' writes the nurse. 'I just feel that up to the present time I have never truly lived! But, indeed, I am living now, and am enjoying it all immensely, although we are running very great risks of being blown to atoms. At any time we may strike a mine or be torpedoed by Germans or be fired upon by their ships.'"

War topics began to regularly appear in Adair's column: the war-awakened women of England, children in the war zone, women leading protest riots after the sinking of the liner *Lusitania*. Growing interest in such topics culminated with an announcement by the *Ledger* that its Women's Page editor, Ellen Adair, would travel to warring Europe to write about issues of interest to women. Adair would not penetrate to the fighting line, it explained: "It is no time for noncombatants, even though they are newsgatherers, to go into the thick of battle. The war correspondent of that sort has passed." However, it continued, "American women are entitled to a faithful picture of what their sisters abroad are

6. May Christie, who wrote under the name Ellen Adair, was the editor of a newspaper Women's Page when the war began. She traveled to warring Europe several times to report on the role of women. George Grantham Bain Collection, Prints & Photographs Division, Library of Congress, LC-DIG-ggbain-37599.

doing, of how they are proving themselves and demonstrating their right to participate in the government of their countries." "Finally, true to the wants of womankind," the *Ledger* assured readers, Adair would also visit the great dressmakers of Paris and learn what effects the war has had on fashion.

For two months Adair sent weekly articles from England and France that dealt with the war mood, the growing influence of women, visits with convalescing soldiers, and a tour of the Marne battlefield. When she returned, she continued to draw attention to the relevance of war issues for the readers of her Women's Page, even for the women of the neutral United States.

3

The *Saturday Evening Post*'s Women's War

The big story of a war is never at the front, but in the hospitals
and homes. War is largely a woman's affair, and a woman, I think,
best understands the little things that go to make up the big story.

—GEORGE LORIMER, "Four American Women Who Have Been to
the War," *New York Tribune*, August 1, 1915

T he genius of George Horace Lorimer, the legendary editor of the *Saturday Evening Post* magazine, amounted to knowing what Americans were thinking before they themselves did. Lorimer took editorial control of the magazine in 1899, when it had only sixteen hundred readers, and quickly built a stable of popular writers that helped to grow readership past the one million mark by 1908. By the time war came to Europe, in 1914, the *Post* had become the largest-circulation magazine in the United States, with a weekly readership of nearly two million.

In part Lorimer accomplished this dramatic growth by broadening the focus of the publication beyond its traditional male readership to appeal to women as well. The *Post* embraced the cause of women's suffrage and highlighted the expanding role of women in the workforce. Its pages featured the work of popular novelists such as Mary Roberts Rinehart and brought to national attention lesser-known women writers, such as the southern regional writer Corra Harris. The *Post*'s more enlightened view on women was also aided by the addition of the first woman to its editorial staff in 1909, Adelaide Neal.

How America's largest magazine would cover the largest event in world history—a world war—became an immediate question in August 1914. "I'm going to play this war hard for six months," Lorimer told *Post* writer Will Irwin, "in case it lasts as long as that, and then I'll drop it. By then the American people will grow sick and tired of reading about it."

Lorimer immediately recruited as his war reporters veteran newsman Samuel G. Blythe and frequent *Post* contributor Irvin Cobb. Blythe would cover the war from the capital cities and Cobb from the front lines. On August 3, the day after Germany and France declared war on each other, Lorimer also sent a telegram to Corra Harris: "How would you like to spend a few days in London for us doing woman's side of war. Can send you over on steamship with Irvin Cobb to chaperone you. Wire answer."

The selection of Cobb and Harris made perfect sense since both had recently written about visits to Europe. Cobb's book *Europe Revisited*, which appeared earlier in 1914, focused his satirical wit on the customs and idiosyncrasies of England, France, and Germany. Harris had been introduced to *Post* readers through the serialization of her novel *The Circuit Rider's Wife*, beginning in 1899. Her writing focused on women who steadfastly maintained their traditional role in society as guardians of home and family. In 1912 Harris wrote several articles on the evolving role of women in Europe. Both Cobb and Harris would be able to compare what they had seen in prewar Europe to the current state of affairs.

Harris accepted the war assignment but asked for a delay while she dealt with family objections. Cobb sailed on August 7 and was among the first correspondents to reach Brussels before it fell to the Germans. He traveled in the wake of the German army until evicted from the country and then covered the war from the German side of the line. Harris sailed on September 23 and wrote a series of articles about the women of England and France. Meanwhile, Lorimer recruited three other women for war assignments, a move that elevated his intuition to a conscious declaration of policy.

A "Woman's Side of the War"

One year into the war the *New York Tribune* ran a feature article about the remarkable fact that the *Saturday Evening Post* had used four women to cover the war. While other publications, including women's magazines, considered war a "man's affair," George Lorimer wanted to uncover the role played by women. According to the article, the *Post*'s four women war correspondents revealed in their coverage that the hard part of war was not in dying gloriously at the front but in surviving ingloriously on the home front. The hard business of living through this war had been assumed by the women of Europe. Not only did they endure the loss of loved ones and the security of marriage; they also faced the challenge of learning a trade other than homemaking, the assumption of additional costs and taxes, the support of the country's educational and charitable efforts, and the burden of care for the wounded and maimed. While the *Post*'s coverage included the military, political, and economic components of war, its women correspondents showed the human interest side of war, the impact on the home, family, and individual lives. Such articles brought the most laudatory reader letters, a measure of success that meant a great deal to George Lorimer.

By the time Corra Harris sailed for England, on September 23, the *Post*'s editorial calendar had finally caught up with the war. That week's *Post* carried Samuel Blythe's report about London crowds watching solemnly as their men marched off to war and Parliament passing sweeping wartime legislation. In the following issue Blythe had two articles about the transformation of Paris: streets and hotels empty, shops closed, citizens paying every possible price to support the war. "The war has reached in and grabbed the vitals of Paris."

Unlike Blythe, Harris found England curiously unaffected by the war. The country faced preparation for war with quiet confidence and courage, she noted, but the signs of war seemed purely ornamental, in displays of bunting and recruitment post-

7. Writing for the *Saturday Evening Post* in the opening months of the war, Corra Harris drew attention to the large role being played by women in the war. *Independent*, November 20, 1913.

ers. Shops and theaters were open. Censorship shielded the public from the details of the fighting. Life went on.

Curiously, women appeared to be the most energized and visible force in England. In the opening days of the conflict, 160,000 women mobilized in London to form the Women's Emergency

Corps, an army on the home front. Unlike the government, they moved quickly in various humanitarian endeavors. They raised money for war relief, equipped hospitals in France and Belgium, supported the flood of refugees from the war zone, and even made toys for British children, who could no longer get toys from the traditional source of Germany.

Harris's first war article, "The New Militants," featured the Women's Emergency Corps, particularly its work with Belgian refugees. Four to six thousand destitute, traumatized refugees poured into England every day: women and children, old people, and young men maimed from battle. To get a feel for the crisis, Harris volunteered with the organization at the Liverpool Street rail station. The emergency corps pinned a white armband onto her sleeve and sent her off to meet the five hundred refugees expected on the first train.

A terror-stricken tableau of faces peered from every window as the train pulled into the station. As the refugees staggered off the train, drooping under the bags and bundles of possessions, Harris thought them the "most miserable multitude" she had ever seen. For Harris this was the real face of war: "Nearly all the women seemed to have babies. Young children bent beneath the weight of large packs. Senile old men tottered out whimpering. They did not understand. They were afraid. . . . There was not a tear upon any woman's face, however. They had been exalted beyond tears by the horrors they had endured. Most of them were widows whose husbands had died in battle. Some had seen their sons shot in the little villages where they lived. Their homes had been burned and they had been robbed of everything they possessed; so they were tearless. You weep for one loss, but when all is lost you rise forlornly above the tide of tears."

Every refugee told a story of hardship and loss, and many also shared an atrocity story, which in turn became the whispered orthodoxy of the British volunteers and fodder for sensational news stories. Someone had seen a British soldier in a hospital whose eyes had been gouged out by the Germans. Supposedly, there were two Belgian boys in London whose hands had been cut off by the enemy so they could never take up arms against Germany. Somewhere there was a demented woman who had seen Germans cut off the heads of her two children. Harris made a point to search out evidence of such occurrences but never found it. "It is difficult to keep one's senses," Harris conceded, "in an atmosphere charged with the horrible annals of this war as related by these women."

The war also caused conditions for women in Britain to deteriorate, Harris reported. Many were impoverished and malnourished. With so many doctors gone to the army, child mortality rates climbed, and more women died in childbirth. Harris presented herself at the War Office, determined to ask Britain's war leader, Lord Horatio Kitchener, exactly how many British women had lost husbands and sons, but she was turned away.

However, Harris didn't need War Office statistics to draw a powerful conclusion from her observations: women were the unsung victims and heroes in this conflict. It was an important shift of focus in the early reporting of the war. "What men suffer in war is written in histories," she remarked. "It is remembered. They earn something which is handed down to generations that come after them, which praise them. . . . When one writes of the women's side of the war one cannot tell of battles won, or of the glories that crown the heads of victorious men. It must be a story of sorrows; of despair; of poverty; of privations patiently endured; of defeat in the tender hearts of all women; of the suffering of little children."

Harris was inclined to editorialize a good deal more than Lorimer preferred. One of the articles she submitted to him never saw print for this reason. But the lesson she took from this first stop in her "Women's Side of the War" tour was that "so long as women cannot fight or have any voice in determining whether the nation shall go to war, it is immoral and unjust to force them to endure the burdens and sorrows that war brings chiefly to them." Harris was the first to wrestle with the concept that women were not just passive victims on the periphery of the real war that happened at the fighting line. Rather, they were active participants, fully engaged in the war, only with different burdens, sacrifices, and heroism than men.

When Harris left for France on October 16, the English Channel was crowded with every type of vessel, heavily laden with refugees. She compared it to the River Styx, dividing life from death. France itself felt like a "house where guests are not expected . . . as if to come here at all is an intrusion." At her landing point at Dieppe, she saw only women with their heads covered in shawls and bent old men moving like ghosts along the pier. On the train to Paris she asked the guard if there would be a restaurant car, and he replied that the restaurant cars were now used for hospitals. Doddering grandfathers served as porters at the Paris station and carried passengers to their hotel in cabs pulled by skeletal horses, through dark and deserted streets.

France gave Harris her first sense of being in a country at war. Long lists of the dead and wounded appeared regularly in the newspapers. All the women she met had husbands or sons in the army; many did not know the fate of their men, and many wore the black of mourning. And yet none complained, only stoically endured the hardships and losses. "It is not natural or even sane for women to believe in an order of things that inflicts death upon their own children," Harris declared.

Corra Harris met those husbands and sons when she visited hospitals in Paris. "It is incredible that one should stand in such a place, surrounded by mutilated men in the prime of their youth and strength, without realizing that war is a ferocious form of insanity. Nothing can justify it." None of the soldier patients or the women who cared for them grumbled or complained. It gave testament to the power of patriotism to animate a nation, Harris thought. But as an outside observer, she could not see beyond war's mindless destruction of lives and culture: "That which remains of it at the end of a century is a history, a few monuments, a generation impoverished and stunted in mind and body by the blood that was lost."

Before leaving the United States on her war assignment, Harris told *Post* editor George Lorimer that she intended to write better war stories than Irvin Cobb. However, while Harris was bottled up in Paris, Cobb had wound up on one of the first official war tours offered to the press by the German army, giving him some remarkable eyewitness stories.

Such opportunities did not exist on the other side of the line. Reporters were "as thick in Paris as zooming insects on fly paper in a village bar," wrote Harris, but at this point in the war, the French did not offer press tours. In fact, France shared virtually nothing about the war with the public. Any enterprising reporter, attempting to reach the front, could count on being arrested. Despite this risk, many American reporters were not overly deterred by military restrictions. If you had to be arrested to get your story, then so be it. Your attempt to breach the secrecy surrounding the fighting became part of the story.

To evade military restrictions, Harris hit on the plan of joining a trainload of refugees returning to the recently liberated village of Senlis. She arrived without incident at the ruined village. The Germans had occupied it in the first month of the war, when they pushed so close to Paris, but lost it back to the French. In her article "When the Germans Came," Harris told stories of French citizen heroism and described the horrible conditions of hunger and disease faced by the survivors.

War reporting seemed to have gotten into Harris's blood by this point. She took an even more daring train ride, closer to the fighting. When Harris learned about the exceptional heroics of Madame Jeanne Macherez (aka Marcherez), who had stood up to the German occupiers of her town and now ran a hospital at Soissons, she set off in search of her. Travel in the war zone for a correspondent at this point in the war required a healthy dose of courage and chutzpah. Along her route Harris had to stop repeatedly to argue a pass from local officials, who could not understand why a woman would want to move so close to the fighting. The mayor of one town accused her of being an American war tourist, a considerable insult.

She hired an old man with a wagon and tottering horse to carry her closer to Soissons and the fighting. They passed through destroyed villages, past many suspicious sentries, along roads choked with war traffic that carried fresh soldiers and supplies to the front and wounded men to the rear. "There is a difference between seeing wounded men lying in clean hospital beds, surrounded by every possible comfort and seeing these other wounded, just dragged from the trenches where they fell, still wearing their uniforms, with the grime of powder and blood sticking to them. And the latter sight is infinitely more horrible," she reported.

As was so often the case with war correspondents, the personal quest, with its many hardships and dangers, proved an exciting part of their reporting. The fact that a woman experienced such perils made it even more compelling. Harris repeatedly ignored advice that her next step was too dangerous or forbidden under military law. She persisted, passing through the eerie forest of Compiègne at night, crossing a temporary military bridge, coming upon abandoned trenches and freshly dug graves and an encampment of French soldiers, as the sound of cannonading grew ever louder.

Finally, the imminence of danger proved too much for her wagon driver, who refused all inducements to travel any farther. Harris spent the night at a village hotel, nursing her frustration. She had gotten so close. The thunder of the guns at Soissons kept her awake most of the night. "I thought of the men falling out there somewhere in the dark," she wrote. "I had seen the trenches. I knew now how they must drop down in them; how crowded it must be in there between the living and the dead. What scenes of horror the dawn must bring! The something dreadful I had heard of so often was happening."

Two days later, back in Paris, Harris finally met Madame Macherez, who had escaped from Soissons under heavy artillery fire to come to Paris for medical supplies. She was a no-nonsense woman of sixty-four who had assumed the position of mayor of Soissons to act as intermediary and advocate for its citizens with the German occupiers, thus saving many lives. She continued as mayor but now also ran two hospitals and employed dozens of women in Soissons to clean and repair the clothing of the soldiers. Harris had found her Joan of Arc, the symbol of the strength of Frenchwomen, and women in general, in their response to the war.

Harris returned to England, where she wrote two more stories before sailing for home on December 23, 1914. One of those articles made a robust attack on England for allowing the lower classes to bear the brunt of the war. Her final article was an abstract condemnation of war. It was a weak conclusion to an otherwise valiant effort to capture the impact of the war on women. As the war progressed, the suffering on the home front in the belligerent countries would gain increasing attention from reporters. But it was Harris, in the chaos of the early months of the war, who first focused on how squarely the burden of war fell on women.

Harris's war articles did not draw many reader letters. Lorimer thought they contained too much personal opinion unsupported by facts. Although Harris asked Lorimer for another war assignment, he instead sent three other women to report on the war.

Canada Mobilizes for Another War

While Corra Harris explored the expanded role of women in England and France, George Lorimer sent women on war assignments to two other warring nations: Canada, as it mobilized for war; and Russia, which had plunged into the war simultaneous to adopting prohibition. America might feel confident that three thousand miles of ocean shielded it from the European conflict, but just across its border, Canada was in the full grip of war fever. Lorimer assigned the journalist, novelist, and short story writer Maude Radford Warren to capture a picture of this U.S. neighbor.

Maude Lavinia Radford Warren seemed a natural choice to chronicle Canada's mobilization for war. Not only was she a veteran Chicago journalist who had previously written for the *Post*, but she had been born in Canada. Her 1910 *Post* article "Petticoat Professions: New Women in Old Fields" noted the barriers women faced in newspaper work: "The authorities seem to think that women lack the news instinct and often fail in the luck of being on the spot when something happens. In the newspaper world man's prejudice against the woman worker is injurious. . . . It is hard for her to get hold of political, financial, military, or waterfront news." However, magazine journalism put women on a more equal footing, she explained. "The woman who writes for the magazine enjoys something as near to professional equality with men as is possible in this world where all the laws and all the important customs are made by men."

The enthusiasm of the young men volunteering for the army was the most visible sign of the war in Canada: new recruits heading to training camps, soldiers embarking for Europe. From politicians to raw recruits, everyone Warren spoke to reflected the firm resolve to fulfill their responsibility as loyal subjects of the British Empire.

However, just as censorship in the war zone prevented Canadians from knowing what was happening in the conflict, so, too, their own mobilization happened largely under a veil of secrecy. An army officer Warren met on the train refused to talk about the troops because, he claimed, the country was awash in spies. He told her that one female American reporter had already been deported for asking too many questions. In Quebec in late September, Warren watched men, horses, and artillery load onto ships. Thirty-one vessels under warship escort sailed off to war— and no mention of it appeared in the press.

Everyone Warren spoke with voiced the same steely resolve about national mobilization. "This war was not our seeking, but became our duty," Home Secretary Reginald McKenna told Warren. In every music hall and moving picture show, she heard rousing patriotic songs. But the sacrifice that underlay mobilization existed on a more personal and painful level for one elderly woman, who had repeatedly paid the price for citizenship in the empire. Warren found her in Ottawa, walking beside a parade of recruits that included her grandson. "It seems to me now that's been my whole life—watching men march away," the woman told her. The woman's father had marched off to fight in the Crimea and never returned. Her husband had fought with General Gordon in Khartoum and came home a broken man. Her youngest son had joined the forces sent to South Africa and never came home. Now her grandson, the only one who could carry on the family name, was going to war.

"You didn't try to hold him back?" Warren asked.

"No," the woman confessed. "If a man sees his duty to his country in that way it's a woman's place to do her share for the country too. I'm glad I'm a British subject, but there is surely no harm in saying that any woman is lucky who belongs to a country that doesn't ask her for the lives of her men."

Russia Goes to War Sober

News that the Russian Empire had taken the extraordinary step of instituting the prohibition of alcohol simultaneous to mobilizing for war first broke in American newspapers in September 1914. The Russian development combined two topics of paramount interest to the American public—prohibition and the war. The prohibition movement had been gathering steam in the United States for decades. New organizations and more aggressive tactics had succeeded in bringing statewide prohibition to thirty-three states. George Lorimer saw the story potential and promptly sent to Russia former *Chicago Tribune* reporter and *Post* contributor Mary Isabel Brush. She had been the *Tribune*'s expert on "women's political problems."

The *New York Tribune* article about the four *Saturday Evening Post* women who went to war described Brush as a "newspaper woman to the bone," with the "steel construction" to prove that a woman can do what a man can do. It added that the telling anecdotes that filled Brush's Russia article could be attributed to a "woman's gossipy human manner carried over to epoch making history."

When Mary Isabel Brush arrived in the Russian Arctic port of Archangel in October 1914, two months into the war, she received a stern warning from a customs official that the czar had decreed

an end to the consumption of vodka. It was the most important thing the official had to share with a visitor to the Russian
Empire—not news of the fighting in Prussia and Galicia, not
security measures being taken against German spies, but that
the country had gone dry. It was one small indication of the bold-
ness of the social experiment.

From her fellow travelers, British businessmen who regularly visited Russia, Brush learned how vodka had been so deeply
rooted in Russian life that every social occasion, political event,
and business transaction had to be lubricated with the drink.
Some factories did not open on Mondays because too many of
their employees had hangovers.

Rumor held that before the war Germany believed that the
Russian army would be too drunk to fight effectively. In fact,
the painful memory of how vodka had impaired the fighting
effectiveness of the Russian army during mobilization for the
Russo-Japanese War, in 1904, motivated the implementation of
prohibition as the country mobilized for this latest war. The day
that mobilization of the Russian army began, special policemen
visited every location where vodka was sold, locked up the supply, and placed an imperial seal on the shop. Since the government enjoyed a monopoly on the manufacture and sale of vodka,
prohibition proved easy to enforce.

Brush spent seven weeks in Russia, wrestling with the enigma
of Russian culture and character. Russia clearly unsettled her,
from its "incomprehensible tongue" to the illiteracy, isolation,
and lack of discipline and motivation to the twilight of a Petrograd afternoon. "Long nights seem to sap the coloring pigment
of an individual and a nation," she observed. "To bring up a people subject to lengthy periods of darkness is something like trying to raise grass under a board." But therein lay the problem
with prohibition. "For centuries the vigor and cheer of Russia has
been supplied artificially, and suddenly to stop the stimulating
fluid would be to invite a first-class revolution." How would the
population react to life without vodka? What would the state do
without the enormous income it had received from taxing vodka?

Brush filled her articles with anecdotes about peasants who had turned around their lives once they embraced a life of sobriety. Individuals and communities that barely functioned under the influence of vodka regained vitality and a sense of purpose once the ban was imposed. Authorities in Moscow gave her the name of the city's heaviest drinker, a "public character" whose life had been transformed. Brush found him working in an electrical shop. He confessed that prior to prohibition he typically missed more than half of his workdays because of drunkenness. Now he was an exemplary worker, had saved enough money to buy his son new shoes, and had signed the petition to the czar requesting the continuation of prohibition. "I couldn't give it up myself, but I'm glad it's been taken away," he told Brush.

If individuals quit vodka, they would have more money, but how could the government wean itself off the addiction to alcohol tax revenue? How could it sustain the war effort without that income? Brush took her questions to the minister of finance. The minister seemed amused by the question and even more amused by the young lady posing it. He pulled a chair up close to Brush. He had never before seen a journalist. What a curiosity. When he had adjusted to the new experience, he asked indulgently, "And now, young woman . . . what points did you want cleared?"

She had heard that a considerable portion of the state budget came from taxing vodka. How would it make up that lost revenue? The minister of finance confirmed that the government would lose a billion rubles annually from vodka taxes, nearly a third of its budget. However, the tax on vodka had been a drain on the economy and removing it had been a great economic stimulus. Now the population was healthier, more productive, and had a greater income that it was spending and saving. Alcohol had been Russia's real enemy, not Germany.

Again, he called her "young woman," in the tone of explaining a complex problem to a child. "Money is unimportant," he assured her. "We have not yet begun to think of it." Brush had to confess to her readers that she did not understand Russia. She felt like a "fly on a plate-glass window of a department store. I was an atom in millions of square miles of Russian land." She had investigated prohibition, but pulling one thread of the Russian knot loosed a dozen dizzying lines of inquiry. With her prohibition articles concluded, she wrote one final report on her Russia experience to explain why it had entered the war.

One day Brush sat in the lobby of Petrograd's Astoria Hotel, people watching and pondering the inscrutability of the Russian character. She was simultaneously scanning an article by Arnold Bennett about Russia's rationale for entering the war while watching the wartime melodrama around her. A bevy of young ladies fussed around a young man in uniform. A general entered the room, and when he saw the soldier, the two of them "flew at each other like schoolgirls," embracing and kissing. Nurses circulated in the lobby, collecting money for wounded soldiers. From outside came the sound of marching troops. They would be going to St. Isaac's Cathedral, across the street, to receive a blessing before heading to the front.

On this day she was meeting with a Frenchman who had lived in Russia for twenty-five years. People said the Frenchman knew more about the political and social conditions in Russia than anyone else. She wanted his thoughts on why Russia had entered the war. She had to listen patiently to the Frenchman's theories about the fundamental difference in character between Slavs and Teutons, but as for what drove Russia to declare war on Germany? Russia had been incited to fight by the British, the man assured her. They promised Russia what it had so long desired, access to the Mediterranean through the Dardanelles Straits, controlled by Turkey.

Brush had been accumulating the tantalizing backstory on Russia in the war from other sources, theories related to the governing style of the czar, stalled efforts at democratic reform, and the influence of German advisors in the Russian court. Whichever opinion you took suggested deeper intrigues and conflicts in the empire. She added the Frenchman's theory to the mix, "for what it is worth, a contribution of something that will perhaps never go into the recorded history of the world, a bit of narrative which may not be authentic in all details."

To complete the picture, she interviewed workingmen in the shops, asking dozens of them the same question: Why do the workingmen go to fight? To gain more freedoms, they all said. There had been considerable unrest in recent years, with protests and strikes against corruption and the lack of progress on democratic reforms. "Report has it that never in the history of Russia had the autocracy been so close to tottering," Brush wrote. The czar and his ministers believed that war would revive patriotism and put an end to all the talk about representative government. The working class, however, supported this war because it had gained so much from the last one. After Russia's humiliating defeat in the Russian-Japanese war of 1904–5, Russia's legislative body, the Duma, had come into existence.

In 1915 Brush posed a prescient question about how that rift would ultimately play out: "Let Russia win, and she thought her autocracy would be stronger than in the days of its strength. But the workingman thinks not. He says, let Russia win, and it will mean more rights for him. He will then be in a position to command. One of the large questions is: Which of them knows what he is talking about—the autocracy or the workingman? The answer will be heard round the world." Two years later Russia would be taken out of the war by revolutions that brought down the monarchy and gave power to workers.

A Writer of Mystery Fiction Takes on the War

Unlike the other women given war assignments by the *Saturday Evening Post* in the first year of the war, Mary Roberts Rinehart had to persuade George Lorimer to send her into danger. She did not seem a natural fit for the job. She was a middle-aged wife, a mother, and a writer of fiction. She had trained as a nurse but had no special expertise in military matters or experience in war reporting—or in reporting of any kind. She rose to national prominence with her best-selling novel *The Circular Staircase* (1908), which sold a million and a quarter copies. Her comedy play *Seven Days*, a big hit on Broadway in 1909, was currently in rehearsal in London. In recent years her short stories had regularly delighted the readers of the *Saturday Evening Post*.

"Frankly, I do not care to take the responsibility of sending anyone over there except old maids, widows and our really tough boys like Cobb and Blythe," Lorimer responded to her request in a telegram. "Personally, I should urge you not to take the risk." Many years after the fact, Rinehart would explain in her autobiography, *My Story* (1931), why she had been so adamant about taking that risk: "All of my suppressed sense of adventure, my desire to discover what physical courage I had, my instincts as a writer had been aroused. . . . I do not intend to let the biggest thing in my life go by without having been a part of it." Her resolve finally persuaded Lorimer and her family.

It is doubtful that any correspondent ever headed off on a war assignment with more fanfare than Mary Roberts Rinehart. On January 3, 1915, photographers captured her backing out of the driveway at her home in Sewickley, Pennsylvania. Newspapers reported that the popular novelist was heading directly to the front to work as a nurse and report on the war. Her New York publisher waved goodbye to her from the pier. Her stateroom on the steamer *Franconia* overflowed with bouquets of flowers, baskets of fruit, and congratulatory telegrams, not to mention her giant steamer trunk, hat boxes, and suitcases, containing her furs, jewels, and a white velvet evening gown, along with a khaki trench suit. As a sensible precaution, she had also purchased a rubber survival suit. Should her ship be torpedoed, she was to don the suit and inflate it by blowing into the attached rubber tube.

She had overcome her own reservations, those of her husband, and George Lorimer. She was now a war correspondent, about to sail into the danger zone, traveling on her own for the first time in her life, the only woman on the voyage.

Rinehart found London overflowing with American journalists. During the early months of the war, enterprising reporters could range across the developing war zone, picking up pieces of the action. But the fluid war of movement and siege had set-

8. Mary Roberts Rinehart, a famous writer of mystery fiction, became a war correspondent for the *Saturday Evening Post*. With the endorsement of the Belgian Red Cross, she won unprecedented access to the war zone and became the first journalist to visit the frontline trenches. George Grantham Bain Collection, Prints & Photographs Division, Library of Congress, LC-B2-4007-13.

tled into the static trench warfare that would predominate for the next four years. This type of war was nearly impossible to cover without access to the fighting zone, and both the British and French adamantly excluded reporters from their armies.

Resourceful reporters arrived in London armed with letters of introduction from editors, publishers, politicians, diplomats, and famous people, which they presented to the War Office, in the hope they would open the door of access. But they did not. Most reporters had to be content to report on the British home front and what little of the war they could distill from official government communiqués and often unreliable newspaper accounts.

Rinehart's plan to bypass this hurdle grew from a serendipitous conversation with a fellow traveler, who suggested that she appeal to the Belgian Red Cross for entry to the front. Rinehart pleaded her case to that organization, which had offices in London. In the book Rinehart published about her war experiences, *Kings, Queens, and Pawns: An American Woman at the Front* (1915), she detailed this important meeting as the key that opened the secret door.

Americans were sending large amounts of money and supplies to aid Belgium, she reminded organization officials, but America knew little about what became of them. They were "swallowed up in the great silence." If this resource was to be continued, Rinehart suggested, America needed to learn what Belgium had already done in the war and what yet needed to be done. If the Red Cross would help her to visit the hospitals and see the front lines, she would tell Belgium's story to the two million readers of the *Saturday Evening Post*.

"The idea was a new one; it took some mental adjustment," Rinehart explained. But to her astonishment, she won their full and immediate support. She received letters of introduction to the right people in Belgium and a high-level pass issued by the Red Cross.

So began the extraordinary two-month war adventure of the fiction writer–turned–war correspondent Mary Roberts Rinehart. She would record the first wartime interviews with British and Belgian royalty. She would be granted unprecedented access to the war zone. She would meet the commanders of the British and French armies. General Ferdinand Foch, commander of the French army in the north, would personally mark her war map, recommending places to visit. She would get a harsh introduction to the fighting war and see its many permutations of horror.

She would slog through the mud of the frontline trenches; venture into the perilous no-man's-land, within a few hundred yards of the enemy; and come under both shellfire and aerial bombing attacks. She would see the ceaseless flow of wounded, the ill-equipped hospitals, and the laudable work of the Red Cross. In the process her attitude toward war would change from one of adventure to "deadly loathing."

She had told the committee that she wanted to see everything, and the Red Cross took her at her word. No other correspondent ever had such a full picture of the war, concentrated into one blue-ribbon agenda. Belgium, Britain, and France used her as a vehicle to introduce more openness into press coverage of the war, allowing her to write eleven hugely popular articles for the *Post* in the spring and summer of 1915 that helped to define the war for the American public. She had been the magazine's most popular fiction writer, and now she became its most popular war correspondent. Her extraordinary experience inspired other female journalists and writers eager to involve themselves in the war.

Mary Roberts Rinehart's Blue-Ribbon War Tour

Rinehart's introduction to war came in the first remarkable twenty-four hours of her journey to the Continent. It began from her plush room at London's Claridge Hotel. At the train station a woman from Scotland Yard searched her person and luggage, demonstrating the wartime obsession with spies. During passage on a Channel boat, she kept vigilant for submarine periscopes.

Immediately on her landing in Boulogne, she experienced her first shock of war when she watched a hospital train unload British wounded. When the train pulled into the station that night, "the first man was lifted down and placed on a truck, and his place was filled immediately by another. As fast as one man was taken another came. The line seemed endless. . . . One by one the stretchers came; one by one they were added to the lengthening line that lay prone on the stone flooring beside the train. . . . The car seemed inexhaustible of horrors." It was "one of the pictures that will stand out always in my mind. Perhaps it was because I was not yet inured to suffering: certainly I was to see many similar scenes, much more of the flotsam and jetsam of the human tide that was sweeping back and forward over the flat fields of France and Flanders."

The busy Channel port of Dunkirk served as her base of operations for the next three weeks. It was conveniently located near the Belgian border, the battlefield at Ypres, and La Panne, the seaside village that had become the temporary capital of what little remained of a free Belgium. Dunkirk proved a good location to watch the traffic of war. Ships unloaded men and war materials, and continuous truck caravans drove them off to that mysterious, inaccessible region known as the "front." The dead and wounded returned in a ceaseless flow of ambulances and hospital trains.

It did not take long for Rinehart to realize that being this deep in the war zone carried risk. While she was dining with some officers in her hotel, gunfire suddenly exploded outside, and an alarm bell rang in the hotel. The officers jumped to their feet, and the lights went out. A waiter appeared next to Rinehart and lit a match. "Aeroplanes!" he said. One of the regular German bombing raids had commenced. The dining room was as safe as anywhere, he informed her, but she might wish to join the others in the cellar.

"I wanted to go to the cellar or to crawl into the office safe. But I felt that, as the only woman and the only American about, I held the reputation of America and of my sex in my hands." It would not be the last time that personal danger tested Rinehart's resolve or that she felt the burden of being the only woman.

Rinehart began her official war tour with a visit to the Ambulance de l'Océan, in La Panne, *ambulance* being the French word for a military hospital. It was the base hospital for the Belgian lines and one of the premier war hospitals in Europe, operating at standards as high as the best hospitals in the United States. It was clear why the Red Cross wanted to show it off.

As a trained nurse, Rinehart would have felt familiar with

such a facility but not with the patients it served: "The men come here with the most frightful injuries. As I entered the building to-night the long, tiled corridor was filled with the patient and quiet figures that are the first fruits of war. They lay on portable cots, waiting their turn in the operating room, the white of coverings and bandages not whiter than their faces. The Night Supervisor has just been in to see me. She says there is a baby here from Furnes with both legs off, and a nun who lost an arm as she was praying in the garden of her convent. The baby will live, but the nun is dying." Rinehart suited up to watch a surgeon remove a piece of shrapnel from a soldier's brain. Twelve minutes elapsed from the initial incision to the moment when the surgeon dropped the shard of steel into Rinehart's hand and the wound was being closed. She would keep the piece of shrapnel as a grisly souvenir.

Since Rinehart was a trained nurse, a member of the American Red Cross, and her husband a doctor, it made sense for her to report on conditions at hospitals. But she had asked to see everything, to pass through that jealously guarded barrier that hid the fighting line. Rinehart's appearance on the scene coincided with Belgium's decision to tell its story to the world. Rinehart was the vehicle it chose. She was handed off to the army.

As 1915 dawned, coverage of the war was in a curious phase of transition, just beginning to move out of what correspondents called the "dark ages." All the belligerents had belatedly concluded that publicity was as valuable a resource of war as weapons and ammunition and therefore required careful management. Germany came first to that realization the previous fall and began to conduct official war tours for neutral journalists. *Saturday Evening Post* writer Irvin Cobb landed on one such tour. These carefully orchestrated excursions showed reporters the war from the German point of view. Generals explained their actions and refuted Allied propaganda. Glimpses of army life humanized German soldiers, who were being vilified in the Allied press. In fact, the amount and success of such publicity, particularly in the United States, the major neutral power, motivated Britain and

France to follow Germany's lead. At the start of 1915, the Allied governments slowly began to set aside their policy of silence and allow limited access to select correspondents. Rinehart arrived on the scene at the front edge of that movement.

Rinehart in the Trenches

Belgian army headquarters prepared a map to show Rinehart the disposition of troops on its front, which stretched along a railroad embankment between Nieuport and Dixmude. In her best fictional style Rinehart dramatized her briefing by a Belgian officer: "Twilight had fallen by that time. It had commenced to rain. I could see through the window heavy drops that stirred the green surface of the moat at one side of the old building. On the wall hung the advertisement of an American harvester, a reminder of more peaceful days. The beating of the rain kept time to the story Captain F—— told that night, bending over the map and tracing his country's ruin with his forefinger."

The captain described for Rinehart the Battle of Yser, fought the previous October, in which Belgium's diminutive army, with French and British assistance, finally halted the German advance by flooding the country's fertile lowlands with seawater. Two weeks of ferocious attacks and counterattacks, and more than one hundred thousand casualties, had left Belgium in possession of a narrow strip of land along its northwestern coast, about 5 percent of its territory, and made army commander King Albert a national hero. Fighting then moved south on the Yser River to the city of Ypres. To this point in the war, no reporter had received so detailed an explanation of the status of fighting in Belgium. To Rinehart it offered a picture of how valiantly tiny Belgium had persevered against the German invasion and how worthy it was of American sympathy and support.

The captain read to Rinehart passages of a diary taken from a dead German officer in which he told of the incessant fight to cross the Yser, suffering in the cold and rain, and the fearful loss of life. The brief entry for October 27 ended in the middle of a sentence, the moment he died. Rinehart reproduced long passages from the diary in one of her articles. Sometimes the raw facts of war carried more pathos than well-wrought narrative.

Armed with a clear battle map understanding of where things stood in the Belgian fighting, Rinehart and the captain began their approach to the trenches. In pitch darkness, in a driving rain, along shell-pocked muddy roads, a car carried America's most famous mystery writer parallel to the Belgian front line. After a courtesy visit to the local commander and a meal of biscuits and bully beef, they headed for the trenches. Here the railroad embankment, rising only shoulder high, served as the barricade. German snipers and artillery batteries lay in the darkness a few hundred yards away. In moonlight Rinehart's group walked behind the trenches for a mile, frequently stopped by nervous sentries. Red flashes of artillery fire marked the horizon in the direction of Dixmude.

From a shielded position in the trench, she gazed toward the German trenches, across the lagoon of floodwater the Belgians had let in from the sea. It shimmered silver with moonlight. "It is beautiful," Rinehart remarked to her officer escort. He replied: "But it is full of the dead. They are taken out whenever it is possible; but it is not often possible."

Rinehart built tension in her reporting by juxtaposing images of beauty and horror. She described a German magnesium flare lighting no-man's-land as "beautiful, silent, and horrible," and she contrasted the conditions of life in the trenches with the attractiveness of the landscape. Her "beautiful" lagoon gave off a horrible stench that was "best forgotten." Rinehart observed, "Any lingering belief I may have had in the grandeur and glory of war died that night beside that silver lake—died of an odour, and will never live again." Such observations appear throughout Rinehart's articles, as harsh reality continued to harden her perceptions of war.

Toward dawn she made it back to her hotel, stripped off her muddy shoes and wet clothing, then wrote notes on the day. Every detail and impression got recorded, like a travelogue of her personal adventure: driving on the nighttime roads without headlights, the line of somber soldiers getting rotated out, the stories told by her escorts, an explanation about the work of spies, a stop at a mass grave of fallen soldiers. These notes became the fodder for her articles that would be written when she returned home. In fact, some articles began with "From my journal," and reproduced her notes verbatim, to capture the immediacy and rawness of the experience, without having to explain or interpret. "This is a narrative of personal experience," Rinehart wrote. "It makes no pretensions except to truth. It is pure reporting, a series of pictures, many of them disconnected, but all authentic."

Hospital visits in the morning and trench visits at night became her daily schedule. A nurse told her of treating one thousand wounded in one night, until her uniform became blood soaked. In the trenches Rinehart stumbled over muddy ground pocked with shell holes filled with foul water, tripping over the telephone and telegraph lines that ran to the rear, tearing her clothes on barbed wire, in the numbing cold and wet, all the while exposed to the danger of snipers and errant shellfire. Occasionally, cannon fire became too lively, forcing her to turn back.

The Belgians made certain to show her a town that had been blasted to ruins, evidence of Germany's crimes against their country. Churches always took a beating because their steeples were used for observation. Their nearby graveyards showed the ghastly effect of bombardments: graves blown open, caskets and skeletons exposed. Rinehart nearly fell into an open grave one night. To her horror she developed a case of head lice, some of the infamous vermin that so bedeviled the men in the trenches. She begged some disinfectant from a hospital and for days after radiated an antiseptic smell.

In one of her articles she confessed that it "becomes a little wearying, sometimes, this constant cry of horrors." It was less a personal lament than a realization of the impact on her readers and an acknowledgment of the role being thrust upon neutral America—"the ever-recurring demands on America's pocketbook for supplies, for dressings, for money to buy the thousands of things that are needed."

whole again. It is all so tragic &
so useless.

Coming back to the hotel
we learn that 48 bombs were
dropped on us last night.
That the destruction is great.
That two women were killed
outright & many wounded. This
is not war. It is intimidation.
To terrorize, to demoralize the
morale of a people, women &
children. Helpless non-combatants
are killed.

Sitting in almost complete
darkness, an ~~noble~~ officer, a member
of the Belgian nobility, told some of
the things he had seen. He had
picked up a girl's hand by a
roadside. A little girl running
from terrible injuries had held up—

9. A page from Mary Robert Rinehart's war notebook, in which she
recorded that forty-eight bombs had fallen on Calais the previous night,
killing two women: "This is not war. It is intimidation. To terrorize, to
demoralize, the morale of a people, innocent children, helpless non-
combatants are killed." Mary Roberts Rinehart Papers, 1831–1970,
SC.1958.03, Archives & Special Collections, University of
Pittsburgh Library System.

In February 1915 a small group of British correspondents was granted a much-coveted opportunity to visit the Belgian front. They would be permitted only a twenty-four-hour stay but would get to see the frontline trenches. It was a dream come true for war reporters at this stage of the war. Since there had not yet been any sanctioned visits to the front, they would get an exclusive eyewitness glimpse of the war. Imagine their surprise when they arrived at the front and discovered a middle-aged, female, American writer of mystery fiction already on the scene. "How long have you been up here?" an incredulous Ward Price of the *London Times* asked Rinehart. "Three weeks," she replied cheerily.

Admittedly, hosting groups of journalists was a novel experience for the Belgian officers serving as guides. That may explain why they chose to give these reporters the most raw and dangerous exposure to the fighting, a nighttime stroll into no-man's-land, the free-fire kill zone between the opposing trenches. The five British correspondents, Rinehart, and their officer guides stepped carefully over fascines, bundles of sticks that provided a narrow, slippery path through the mud of the frontline trenches. Soldiers whispered to them that it was quiet now but fighting had been heavy in recent days.

They paused where the trench seemed to end, rising up to near ground level. Here only one thousand feet of flooded lowland separated the opposing trenches. Moonlight glinting off the water outlined the silhouette of a ruined church steeple halfway out. That was their objective. In it a Capuchin monk–turned–soldier served as a lone observer.

They had to pass single file from the protection of the trench across exposed ground to reach the church steeple outpost. If a flare goes up, freeze, an officer cautioned, or they will fire at you. The correspondents went first, exposing themselves to the view of the enemy. When Rinehart's turn came, she experienced a moment of panic. Additional fascines extended a narrow, muddy path through the flooded terrain. Moonlight painted the water with a beautiful silvery sheen, but she knew that it was a pond of corpses.

This was rather more of the war than she had expected. One fleeting moment of sanity assaulted her: thoughts of her family and that she had no business courting such danger. But she had come to the war to feed her sense of adventure and test her nerve, and this was the supreme test. Besides, the men in her group had all started off already, so she could not show fear. At one point she fell and nearly slipped into the foul water. Farther along, the Germans sent up a parachute flare that etched the whole eerie landscape in harsh, flickering light. The correspondents froze until it ended, then went on.

At the ruined church steeple the soldier-priest descended from the tower on a rope ladder to greet them in whispers. He used a telephone to serve as an artillery spotter and give alerts of raids, he explained. He showed them a cross-marked grave where he had buried several German soldiers. Just six hundred feet away, the German trenches stood in clear outline. The crackling of rifle fire sounded farther down the line, sharp against the continuous rumble of the big guns. Though none of the correspondents spoke it, it seemed obvious to all that the priest's days were numbered. One day German artillery would find its mark on his position, or a raid would overwhelm him. But he exhibited the same fatalistic courage as all the other Belgian soldiers Rinehart met.

Rinehart returned to her car and covered many more miles that night, visiting other sections of the front. Though a bitter cold wind blew, a "glow of exultation" kept her warm. This would prove to be the most frightening and exhilarating experience of her time in the war zone: "I had been to the front. I had been far beyond the front, indeed, and I had seen such a picture of war and its desolation there in the center of No Man's Land as perhaps no one not connected with an army had seen before; such a picture as would live in my mind forever."

King, Queens, Generals, and Pawns

It's not clear what pieces fell into place behind the scenes to orchestrate the rest of Rinehart's extraordinary war excursion. But the catalyst seems to have been the interview she managed to get with Belgium's King Albert, the first interview he granted during the war. It served as a vehicle for the king to speak to America about Germany's violation of Belgian neutrality, the destruction of Belgian cities, the question of German atrocities, and his esteem for President Wilson. The king had heard about Rinehart's foray into no-man's-land, and doubtless that opened the door for this interview. Rinehart would later interview the Bavarian-born Belgian queen Elizabeth.

The interview with the king was the first of her articles to appear in the *Saturday Evening Post*, the only one published while she was still in Europe. Following that interview Rinehart was unexpectedly summoned to England to interview Queen Mary and Winston Churchill, First Lord of the Admiralty. Armed with letters of introduction to British and French commanders, she then returned to the Continent to visit the French and British lines.

Rinehart would spend several weeks visiting the French and British armies. These visits included none of the nerve-wracking trench tours from her time with the Belgians, but they filled out the picture of the Allied efforts. She met General John French, commander in chief of the British Expeditionary Force. She lunched with the French commander General Ferdinand Foch, who questioned her about U.S. public opinion of the war, the very thing he expected Rinehart's articles might influence. Foch gave her a map of the western front, marked with places for her to visit.

It's hard to exaggerate just how extraordinary and unique was the level of access given to Mary Roberts Rinehart. Correspondents were still being arrested if they got near the front. A few authorized journalists, on brief conducted tours, received a quick glance at the workings of the war. But clearly, the Allies were convinced that they had struggled on in silence long enough. Rinehart appeared on the scene at the very moment of changing policy. The Belgian Red Cross had opened the door, but Rinehart's fame and connection to the influential the *Saturday Evening Post* convinced wary governments to select her to tell the United States about their heroic struggle.

And she did just that by providing the first woman's perspective on the fighting war on the western front. Rinehart drama-tized her experiences in the war zone in eleven *Post* articles that were collected into a hastily published book, *Kings, Queens, and Pawns: An American Woman at the Front*. She was not a trained military observer, she confessed to readers, but "to the reports of trained men must be added a bit here and there from these untrained observers, who without military knowledge, igno-rant of the real meaning of much that they saw, have been able to grasp only part of the human significance of the great trag-edy of Europe."

4

Novelist Journalists

Here we were, then, actually and literally in the front lines!
The knowledge made one's heart tick a little.

—EDITH WHARTON, "In Lorraine and the Vosges,"
Scribner's Magazine, October 1915

On July 30, 1914, four days before France entered World War I, American expatriate novelist Edith Wharton stood inside the cathedral in Chartres at the very moment when the sun emerged from behind a bank of thunderclouds. In one enchanting moment sunlight splashed through the famous stained glass window and painted the interior with prismed colors. "All that a great cathedral can be, all the meanings it can express, all the tranquilizing power it can breathe upon the soul, all the richness of detail it can fuse into a large utterance of strength and beauty, the cathedral of Chartres gave us in that perfect hour," she observed. In her first war article for *Scribner's Magazine* she used that ethereal moment as the dividing line between the well-ordered world of the past and the cataclysm of war. That article also marked her temporary hiatus from fiction writing to take on the role of journalist through sanctioned visits to the front.

The fifty-two-year-old Wharton, who enjoyed an international literary reputation, had been living in Paris for seven years. On her return from Chartres, "thundery" rumors of war quickly exploded to reality with the announcement of general mobilization. That night she watched from a restaurant window as the first flood of young men trudged through the streets to join their military units. The restaurant band played unceasingly "La Marseillaise" and the British and Russian national anthems. Outside, crowds gathered to sing patriotic songs. This "sudden flaming up of national character," as Wharton would call the stoic commitment to sacrifice, forged all segments of society behind one clear purpose of confronting an invader.

Wharton had been working on her next novel, tentatively titled *Literature*, but that project suddenly seemed inconsequential. It would never be finished. She cabled her publisher Charles Scribner: "Detained in Paris. Extraordinary sights. Do you want impressions?" The company Charles Scribner's Sons included both her book publisher and *Scribner's Magazine*, a successful monthly that reached some two hundred thousand readers. Wharton was one of its leading writers. Scribner absolutely did want her impressions, but his cable requesting them got lost in the chaos. Six months would pass before she captured her war impressions.

As a true citizen of her adopted homeland, Wharton quickly devoted herself to numerous wartime charity projects. She created a sewing workroom for unemployed women. When Belgian refugees flooded the city, she helped establish the American Hostels for Refugees and the Children of Flanders Rescue Committee. And she worked tirelessly to raise funds for these projects.

When Wharton finally put her wartime impressions on paper in February 1915, she titled the article "The Look of Paris." It cameoed moments from the first six months of the war that defined the French mood and character. She recalled "the morning when our butcher's boy brought the news that the first captured German flags had been hung out on the balcony at the Ministry of War." Wharton hurried to the ministry, more to see the crowd than the flags. Citizens of every rank gathered, family groups and mothers holding up young boys, to view the captured banners from the first modest successes in Alsace. "There was hardly a man or woman of that crowd," she noted, "who had not a soldier at the front and there before them hung the enemy's first flag. . . .

It symbolized all they most abhorred in the whole abhorrent job that lay ahead of them; it symbolized also their finest ardour and their noblest hate. . . . And there they stood and looked at it, not dully or uncomprehendingly, but consciously, advisedly, and in silence; as if already foreseeing all it would cost to keep that flag and add to it others like it; foreseeing the cost and accepting it."

After the flags came the wounded. "Day by day the limping figures grow more numerous on the pavement, the pale bandaged heads more frequent in passing carriages," she wrote. Wharton took the expression on the face of the wounded as her final image of the article: "They are calm, meditative, strangely purified and matured. It is as though their great experience had purged them of pettiness, meanness and frivolity, burning them down to the bare bones of character, the fundamental substance of the soul, and shaping that substance into something so strong and finely tempered."

The article was a paean to the French character forged in those first months of the war. An articulate observer had given American readers a front-row seat on the exact moment when her beloved France tipped from peace to war.

When Wharton mailed "The Look of Paris" to *Scribner's Magazine* on February 20, it must have already felt like an anachronism, a too-precious moment trapped in amber. At the start of her article she enthused about sunlight in Chartres Cathedral and observed that "the Seine trembled with the blue-pink lustre of an early Monet." By the end Paris overflowed with makeshift hospitals, and limping figures of the wounded haunted the city. Dozens of battles had already written a harsh new chapter in this conflict that required a different style of writing.

By February, Wharton had already gained fame for her work with war charities and her fund-raising efforts. In several American cities Edith Wharton Committees collected money and supplies. The French Red Cross asked her to take on one more cause. Would she visit some of the hospitals near the front in the Argonne and inform the American public about their needs? "Common prudence should have made me refuse to beg for more money,"

Wharton noted in her autobiography, *A Backward Glance* (1933), "but in those days it never occurred to anyone to evade a request of that kind."

As happened with Mary Roberts Rinehart, Wharton's initial rationale for venturing into the war zone, to publicize the work of the Red Cross, transformed into a thorough exploration of the front. For a brief period in early 1915, Wharton's travels in the war zone overlapped those of Rinehart. Wharton set out for her first visit to the front at the end of February, at just about the same time Rinehart returned from England to the Continent to finish her war adventure with visits to British and French troops. Allied governments had clearly identified both women as having the stature and the sympathies to plead their case in the neutral United States. Thus, two of America's most popular novelists gained more privileged access than any journalist to that point in the war.

Throughout 1915 their war narratives played out in the large-circulation *Saturday Evening Post* and *Scribner's Magazine*, providing the first accounts that so thoroughly mapped the landscape of the war. From the familiar cities of London and Paris, through every intermediate point, to the front lines, they captured the people caught in the tragedy. They suffered innumerable dangers, came under enemy fire, witnessed combat, interviewed royalty and generals, and made it to the most advanced frontline trenches. Their mix of emotions—shock, awe, excitement, compassion, horror, and glory—so perfectly reflected the response of an innocent observer learning about the war, a response that mirrored that of their readers. In the process these two novelists helped to shape American public opinion at this critical juncture in the conflict. The telling of their war experiences, in two of America's premier magazines, also revealed to other female journalists that being a woman was no bar to reporting the biggest war in history.

A semblance of normalcy had returned to Paris by the time Wharton set out on her first war excursion to the Argonne on February 28, 1915. Traveling due east, in a car packed with medical supplies, Wharton and her friend Walter Berry cut a cross section through the war zone, from the familiar world of Paris to that otherworldly region devastated by fighting and inhabited by vast armies.

Twenty miles out of the city, she encountered the first signs of war in abandoned farms and depopulated villages. Soon military and Red Cross vehicles appeared on the road, and sentries stopped their car at every bridge and rail crossing. The first full sense that she had entered the war zone came when she descended a hill outside Montmirail and drove into the unbroken flow of military traffic: "First the infantry and artillery, the sappers and miners, the endless trains of guns and ammunition, then the long lines of grey supply-wagons, and finally the stretcher-bearers following the Red Cross ambulances. All the story of a day's warfare was written in the spectacle of that endless silent flow to the front."

Army headquarters in Châlons seemed the very nerve center of the war. It buzzed with busses, cavalry units, the constant coming and going of messengers, orderlies hurrying about, Red Cross ambulances, troops on the move, and "much-decorated military personages in luxurious motors." Here, too, Wharton found thousands of the poor wretches known as *éclopés*, "the unwounded but battered, shattered, frost-bitten, deafened and half-paralyzed wreckage of the awful struggle."

Sixty miles from Paris, she encountered a desolate landscape of villages, utterly destroyed during the fighting the previous September. No one any longer remembered the names of some of the empty villages. War had wiped them from existence. Wharton felt haunted by the destruction of the French way of life and the traumatized lives of the residents, all the "separate terrors, anguishes, uprootings and rendings apart involved in the destruction of the obscurest of human conditions."

German artillery had pounded to ruins the hill town of Clermont-en-Argonne, except for one small cluster of houses. What had once been a hospice for old men now doubled as a battlefield hospital. There Sister Gabrielle Rosnet and her nuns

10. Expatriate novelist Edith Wharton at the front with two French officers. The French army took Wharton on several war tours in 1915, which resulted in a series of articles and a book that helped to publicize the French war effort in the United States. Edith Wharton Collection, Beinecke Rare Book and Manuscript Library, Yale University.

remained to care for the old men and to nurse soldiers wounded on the battlefield.

The world had not yet learned about the many courageous women working at or near the front. Impressed by their courage and devotion to duty, both Wharton and Rinehart rescued some of them from obscurity by weaving them into their narratives like characters in a novel. Wharton introduced Sister Rosnet as "a small round active woman, with a shrewd and ruddy face of the type that looks out calmly from the dark background of certain Flemish pictures." Over lunch Sister Rosnet regaled

Wharton with stories of the invasion: how German officers broke down the door of the hospice and burst in with pistols drawn to confront Rosnet and her nuns. Through the destruction of Clermont, and while battles swirled around the town, the nuns remained to care for the old men and the wounded.

The sounds of battle interrupted Sister Rosnet's stories. The nuns led Wharton to the hospice garden, where the scenic view revealed fighting across the valley: "the feathery drift of French gun-smoke lower down, and, high up, on the wooded crest along the sky, the red lightnings and white puffs of the German artillery." Wharton had just stumbled upon a small piece of the Battle of Vauquois Hill, fighting for an entrenched position taken up by the Germans after their failed thrust to Paris. The German position was nearly impregnable, but that day French troops gained the ridge and occupied part of the town. Although Wharton thought the battle awe-inspiring, Sister Rosnat had already been notified to expect four hundred more wounded.

The valiant work of these nursing nuns marked but one of the many battlefield care stations. A few miles distant Wharton came upon a small village of cottages and stables converted to makeshift infirmaries, every dwelling packed with patients. It was typical of the improvised care for the sick and wounded to be found all along the front. The village church held the worst cases, the severely wounded, plus those stricken with "fever, bronchitis, frost-bite, pleurisy, or some other form of trench-sickness." In the dark interior, lit only with flickering altar candles, a priest waved incense, while the few women remaining in the village ministered to the patients.

Wharton finished her medical mission by driving to Verdun. Fourteen hospitals operated in that half-destroyed, fortified city. All were overcrowded and their arrangements primitive. She was informed that the greatest need was for blankets and underclothes, as the men came from the trenches encrusted with mud. "What I saw there made me feel the urgency of telling my rich and generous compatriots something of the desperate needs of the hospitals in the war-zone," she explained.

Wharton wrote of her Red Cross mission for *Scribner's Magazine*, but it seemed to her that she had only scratched the surface of this drama. She cabled Charles Scribner, proposing a series of articles based on additional visits to the front. Through her network of highly placed friends, she gained unprecedented permission to visit the entire French front that stretched over four hundred miles, from the English Channel to the Swiss border.

Four additional war tours resulted in four articles in *Scribner's* and one in the *Saturday Evening Post*, plus two essays about the spirit of France. They were collected into the book *Fighting France, from Dunkerque to Belfort*, published later in 1915. Critics cannot agree how to categorize Wharton's war articles—reportage, essays, travel articles, memoirs, participatory journalism. She adopted a deeper sense of commitment and urgency on her next visits to the front, more fully embracing her role as war correspondent, more willing to accept inconvenience and hazard to give her perspective on the conflict and "bring home to American readers some of the dreadful realities of war."

When Edith Wharton set off to the Argonne, Mary Roberts Rinehart stood on a cold and rainy quay in the English port of Folkestone, in the middle of the night, staring at two boats about to cross the Channel, one to Boulogne, the other to Calais. She had arranged for a military car to meet her in Calais, to take her on her next war tour. But a security screening officer in the terminal had just informed her that she could travel to Boulogne but not to Calais, which was closed tight to all except military personnel. That was a problem. Arriving in Boulogne would throw off her well-laid and tightly scheduled plans. She would have no way to contact the officer set to receive her in Calais.

Summoning her courage, she boarded the Calais boat and pleaded her case with an officer. He was sympathetic but unmoved. She showed her letter from the French ambassador in London, to no avail. Mentioning that she had just interviewed the queen and Winston Churchill, First Lord of the Admiralty, made no impression. Her pleas for mercy were equally ineffective. When the officer was finally called away, Rinehart snuck into an empty cabin and locked the door. She woke a few hours later in Calais. The trick would have done credit to any war correspondent. Choosing to disobey a strict military order marked a turning point in the mind-set of Mary Roberts Rinehart. She, too, had found a deeper commitment to her assignment.

The military car that met her in Calais arrived directly from the front, covered in mud inside and out, dotted with bullet and shrapnel holes. The mud shield had been torn away, and tattered curtains flapped in the wind. "Even in that region of wrecked cars people turned to look at it," Rinehart noted. Days earlier she had dressed in her best traveling clothes to interview Queen Mary of England. Now she settled into this battered limousine to be driven south to the headquarters of French general Ferdinand Foch.

Part of Rinehart's war adventure was to collect snapshots of the principal personalities. She would devote one article to each of the three royals she interviewed, plus one about General Foch and another about Sir John French, commander in chief of the British Expeditionary Force. The fact that all of these VIPs now opened up to an American journalist was both a testament to the gravity of the war situation in early 1915 and evidence of a new strategy to counter it.

The war had not ended in one climactic battle in the fall of 1914. The opposing armies had not spent themselves within six months, as many had predicted. Instead, fighting had settled into the stasis of opposing trench lines, punctuated by cataclysmic battles. Rinehart's muddy limousine was returning her to the area west of the legendary battlefields of Ypres, which had claimed one hundred thousand casualties the previous fall. Edith Wharton would visit Ypres later in 1915, after the second Battle of Ypres had claimed an additional hundred thousand. For their long-term viability the Allies needed the good graces of the neutral United States. They needed to tell their story.

Using an engaging form of literary, participatory journalism, both Rinehart and Wharton explained to readers in America how to feel about a war that they barely understood. Rinehart reminded readers of French support for the American Revolution and that France was a sister republic: "The French adopted the American belief that liberty is the object of government, and liberty of the individual—that very belief that France is standing for to-day, as opposed to the nationalism of Germany." Both Wharton's article about her Argonne visit and Rinehart's about her visit with General Foch were published in June 1915, only one month after the sinking of the British passenger liner *Lusitania* turned American sympathies sharply against Germany.

Rinehart traveled some twenty miles south to Foch's headquarters in the town of Cassel to see what she could learn about "The Man of Ypres." When she arrived, General Foch was not at his headquarters but at a local church. Thinking there might be a service in progress, Rinehart went to the church but found it empty, except for Foch. "The Commander of the Armies of the North, probably the greatest general the French have in the field to-day, was kneeling there alone," she wrote. "He never knew I had seen him. I left before he did. Now, as I look back, it seems to me that that great general on his knees alone in that little church is typical of the attitude of France to-day towards the war. . . . The enemy is on the soil of France. The French are fighting for their homes, for their children, for their country. And in this great struggle France daily, hourly, on its knees asks for help."

The next day she lunched with General Foch and a dozen of his staff. The fact that the meeting was happening at all marked a sea change in French attitude toward the press. The French army preferred to keep its activities secret, even from its own government. No other reporter had dined with Foch. None had been privy to the insights he would share. None had been asked to satisfy his curiosity about the mood in America. The commander of French armies of the north, hero of the pivotal Battle of the Marne, faced across a table America's most popular crime novelist. It was a telling moment. Although they used a translator, Foch kept his gaze fixed squarely on Rinehart as he began with a barrage of questions. Rinehart clarified the situation for her readers: "I did not interview General Foch. General Foch interviewed me."

How many Germans lived in America? he wanted to know. How many French? How was America affected by the war? How much did America know about the efforts of the French army? What did America think would be the outcome of the war? Did the press endeavor to be neutral in its reporting?

The American press was not neutral, Rinehart conceded. "Sooner or later they become partisan. It is difficult not to. In this war, one must take sides." When she finished answering his other questions as best she could, the general took his turn at information sharing. He led her to his office and opened his map book from the Battle of Yser the previous October, when France and Britain supported Belgian troops in holding off fierce German attacks. His day-by-day charts of the fighting were bound in a great book. Each day had a fresh page, with the German army marked in black and the French in red. Earlier that month, in Belgium, Rinehart had walked the first-line trenches on that battle-front, even ventured into no-man's-land. But now she could relive the battle itself, page after page watch the black line advancing "like waves in the sea" and the blue of the British waver against overwhelming numbers, while the red line of the French advanced to reinforce the British.

Foch shut the book and sat for a long moment with his head bent, "as though in living over again that fearful time some of its horror had come back to him." Then he added, "I paced the floor and watched the clock." A novelist like Rinehart could distill the emotion from this exclusive glimpse into the character of the man who held the fate of France in his hands. During their luncheon conversation Foch had been surprised how little America knew about the efforts of the French army. It pleased him that through Rinehart "America is to know something of [its] spirit, of the invincible spirit and resolution of the French to fight in the cause of humanity and justice."

Mapping the Landscape of the War

The war articles of Edith Wharton and Mary Roberts Rinehart ran April through November 1915. Such adept observers of the human condition, and so capable of dramatizing it, these novelists became travelers in the war. Their articles have the feel of travel narratives. Sections were prefaced with "From my journal" or carried the location and date. They featured the places they visited, things they saw, people they met, and their experiences along the way. They shared what it was like to travel by ship, train, and automobile in a time of war as well as their lodgings and meals. Since neither of them had experience with war, they came to their adventure as naively as any of their readers.

The fact that they were often the first correspondent to be somewhere or to do something added uniqueness to their reporting. And each would often point out that she was the only woman to visit an area or have such an experience. When Wharton visited some of the hospitals outside Verdun, she mentioned that no women nurses worked in any of those facilities. Rinehart was the only woman aboard the ship crossing the English Channel to France. She was the only woman in a Dunkirk hotel dining room full of officers when the city came under a bombing attack.

They were women in a dangerous and almost exclusively male world. But they were not just any women. They were not hardscrabble newspaperwomen, toughened by the daily grind of covering the grittier stories of the day—not war nurses devoted to tedium and hardship or female ambulance drivers, fatalistic about life near the front. Mary Roberts Rinehart and Edith Wharton were monied, cultured, famous, and articulate reporters of the human condition. They could enthuse about a Gothic cathedral, interview royalty, or slog through a frontline trench. To see them wallow through muddy battlefields or face the dangers of snipers and errant artillery fire was more of a shock to the reader's sensibilities.

For years Edith Wharton published fiction about high society and travel pieces describing Europe's charms and cultural heritage. Now she drew an eyewitness picture of its destruction. Rinehart wrestled with her fears of walking into no-man's-land as barbed wire tore at her clothes, and she stepped gingerly through flood waters polluted with corpses. These were jarring images that demonstrated their pluck and challenged conventions of the period.

The war terrain included not just the front but everything that separated it from the capital cities of Paris and London: the dangerous English Channel, ports, train stations, stifling security and spy mania, roads crowded with war traffic, suspicious sentries, ruined towns, staging areas, army headquarters, wounded soldiers and the crude clinics that cared for them. Both writers gave cameos of the people who by chance or choice found themselves in the war zone, including many women. Along with their novelist guides, readers became immersed in the ghastly, confused world of the war.

France Starts War Tours

By the summer of 1915, as more journalists and private individuals visited France to cover the war or just to see it, France developed procedures for giving war tours. They were learning how to package the war. When the news team from the *New York Times*, illustrator Walter Hale and novelist-turned-reporter Owen Johnson, arrived in Paris that summer, they had to abandon plans to drive to the front on their own. There were no more freelance excursions, as there had been early in the war, only conducted tours. The handling of war correspondents had become "regulated, systemized, and standardized," Hale lamented. Journalists arranged a visit to the front by presenting their credentials at a small office in the Ministry of Foreign Affairs and waiting impatiently for four to six weeks.

When Hale and Johnson finally got their war tour, it felt as choreographed from start to finish as a summer travel excursion. Hale complained: "The precise duration of the trip, the precise route to be taken, the precise place at which each meal is to be eaten, the precise room in the precise hotel in which each night is to be spent, the precise General to be met and trench to be visited, are all inexorably fixed in the schedule of the trip."

While Hale, Johnson, and other journalists struggled to catch a glimpse of the front on an official press tour, Edith Wharton was being chauffeured along the four-hundred-plus miles of the battle line. In tours during May and August 1915, she chronicled trips to the regions of Alsace and Lorraine. These provinces along France's eastern border had been ceded to Germany in 1871, after its victory in the Franco-Prussian War. In the opening days of World War I, France recovered some ground in the region, but 1915 brought a brutal back-and-forth struggle that eventually became an entrenched standoff.

Wharton was pleased and flattered to be given an exclusive glimpse of this region. At the start of her article "In Lorraine and the Vosges," she mentioned that "this corner of old-new France has hitherto been inaccessible—even to highly placed French officials: and there was a special sense of excitement in taking the road that led to it." As she traveled along the route of the invasion, she saw signs of life returning to the ruined towns: roads and buildings being repaired, children playing in the villages, women planting crops.

At the town of Gerbéviller, Wharton was horrified by the ruined houses, a reaction often repeated on her other war tours. The wanton destruction wrought on civilian lives had emerged as a major theme of war reporting, and Wharton brought out her most colorful prose for the occasion: "Her ruins seem to have been simultaneously vomited up from the depths and hurled down from the skies, as though she had perished in some monstrous clash of earthquake and tornado."

Like so many of the towns that suffered the invasion, Gerbéviller had its own courageous nun, Sister Julie, who had stood between the townspeople and the fury of the Germans and now championed the town's revival. Wharton's reporting immortalized the heroic work of numerous nuns, in nursing and as the sustaining heart and soul of ruined communities. Included on many of the French war tours, Sister Julie would become an iconic figure of French strength and renewal.

After lunch with a general, Wharton reached the front lines at a hilltop fortress overlooking the river town of Mousson. Her officer guides did not always appreciate the danger to which they exposed their famous guest. An officer pointed out enemy positions on the surrounding slopes. The hazards of such frontline sightseeing were brought home moments later when a sniper's bullet struck a tree only a few yards away. Although they had not been exposed, the sniper had fired at the location of their voices. Do not go any farther, soldiers cautioned, but the obliging officer led Wharton to the edge of the cliff, where soldiers with machine guns kept watch at peepholes.

"Do you want to look down?" one sentinel asked. His lookout projected over the cliff. Through an observation hole, Wharton peered down along the ravine. Halfway down, she caught sight of a gray uniform in a dead heap. "He's been there for days," the sentinel explained. "They can't fetch him away." Despite her access, Wharton had been largely shielded from the fighting. This was the first dead enemy soldier she had seen, and it evoked no emotional response, just another occasion to praise the French character: "On the far side of the dividing line were men who had made the war, and on the near side the men who had been made by it."

By the time of Wharton's August war trip, the French had gained more experience in conducting press tours. The tours could be as arduous and dangerous as before, but they now included a fuller itinerary of stops to educate and entertain. At Reims, which the French had taken to calling the "city of the desecrated cathedral," Wharton could wax eloquent about how fire caused by German shelling had burnished color onto the walls of the famous fourteenth-century cathedral: "The whole blunted, bruised surface recalls the metallic tints, the peacock-and-pigeon iridescences, the incredible mingling of red, blue, umber and yellow of the rock along the Gulf of Aegina." Later on the itinerary would come a tour of a vast subterranean wine cellar and a display of military equestrian riding.

The small Alsatian town of Thann, on the eastern slopes of the Vosges mountains, stood on the front lines, under the shadow of German guns. The town had been German for the past forty years, since the Franco-Prussian War. The recapture of Alsatian territory was a mark of pride for the French. German signs still named the streets, but shop owners had begun to paint over their German-language signs. From there Wharton passed through other mountain villages that served as a perfect showcase for French progress in the war. They represented newly won territory and liberation of the population from German control. A choir of schoolgirls sang "La Marseillaise" for the American writer.

If Wharton's fifty-two-year-old body had not yet wearied of the tour, August 16 tested its limits. "Up and up into the mountains!" she wrote in her journal. Wharton's party drove up wooded slopes as far as possible and then mounted mules to continue to climb the steep hills that here marked the front line. They occasionally dismounted to see a camp or from a lookout point view the zigzag earthworks that scarred the opposing slopes. When they passed an artillery battery in action, Wharton described the four phases of sound: "the sharp bang from the cannon, the long furious howl overhead, the dispersed and spreading noise of the shell's explosion, and then the roll of its reverberation from cliff to cliff."

After a long and tiring day, a deluge drove them off the mountain that night, forcing them to descend on mules over treacherous mountain trails washed in rivers of mud. They had to squeeze carefully past soldiers climbing in the opposite direction to take their turn defending the mountaintop positions, men "who had orders to hold out to the death rather than let their fraction of that front be broken." The trip had been an exciting mix of adventure, danger, and physical challenge, just the sort of thing to burnish the reputation of a literary novelist war correspondent.

The war reporting of novelists must be viewed within the context of the propaganda efforts of the belligerent countries. Britain,

France, Germany, and Austria-Hungary moved quickly to mobilize popular writers for propaganda purposes at the start of the war. Austria created its War Press Bureau on the first day of the war. In the first month Germany began taking journalists from neutral America on visits to the front. Britain's effort began on September 2, 1914, when its War Propaganda Bureau convened a meeting of twenty-five leading authors, including J. M. Barrie, Arnold Bennett, G. K. Chesterton, Arthur Conan Doyle, Thomas Hardy, and John Masefield. The Authors' Declaration, signed by most of the attendees, justified the righteousness of British entry into the war, the sanctity of Belgian neutrality, and the barbarism of the German invader. Germany quickly countered with its own declaration by an even larger group of its artists, authors, and scientists who signed the Manifesto of the Ninety-Three, which denied any German wrongdoing in Belgium.

As the war progressed, other opinion makers were recruited for the cause, including academics, politicians, clergy, and editors, from both the warring and neutral countries, in particular the United States. By selecting largely sympathetic individuals, giving them controlled access to information and the war zone, and censoring their material when possible, countries could largely shape the message to support their cause.

British novelists Arnold Bennett and Rudyard Kipling both visited the front in mid-1915, covering some of the same ground as Wharton. Bennett's wartime travelogue reads much like Wharton's. Though horrified by what he saw at the front, Bennett encouraged men to join the British Army. Kipling's anger over the suffering of Belgian refugees and the horror he saw of trench life caused him to harshly criticize Germany for its uncivilized brand of total war that targeted civilians and cultural treasures. He reserved some of his vitriol for neutral nations that refused to help save civilization. Edith Wharton's war reporting, full of grand nationalism and effusions on French character, mirrored the tone of these other sympathetic writers by glorifying and justifying the Allied cause.

Mary Roberts Rinehart, on the other hand, brought a more

empathetic, human touch to her reporting, proving herself more capable of thinking outside narrow nationalistic interpretations. Although she was sympathetic to the Allied cause, she did not filter every observation through that lens. When she saw a young Belgian soldier die from shock and loss of blood from an amputation, she observed that he was "only a pawn in the great chess game of emperors." She reacted sympathetically to captured diaries and letters from dead German soldiers. While in the trenches near Ypres, she suddenly found them "unspeakably loathsome and hideous. . . . What a mockery, this business of killing men." The horrors of the trenches made her confess that "any lingering belief I may have had in the grandeur and glory of war died that night."

In this sense Rinehart foreshadowed the realism emerging in war reporting. The October 1915 issue of *Scribner's* that carried Wharton's "In Lorraine and the Vosges" also ran an article by E. Alexander Powell, "On the British Battle Line," which gave a graphic account of shellfire, shrapnel wounds, and gas attacks, including one injured man waiting his turn outside an overflowing operating room. "I hope that man is not married," Powell observed, "because he no longer has a face. What a few hours before had been the honest countenance of an English lad was now a horrid welter of blood and splintered bone and mangled flesh." Powell gave one of the first unflinching views of war without heroism or idealism.

Finding Women at the Front

Women journalists had already highlighted the suffering and sacrifice of women in the war, but they also drew attention to the women who worked heroically under the most trying and dangerous conditions at or near the front lines. Corra Harris had found her Joan of Arc in Madame Jeanne Macherez, the savior of Soissons. Wharton highlighted the work of Sister Gabrielle Rosnet, who stood up to the German invaders to protect her hospice, then cared for the wounded within sight of the fighting. But it was Rinehart who gave the fullest accounting of several courageous British women who worked under hazardous conditions. By detailing how she met them and her visits to their house at the front line, Rinehart developed their characters as fully and dramatically as those in a well-crafted novel.

The episode began one cold and stormy night at a British naval aviation field near Ypres. As Rinehart was enjoying a cup of tea with officers, a "well-known English novelist" stopped by because her auto had broken down. She ran a soup kitchen at a rail station a few miles behind the front. This came as a bit of a revelation to Rinehart. Nurses worked at hospitals and aid stations miles behind the lines, but the role of women near the front lines had received little mention in the press.

Rinehart did not name the English novelist, but it was Sarah Broom Macnaughtan, a world traveler, suffrage supporter, and aid volunteer in this and previous wars. In response to Rinehart's questioning, she explained how she fed wounded soldiers while they were being evacuated on hospital trains. But this surprise discovery of women at the front had only begun. No sooner had Macnaughtan finished her story than two other women dropped by unexpectedly. Their car had gotten stuck in the mud, and they wanted to borrow a military vehicle.

Their military-style attire surprised Rinehart: khaki-colored leather coats, riding breeches with puttees, flannel shirts, and knit caps. They were known to the officers for their work assisting wounded in the trenches. Again, the women went unnamed in Rinehart's article, but they were Mairi Chisholm and Elsie Knocker, English aristocrats who had been working with the wounded on the Belgian front since the previous September.

It took considerable cajoling from the officers to learn why the two women were out on such a bitterly cold night. They finally held open their coats to reveal the gleaming star of the Order of Leopold pinned to their shirts. That very afternoon King Albert of Belgium had decorated them for bravery. They had not been more forthcoming about the honor because they knew that the British Army did not officially approve of their work or of any woman's presence at the front.

Rinehart knew a good story when it fell into her lap. When the women invited her to dinner that night, she quickly accepted, despite their warning that the Germans regularly shelled their village. The women left, and Rinehart set off later with some officers for the nine-mile drive. The women lived in a ruined house right on the front line, in a town that had changed hands several times and was always in the thick of the fighting. "They go right into the trenches and take care of the wounded until the ambulances can come up at night," an officer explained to Rinehart.

Rinehart's drive to visit the women in the village of Pervyie, Belgium, illustrates the hardships and risk she undertook for her war articles. As she explained to her readers, she was often frightened or terrified, but "as happened many times during those eventful weeks at the front, my pride refused to allow me to turn back."

Rinehart and a couple officers set off in darkness, in rain. Fog shrouded the muddy roads, slowing progress. Three miles from their destination, but only one mile from the German lines, they had to douse their headlights. Progress became slower and more precarious, as they dodged shell craters and turned off frequently to make way for teams of horses dragging artillery to new positions on the line. One such turnoff landed them in a ditch. Even twenty volunteers from the passing troops could not dislodge the auto.

At this point in the road, only a railroad embankment separated them from the German lines. The enemy regularly lit the night with magnesium parachute flares that revealed "the entire landscape spread out like a map—ditches full of water, sodden fields, shell holes in the roads which had become lakes." They were still miles from their destination when the car made a sickening slide off the road and became hopelessly mired. Rinehart had dressed for tea, complete with high heels. She stepped from the car and sank knee-deep in mud.

Rinehart was "limping, drenched, irritable," when they finally reached the town and found the women's house. It had no roof, and a sidewall and corner had been blasted away. Boards covered what had once been windows. Their dwelling was furnished with cast-off and broken furniture, including a damaged piano. The two women had prepared a meal of mutton, and a few officers had wandered in from the trenches for good food and fellowship. The occasional boom of German artillery or the crack of rifle fire from the trenches went unremarked. An officer gave an impromptu piano concert. "No one seemed to consider the circumstances extraordinary," Rinehart observed. "I had an idea that these people would keep on eating and discussing English politics quite calmly in the event of a German charge."

Rinehart's group had set as their departure deadline 11:00 p.m., when the Germans punctually began shelling the town. Good fellowship had brightened the occasion, but as the deadline approached, Rinehart became chilled and aware of her painfully swollen feet. Suddenly, the whole situation seemed incredibly ghastly and unreal to her that the noise at the foot of the street was really guns; that I should be there; that these two young women should live there day and night in the midst of such horrors. For the whole town is a graveyard. Bodies in numbers have been buried in shell-holes and hastily covered, or float in the stagnant water of the canal. Every heavy rain uncovers shallow graves in the fields, allowing a dead arm, part of a rotting trunk, to show."

Rinehart often injected an unflinching portrayal of the grittiness and gruesomeness of what she saw, something that Wharton rarely did. In part this is explained by the fact that Wharton was on official war tours, with sanctioned itineraries, whereas Rinehart, with the blessing of various officials and generals, had more freedom to pursue news-gathering opportunities that presented themselves.

Rinehart returned to the United States in March 1915 and commenced writing weekly articles for the *Saturday Evening Post* from her detailed journals. They were collected into a book later that year. While expatriate Wharton wrote as an adopted citizen of France, Rinehart branded herself an outsider. "I was an intruder, gazing at the grief of a nation," she explained. Reviewers marveled at all Rinehart had accomplished: enduring a bombing raid in Dunkirk, interviewing royalty, working with Red Cross nurses, walking through no-man's-land, coming under artillery fire, gauging the views of soldiers and civilians. And as one reviewer suggested, "Through all the horror of it, she expressed her woman's sympathy for the boys on both sides."

The *New York Times* review of Wharton's book of collected war articles, *Fighting France, from Dunkerque to Belfort*, listed some of her experiences but gave most praise to her writing. "Makes one think of carved ivory," the reviewer noted. "Whether she is depicting the outward aspects of trench life or the inmost soul of the people, she does it with that calm intelligence and habitual felicity of expression which have made her a peculiarly apt interpreter of the French temperament."

Gertrude Atherton Promotes War Charities and "Does the Front"

Throughout the first decade of the twentieth century, prolific American novelist Gertrude Atherton spent half of every year in Munich, Germany, which she considered the most beautiful city in Europe. Her strong German attachments prompted her to support U.S. neutrality at the outbreak of war. When her German friends pleaded with her their nation's rationale for war, Atherton shared their arguments in letters to U.S. newspapers.

But two events in May 1915 changed her view completely and made her an advocate for American preparedness and its entry into the war. On May 7 a German submarine sank the British passenger liner RMS *Lusitania*, with the loss of 1,198 lives, 128 of them American. Less than a week later the British government released the Bryce Report, an investigation into charges of German atrocities during the first month of the war. The report concluded that the German army had engaged in an official policy of the murder of civilians, rape, and wanton looting and destruction. Although the report would later be largely discredited, it became a powerful piece of propaganda that galvanized public opinion against Germany.

Unlike Mary Roberts Rinehart, who felt war's call to adventure, or Edith Wharton's passionate advocacy for her beloved France, Atherton was not immediately drawn to report on the war. Even with her ire raised against Germany, she struggled with a bleeding ulcer in 1915, while she worked to complete several writing projects.

When her friend, reporter-novelist Owen Johnson, traveled to France in 1915 to report for the *New York Times*, he suggested to Atherton that she should visit France to report on the impressive war work of Frenchwomen. Since Atherton's novels featured strong, intelligent heroines who led independent lives, the assignment appealed to her. "My idea in going [to France]," she explained, "was not to gratify my curiosity but to do what I could for the cause of France as well as for my own country by studying specifically the war-time work of its women and to make them better known to the women of America." Of course, she would certainly have read the wartime articles of Rinehart and Wharton, and they may well have stirred her competitive spirit.

In the opening years of the twentieth century, Edith Wharton and Gertrude Atherton reigned as the predominant female novelists in America. Both wrote novels of manners that featured the upper class. Both lived a restless, international life, traveling often between the United States and Europe, where they lived some years as expatriates. They favored European culture over mainstream American culture. However, Wharton placed higher on the social and literary scale than Atherton. The same critics who ranked Wharton in the first rank of literary novelists criticized Atherton for her romantic, sensational, or "lowbrow" fiction. Literary critic John Underwood once opined that Gertrude Atherton, rather that Edith Wharton, should be considered America's leading female novelist because Wharton was in a class by herself.

But Atherton's fiction won a base of loyal female readers by championing the theme of feminine emancipation. Atherton scholar Carolyn Forrey has suggested that Atherton's heroines "had continually to fight traditional beliefs about women's nature and role—beliefs held by their parents, their husbands and lov-

GERTRUDE
ATHERTON
1909
—"—

11. Popular novelist Gertrude Atherton, pictured here in 1909, went to
France in 1916 to study the wartime work of women. Arnold Genthe
photograph, courtesy of the California History Room,
California State Library, Sacramento.

ers, society, their professions, and more fundamentally, themselves." From what Atherton had read about the women of France,
the war had forced them out of their traditional roles.

By mid-1916 Atherton had finished her other literary commit-
ments and gotten an assignment from the women's magazine
the *Delineator* to write a series of articles about the women of

France. The guarantee of a book contract on the articles sweet-
ened the deal. She would spend May through August on assignment in France.

When she arrived at the Paris train station at midnight, she
saw how completely the city had changed. There was not a por-
ter or a cab to be found, and the city was dark. She might have
spent the night on the dark station platform but for the kindness
of a fellow passenger, who gave her a lift to the posh Hotel Crillon. Her friend, the American architect Whitney Warren, introduced her to the world of the war charities that flourished in the
city. Warren had founded the Committee of American Students
of the School of Beaux-Arts, Paris, a war charity that supported
the French cause by creating and selling art postcards.

Atherton's calendar quickly filled with daily lunches with
women who ran an *oeuvre* (workroom) or a war charity. After-
ward her hostess of the day would escort her to see the activities of her particular cause: "Hospitals, *Éclopé* stations, *Dépôts
des Isolées*, munition factories, canteens at railway stations, doll
factories [the French hoped to recover this lost industry from
the Germans], *oeuvres* for the benefit of widows, orphans, midi-
nettes, lacemakers: women of all sorts and pursuits whom the
War had thrown abruptly out of work."

Many of these charity organizers were members of the aristocracy or leading figures of society. Some were widows or temporarily alone while their husbands served in the army. All had
been galvanized by the war to pursue meaningful work for the first
time in their lives. Atherton must have felt herself surrounded
by her own fictional heroines.

Madame d'Andigné, the former Madeline Goddard of Rhode
Island, who supported hospitals at the front, urged Atherton to
write articles about the hospitals in order to encourage donations from readers in America. Atherton had already been denied
permission by the War Office to visit hospitals in the war zone.
She was a prominent American, they explained. Should anything
happen to her, there would be unpleasant publicity, and they
would be blamed. But now that she had accepted the charge to

publicize the work and needs of the war zone hospitals, she concluded that she was essentially working for France and would be given permission.

"I must have gone to the *Ministère de la Guerre* twenty times," Atherton complained, "climbing several flights of stairs at that." Finally, she won permission to visit a hospital in Meaux, which stood well behind the lines. After that visit she returned in frustration to the War Office and demanded to be allowed to penetrate deeper into the war zone or she would return to America and "their hospitals could take care of themselves." That threat won her approval to visit Châlons and Bar-le-Duc, over one hundred miles from Paris. She traveled there by train, the only woman, the only civilian passenger. At several hospitals in Châlons she "saw enough harrowing sights and heard enough harrowing stories of bombs dropped from above to furnish me with abundant material!" Atherton does not describe her experience in the hospitals but focuses instead on the difficulties of traveling in these areas, with or without military escort. The hotels and meals come in for special criticism.

She pushed on to Bar-le-Duc, even closer to the front, but there encountered the problems of traveling on her own. When she asked for a room at the hotel, the cashier "looked at me with positive hatred." All the rooms were taken by officers on leave from the front. What an impertinence for her to expect accommodations. When she stepped into the dining room full of officers, a dead silence greeted her. She caught a train back to Paris.

The next day she returned to the War Office to complain and negotiate once more for a closer visit to the front, perhaps Reims or Verdun. Officials there countered with suggested visits to Révigny and Nancy. Atherton groused to her readers that she knew several male correspondents who within days of arriving in Paris went off on guided tours of the front lines or to interview General Joseph Joffre, commander of French forces: "I reminded my friends at the War Office that men were as easily killed as women, even American men. But they seemed to think that the explosion of an American woman, especially if she happened to be 'of a prominence,' would make too much noise in the world to be agreeable. They have trouble enough on their hands."

A strong opinion existed at the French War Office that not all journalists and would-be journalists who bothered them for visits to the front warranted the time and trouble needed to accommodate them. Did a lady novelist, writing for a women's magazine, really need to visit the trenches just so she could have an exciting war adventure? Did it matter whether she visited a hospital five miles behind the lines or one twenty-five miles back? If such a journalist had important friends or could persuade the War Office of her influence, then the answer was yes.

The War Office finally agreed to provide Atherton with a military car and a French officer escort to travel to Nancy but only on the condition that she find an American officer to share the responsibility. Fortunately, she managed to find one at the American War Relief Clearing House. On August 25 she set off with two officer escorts, a female traveling companion, a driver, and a mechanic.

As with her other excursions, the Nancy trip provided ample sights and experiences to fill her travelogue-style account. The *New York Times* gave her article about the trip the somewhat touristy headline "Mrs. Atherton Sees the War Ruins in France." She reported that her car had to drive slowly through the debris-littered streets of Nancy. Residents lived in cellars. An old woman sold postcards of the ruins. She met two American women supporting a reconstruction project who hoped to raise money in the United States for rebuilding French towns. She met Sister Julie, the intrepid nun first mentioned by Edith Wharton.

Nancy sat some five miles behind the front lines, but Atherton was still possessed with the notion of getting closer. She wanted to push on to the Alsatian town of Thann but was denied permission, as it was under regular bombardment. "There is but one way by which a woman can get into any of these bombarded towns, Rheims, Thann, Verdun," she explained. "After she is in the war zone, if she happens to know one of the Generals there, knows him quite well, so that he feels a certain degree of friendship for her, and if he happens to be in a very good humor, and if the bombardment at that moment happens to be weak or non-existent, as it was when I was at Châlons and Bar-le-Duc, then he will put her in an automobile and whizz her through the famous target. She will hardly have time to experience the expected thrill before she is out again, but at least she can say she has been there."

A note of frustration simmered throughout Atherton's war zone articles. Every time she was prevented from seeing or doing something, every time circumstance did not meet her expectations, whenever she was vexed by a person or a rule, it violated her expectation of privilege. On her last night in Nancy, she took stock of her situation: "I lay awake part of the night listening to the guns. It was not so much a sound as a vibration that shook the atmosphere, far more uncanny and mysterious than sound. It exercised a curious morbid fascination. And at last I was as close to the front as I would ever get, and closer than any other American woman had been."

It's worth noting that her claim of having gotten closer to the front than any other American woman appeared not in her war articles written at the time but in her autobiography, *Adventures of a Novelist*, published sixteen years later. Atherton, and many of her readers in 1916, would likely have read Mary Robert Rinehart's numerous articles from the Belgian front and Edith Wharton's reports from the front lines, one of them from Thann, the very town that Atherton sought to visit. Those articles clearly disproved Atherton's boast.

But Atherton's excursions to the front are really an aside to her larger effort of chronicling the war work of Frenchwomen, her declared intention of traveling to France. She originally planned to stay a month in France; instead, her visit ran from May 9 to August 19. Her visits to the front accounted for a little more than a week of that time. Those articles appeared in the *New York Times* and in a thin volume titled *Life in the War Zone* (1916).

Atherton's reports of the notable war work of the women of France, first published in the *Delineator* in 1916, appeared the following year as a book, *The Living Present*. One reviewer found her accounts "interesting and gossipy" and praised the book for showing how these women had transformed themselves. From the simplest workingwoman to the "spoiled favorites of French society," Frenchwomen had "found themselves," in ways that no man could.

5

Status of Women in Warring Countries

It was on a summer's day in 1916 that I rushed into the office
of the *Pictorial Review*. "Look!" I exclaimed excitedly to the
editor at his desk. "See the message in the sky written in
letters of blood above the battlefields of Europe! There
it is, the promise of freedom for women!"

—MABEL POTTER DAGGETT, *Women Wanted*, 1918

An auspicious moment unfolded at the office of the *New York Tribune* in 1915, when female reporters descended from the upper-story room, where they had long worked in isolation, to join their male colleagues in the newsroom. The occasion earned only a few sentences in the iconic history of women in the early years of journalism, *Ladies of the Press*, by Ishbel Ross. But the imagination begs to fill in the details of glances, emotions, and the awkward adjustment of duties and interactions.

The newsroom of a metropolitan newspaper had long been considered a rather coarse work environment, where men smoked cigars, cursed, and spoke freely about the gritty topics of the day. News gathering was a sometimes dangerous job, with long hours that exposed journalists to the harsh realities of city life. Editors could hardly be expected to send women on nighttime assignments to bars, sporting venues, or police headquarters, where news so often broke. Many of the women who began writing for newspapers in the decades leading up to the war did so by correspondence, to shield them from the corruption of the all-male newsroom environment.

Women had won this honor at the *Tribune* in part by virtue of having covered a growing list of hard-news stories, such as crime, the suffrage movement, and VIP interviews, and by undertaking high-profile "stunt" assignments. By the time the *Tribune* women began their assimilation into the newsroom, they had also won an assignment to cover the harshest reality of all—war.

The *Tribune* already received war stories from the most famous war correspondent of the age, Richard Harding Davis, who had arrived in Brussels in August 1914 and traveled in the wake of the advancing Germany army. But even the venerable Davis had caught none of the actual fighting. His reporting, and that of others, such as Mary Boyle O'Reilly, instead began to reveal the dramatic toll of the war on the civilian population. Victims of the fighting and the cast-off refugee populations figured prominently in early reporting. Reporters had just begun to turn their attention to the role of women as a separate wartime story line.

In early 1915 the *Tribune* began to publish articles from a freelance foreign correspondent named Ernestine Evans. The twenty-four-year-old Evans set off to Russia in late 1914 on a freelance assignment for a small Boston magazine to write about prohibition. When Russian censors killed her prohibition story, Evans found herself in the unenviable position of being in wartime Russia, on her first foreign posting, learning the ropes of war reporting, without formal attachment to any publication.

Evans had graduated from the University of Chicago in 1912, with a degree in English and having taken a course in journalism. In the two years since her graduation, she had worked for at least four publications, one of which folded and one from which she was fired. The note of dismissal from her post as a literary critic at the *Chicago Daily News* read, "We do not hire little chits from the University of Chicago to demolish America's literary reputations." That quotation appeared fifty-five years later, in her obituary, after her long career in journalism and publishing, perhaps a testament to how often she had repeated that juicy story for friends.

Several other American journalists had made it to Russia by this time. Two worked for British newspapers, Stanley Washburn (*London Times*) and Granville Fortescue (*Daily Telegraph*), and John Bass was there for the *Chicago Daily News*. In their wartime writings these men explained how they cultivated their contacts: visiting the Russian Foreign Ministry, dining with the American ambassador, and receiving briefings from U.S. military attachés. They were soon traveling on some of Russia's first army press tours to the fighting in Russian Poland, where they wrote headline-grabbing stories about the war on the eastern front.

Evans, a young, inexperienced, freelance, female foreign correspondent, would not have had such opportunities. Instead, she saw the war through the grisly apparitions of disabled and disfigured soldiers who wandered the streets of Petrograd by the thousands. "It is a curious sight to see groups of these bearded men on the streets as soon as they are able to be about," she reported. "Always accompanied by a sister [nurse], one sees these little parties making their way about the cities, visiting museums and cathedrals, then the clucking of the little figure in gray gingham, as she marshals her charges and takes them on a tram back to the hospital."

Dozens of war hospitals and makeshift clinics had opened in Petrograd and other cities to handle the many wounded brought from the battlefields. Since Russia had no professional organization for nurses, hundreds of women, including some from the nobility, rushed into a six-week training program that qualified them to wear the uniform of an authorized nurse. A visit to a few facilities in Petrograd gave Evans a glimpse of the massive operation to care for the wounded and of the significant role played by women. She had her Russian story. Her first article for the *Tribune*, "Russia's Women Lovable in War Time," appeared on January 31, 1915. "Miss Evans visits Petrograd and Moscow and writes back the humorous and tragic sides of the world event as it affects that country's women," the subhead explained.

12. Ernestine Evans reported from Bulgaria, Germany, and Russia in 1914 and 1915, with a focus on women. American National Red Cross photograph collection, Prints & Photographs Division, Library of Congress, LC-A6195-5166.

The impact of the war on women was quickly emerging as an important story of the war. The victimization of women grabbed the early headlines. Women in mourning became the most visible signs of that sacrifice, along with refugees from the war zone. Corra Harris first tapped that deep vein. But Harris's reporting also defined the expanded role of women who overcame challenges and stepped into larger social and economic roles. In an age in which women's rights and empowerment were prominent social issues, these stories resonated with American readers.

Evans praised the British hospital in Moscow and the American hospital in Kiev as models of organization, where professionally trained nurses rendered the highest level of care. But such was not the case in the Russian hospitals and clinics, which were understaffed, under-supplied, with minimally trained nurses. Other shortcomings she noted were unique to the Russian Empire. Half the books donated to the English hospital in Moscow were burned by the authorities "because they were too likely to make the soldiers think." However, the absence of books was not too great a problem since many of the soldiers were illiterate. A nurse showed Evans a ward filled with men recently brought in from the fighting in Poland, many with their eardrums burst from cannonading. As was the case with many peasant soldiers in Russia's army, these men could not read or write, and now they could not hear as well.

Throughout the war Russia frustrated and confounded American journalists. The issues of corruption and social unrest seemed to undergird its alien culture. Shortly after Evans wrote about Russian hospitals, Mary Boyle O'Reilly paid a quick visit to Petrograd. Her focus also fell on the role of nurses but through the eyes of a woman of the aristocracy, Marie Nicholovna. Thousands of noblewomen had given up their gowns, furs, and jewelry to wear the gray serge of a nurse. "Call it an outward sign of an inward change," Nicholovna told O'Reilly. The women of the nobility had been asleep before the war, unaware of social problems that are more obvious in wartime. When they volunteered with the Red Cross, they discovered "the war that is behind the war." Nicholovna cited the miserable tenements in Petrograd and the alarming child mortality rate for the poor.

Perhaps this new social awareness would lead women to get the vote after the war, Nicholovna thought. "But," she wrote, "I think we will never forget—never—how much must be done to make life safer and happier for the people who have no furs." Even as the role of women and their voices continued to attract more news coverage, it typically remained isolated on the Women's Page of the newspaper. O'Reilly's article ran as a Women's Page story. Evans's Russia article appeared on the Women's Page, as did the other articles she wrote in 1915, including her article about a woman doctor planning to organize a Red Cross hospital and train nurses.

In Berlin, Evans interviewed Minna Cauer, a pioneering figure in the suffrage movement since the 1890s. Cauer claimed that women in Germany, and everywhere, had lost their public voices because of the war. "I have promised myself not to die," she told Evans, "until the war is ended and some of our old work goes on again." Expressed by Cauer and echoed by other female voices was the notion that things would be better for women after the war, that their expanded responsibilities in wartime would translate into expanded opportunities and rights in peace. Evans had captured an important theme emerging from reporting on women in the war. The interview landed on the *Tribune*'s Women's Page, wrapped around a regular column titled "Are Women People?"

Major developments in the war allowed Evan's March 1915 interview with the queen of Bulgaria to receive more prominent placement. Britain and France had just commenced their Gallipoli campaign to open the strategically important Dardanelles Strait in Turkey. The assault hoped to gain control of the waterway link between the Black and Mediterranean Seas, to allow easier delivery of war materials to Russia. Success against the Turkish army might also knock Turkey out of the war and sway the wavering Balkan states of Romania and Bulgaria to enter the war on the Allied side.

Evans met Queen Eleanore at an American missionary school,

forty-five minutes outside Sophia. The queen arrived "dressed in a short fox coat and a simple purple hat, and carrying a walking stick." The queen explained her country's competing Russian and German loyalties and the lingering enmity toward Greece, Romania, and Serbia for seizing Bulgarian territory in an earlier war. With the outcome of Gallipoli still in the balance and because Bulgaria, Greece, and Romania had yet to enter the war, the interview was especially newsworthy. It was the only article that Evans cabled back to the *Tribune* rather than mailing.

Sophie Treadwell Seeks a War Voice

Any journalist who traveled to France in spring 1915 would have been mildly hopeful of getting near the front lines. Mary Roberts Rinehart's adventures at the front had begun to appear in the *Saturday Evening Post* that April. A few other reporters had also caught a glimpse of activities at or near the front lines. All the belligerents were exploring policies that granted journalists greater access to the war zone.

However, reporters who arrived in Paris that spring and put in their request with the War Office discovered that the veil of secrecy had not lifted very high. When E. Alexander Powell (*New York World*) arrived in Paris in spring 1915, he described the situation: "I wonder if you, who will read this, realize that, though the German trenches can be reached by motor-car in ninety minutes from the Rue de la Paix, it is as impossible for an unauthorized person to get within sound, much less within sight, of them as it would be for a tourist to stroll into Buckingham Palace and have a friendly chat with King George." For Powell getting permission to visit the front required the joint efforts of "three Cabinet Ministries, a British peer, two ambassadors, a score of newspapers—and the patience of Job."

Into this environment came another college-educated woman journalist, Sophie Treadwell, of the *San Francisco Bulletin*. The French and Belgian armies turned down her requests to visit the front, a snub she attributed to her being a woman. Although women certainly faced additional hurdles in dealing with European war offices, that simple explanation misses other obvious factors. Primarily, at this point in the war it was still difficult for anyone to get access to the war zone. Reporters from major urban newspapers, large-circulation magazines, or one of the wire services typically had priority. Wythe Williams, the *New York Times* foreign correspondent in France for many years, earned an early visit to the war zone. Veteran war correspondent Frederick Palmer became the first, and only, American correspondent credentialed with the British Army in 1914. And yet even Palmer did not visit the British lines until May 1915.

Therefore, it is not surprising that a twenty-nine-year-old reporter from a smaller, West Coast newspaper was turned down on her first request for permission to visit the front. Being a woman did not strengthen her cause since authorities did not want to assume the risk or the additional arrangements required for taking a woman into the danger zone. The reason seems more likely that both Treadwell and the *Bulletin* were unaware of how best to plead their case for access.

However, given Treadwell's journalistic background, it seems probable that the *Bulletin* sent her to France not to enlighten readers about the military situation but to write about women. Treadwell was actively involved in suffrage activities and had built a successful career covering women-related stories. She gained public recognition by reporting on two sensational murder trials, both of women accused of murdering or plotting to murder an abusive lover and an adulterous husband.

In the most prominent of these trials, Elizabeth Blair Mohr was accused of hiring three men to murder her cheating spouse. In a sixteen-article series Treadwell covered the trial with a blend of factual reporting and subjective observation. She informed her readers about such things as the expression on the defendant's face, a snippet of conversation overheard outside the courtroom about the murdered husband's good looks, or a woman's gasp in the courtroom as the prosecution concluded its case.

The overall impression conveyed was that a sensitive female reporter was able to observe trifling, yet significant, things that a typical (male) reporter would have overlooked. At the very least these observations suggested that the case was more complex than the prosecutor and the all-male jury realized. Or as Treadwell scholar Jerry Dickey has observed, the larger impressions of Treadwell's reporting on these trials suggests the "crushing weight of an entire society whose masculine laws and orientations stifle the voices and emotional needs of women." Elizabeth Blair Mohr was acquitted.

Later in 1914 the *Bulletin* assigned Treadwell to write about prostitution in the city. Centered in San Francisco's red-light district, the "Barbary Coast," prostitution had been a feature of the city since the gold rush of 1849. By 1914 the city's newspapers were supporting the efforts of Mayor James "Sunny Jim" Rolph to eliminate the district. To go undercover for her assignment, Treadwell posed as May Bertin, a homeless prostitute seeking help from Christian organizations to "get back on the right track." In "An Outcast at the Christian Door," which ran as an eighteen-part series, she analyzed the hypocritical attitude of religious, charitable institutions that were supposed to help such women. The popularity of the articles made Treadwell an overnight sensation in San Francisco and prompted the newspaper to publish the series as a booklet.

As Treadwell sought her bearings as a war correspondent, she likely thought of constructing a series. She had enjoyed success with them, and articles running in a series had the advantage of hooking readers and bringing them back repeatedly to catch the latest installment. One obvious subject might be her interactions with the civilian population and military authorities. Just as her impressionistic rendering of the murder trials revealed underlying complexity, so, too, that approach might work for war coverage.

Treadwell chose to write her series about life in France in the form of letters, a not-uncommon format for some correspondents. Letters, which often read like gossipy travelogues, had the advantage of being more informal and faster to write than articles. In an episodic listing of personal experiences and

13. When Sophie Treadwell (left) reported from Paris in 1915, she tried to find a woman's voice for her war articles. This photo was taken during a 1917 cross-country auto trip in the United States with her childhood friend Esther Barney. Sophia Treadwell Papers, Special Collections, University of Arizona Library.

impressions, the reporter could reveal greater insight into life in a warring country than by chronicling the horrors of battle. The social and economic transformation of a nation, the psychology of a population, the story of one wounded soldier, one refugee, or one woman in mourning, told volumes.

However, Treadwell added a stylistic variation to the letter format. Instead of writing letters to the *Bulletin*, she wrote letters to an imaginary female friend named "D." Treadwell has received some scholarly attention over the years, primarily for her plays, which explore feminist themes. Some scholars have suggested that Treadwell's woman-to-woman war letters were an attempt to find an authentic female voice in the male-dominated field of war correspondence.

From the start her letters suggested that Treadwell struggled to find her war voice and her role as a war reporter. "I'm a real journalist now, D—No more reporter," one letter noted. "I've a passport, and a *'permis de sejour'* [residence permit], and a 'portfolio' in the war office, along with other 'journalists.'" After visiting a café in Bordeaux and seeing so many women in mourning and men maimed by war, she "began to realize a little of what I was getting into."

The letters provided behind-the-scenes anecdotes of her experiences that often sounded naive, gushingly impressionistic, cynical of the correspondent's role, and sentimental about the nobility of war. Of her impressions of the French capital, she wrote: "Paris! I didn't know that anything in the world that man had anything to do with could be as beautiful as Paris. You know something? In my next incarnation I'm going to ask please to be the kind of woman, Paris is a city. Now, don't be shocked, D. She is very beautiful, very noble, without being oppressive about it. There is a soft luminous air about her. She is amusing and gay—Oh, I know they say she is wicked, but aren't they always saying that sort of thing?"

Her editor back at the *Bulletin* was not a fan. He thought her idea about the worthwhileness of war "rubbish." He ran only three of her early letters and killed the rest. On the three published letters he removed the "Dear D" salutation and offered them as straight news reports. To get her back on the right track, he suggested, "Be your old self, and imagine you sit here in the local room, and imagine you are writing a story for today's *Bulletin*, and cut out all irrelevant, inconsequential stuff." And then, by way of a patronizing pep talk, he offered, "You must be big and brave and go ahead and do the best you can and everything will be all right." It was a word of encouragement for someone who had lost her way.

Whether Treadwell thought this good advice, her only other story published in the *Bulletin* was more sober, with no impressionistic descriptions of people and places. It gave a general summary of the war mood in Paris, just after Italy entered the war on the side of the Allies. The names of numerous battles were sprinkled throughout, but no evocative scenes, no individuals, were singled out—only "the women and others left home to wait" the next turn in the war. The "great game goes on." The war correspondents write the big "horror stuff," while the military trains continue to carry men to the trenches, and the hospital trains bring them back.

After promoting Treadwell as their war correspondent, the *Bulletin* ended up running only three of her letters, deep on its inside pages. It fell to *Harper's Weekly* to publish the most memorable article from Treadwell's four-month stay in Europe, "Women in Black." Women in mourning looked out at her from "every nook and corner" of France. Meeting them gave Treadwell the perfect canvas to tell their story.

In two dramatic scenes Treadwell gave a glimpse into the toll of the war on the women of France. In the best of these, she rode a train with a peasant woman who had lost one son and had two more in the trenches. Her large extended family of husband, daughters-in-law, and grandchildren now lived in one small house. The government had confiscated their only horse, so they could not work the fields. The army might yet call up her old and sick husband. In one respect that would be a blessing, for she would then get a government stipend. But it would leave a house of only women and children. She lovingly unfolded a worn letter, the last she had received from her dead son, an object she obviously venerated, and shared it with Treadwell.

In the article's second anecdote, Treadwell dined with three women of the middle class. They seemed a "pitifully inadequate little gathering," she confessed, three women in black. "War death had reached its hand" into their hearts. They spent the evening folding bandages. The call now was for hospital supplies, which made them fear that a great offensive was planned, which would put even more women into mourning.

Women in the Workforce

When Jessica Lozier Payne of the *Brooklyn Daily Eagle* arrived in Liverpool in the summer of 1916, the war seemed locked up tighter than a safe. Before she could even set foot on land, an officer boarded her ship to examine papers and pose many probing questions before the passengers could disembark. Unless a passenger was particularly desirable, the officer explained, England resented that person taking up a seat on a train that might better be filled by a soldier or consuming food that was sorely needed by the English people.

Payne reached her hotel late that night but could not check in until she had registered with the police department. When she complained to the police officer, he replied, "Madame, our orders are to regard every American as a German spy until proof is given us to the contrary."

One feature of the total war being practiced in this conflict was that it encompassed the entire country and everyone in it. Everyone suffered and sacrificed. Cities such as London, Paris, and Berlin, well known to many American travelers, had been transformed: many shops closed, grand hotels converted to hospitals, women in the workforce, spy mania, food shortages, severe travel restrictions, disabled soldiers on the streets, and thousands of war-damaged civilians. Life in the belligerent countries overflowed with dramatic stories about the effects of war. The problem was to observe and record the stories without being suspected of spying.

The level of security got even worse in Scotland, Payne's first destination. Because of coastal naval facilities, Edinburgh fell within a "restricted military area." By the time she arrived there, Payne had accumulated a ream of passes from various police agencies along the way. But the Edinburgh police official insisted that she also have an identity book. That required another thorough examination of her character, an endorsement by two local residents, and a stamp of approval from the American consulate. Then she had to reveal any identifying marks on her body, such as a blemish, mole, or scar. Fortunately, she had a recent scar on her wrist that was duly measured and described and logged into her identity book. Her experience passing security in Great Britain became Payne's first war "letter" to the *Eagle*. To venture into a belligerent country was to become a character in a war story.

The first thing that struck Payne in Edinburgh was the novelty of women working in so many occupations previously held by men. Young women in sharp blue uniforms served as conductors on trams and buses. One of them told Payne that she liked her job and expected to keep it even when the men returned home.

The city's munition factories saw the largest influx of women into industry. The longer the war continued, the more it drained men from the civilian workforce and the greater the appetite for materials of war. When the British Army experienced a severe shortage of artillery shells in 1915, the "shell crisis," the government called for every machine shop and foundry to produce munitions. With the men away at the front, a "tremendous army" of women mobilized for the work—the "munitionettes."

Visiting one engineering shop, Payne found herself "surrounded by the hum and throb of speeding machinery. Long aisles of electrically driven tools, each with a woman worker before it absorbed in her task." To grasp the novelty and gravity of this sight required an adjustment in one's thinking about women. This "army" of women had mobilized for the war, just like the men, laboring fifty to sixty hours a week, under dangerous conditions, to serve their country.

"I like to watch my machine cut the metal, just like it was cheese," said one young woman working on a lathe, "and every shell I pass along I say, 'There goes another one for our boys at the front.'"

The women dressed in smocks and trousers, their hair pulled under a cap for safety, and bent over heavy equipment as though it was their natural state. "Three young Amazons" operating hydraulic presses that forged copper bands onto artillery shells joked and laughed, completely at ease with the heavy work. They reflected the high spirits of the women who had met the wartime demands of heavy industry.

The story was the same at the shipbuilding works in Glasgow, the dye factories in Manchester, and a hospital in London. Women were working in positions from which they had previously been excluded, bringing home their first paychecks, living on their own, and enjoying their newfound independence. It was a truly astonishing social development. Payne couldn't help but wonder what would happen after the war, when the men returned. How would the economy readjust? Having gotten their first taste of economic independence, would women be content to return to the home? Would companies keep their female employees or allow returning soldiers to take their jobs? Would society continue to insist that women were unsuited for some employment?

In France there was no ignoring the war. "Paris is no longer gay and sprightly," Payne reported, but was now overflowing with soldiers. What a contrast they presented: new recruits, veterans on temporary leave from the trenches, and the wounded. The recruits looked eager and erect in their fresh uniforms. The bearded veterans sagged with weariness, their uniforms mud stained, their helmets dented. "Then there are the wounded, men without arms, or lacking a leg, or with parts of their jaws shot away—and saddest of all, the blind . . . you see them on the boulevards, being taught to walk and given courage by some young woman who chats and laughs with them and tries to inspire them to step briskly and have confidence."

The *Eagle* had a foreign correspondent in Europe, Henry Suydam, who arranged for Payne to visit the iconic battleground on the River Marne and made the trip with her in September 1916. A twenty-eight-mile train ride took them to the spot where France had finally halted the German invasion two years earlier. Villages in the area still bore the damage of the fighting. Payne walked among the white crosses and miniature flags dotting the surrounding fields, marking where soldiers had fallen and been buried. By following the advancing line of German graves until they met a cluster of French graves, Payne could visualize the attack and repulse of the fighting.

A corked bottle dangled from many of the graves. Inside, Payne found a note from a French mother asking for news of her son, who was missing and whom she believed to have been killed at the Battle of the Marne.

Payne's driver took her to a small stone house for a peak at three German prisoners and then to some abandoned trenches. "I climbed down into them and walked along in the slippery mud, for I wanted the experience of being in a real trench," Payne wrote.

Along with the shell-damaged cathedral at Reims, the Marne battleground had become one of the permitted destinations for correspondents and other curious, and possibly influential, Americans who visited France at this time. Some were already referring disparagingly to the practice as "war tourism," but it served to publicize the Allied cause in the United States.

Noted Lecturer Visits the War Zone

The same month Payne returned home, a flutter of news stories appeared about the noted explorer, photographer, and lecturer Harriet Chalmers Adams in the war zone. A frequent contributor to *National Geographic Magazine*, Adams had gained fame for a three-year exploration of South America and an expedition to retrace the footsteps of Christopher Columbus in the New World. Now she was exploring her most dangerous challenge yet, the Great War. "Shells Burst over Woman Gathering Lecture Material," one headline reported. Another story carried a photograph of Adams holding a bouquet of wildflowers, presented to her by the bedraggled French foot soldier pictured with her.

Adams enjoyed the sponsorship of the American Fund for the French Wounded, which allowed her to join a French army war tour, along with four male correspondents. They followed the typical itinerary of visits to the Marne battlefield, Reims cathedral, and the nearby front lines. Not so typically, she also won permission to photograph military scenes. Adams planned to use the photos for a series of lectures about the French war effort.

As befitted a famous explorer, Adams also traveled on her own deeper into the war zone, to the shell-battered city of Nancy, only five miles from the front. The women of that tortured town impressed this world traveler. She met an old woman who made sandbags for the trenches, a young woman ill from working in a munitions factory, and many courageous women who kept

14. Harriett Chalmers Adams on a French army press tour with other correspondents, visiting Reims cathedral, which had been severely damaged by German artillery. She holds a bouquet of flowers given to her by a French soldier. Note the officer on the right wears an artificial hand and arm. Harris & Ewing Collection, Prints & Photographs Division, Library of Congress, LC-H261-2788.

Nancy functioning even as it suffered near-daily artillery shelling. The obliging Germans dropped shells from their huge siege guns onto the town during Adams's visit. She huddled in a basement shelter with twenty-six townspeople, later writing, "I have never heard anything as ominous as the sound of those Titanic shells, each crushing out homes and human beings."

Her itinerary included a stop in Gerbéviller to meet the iconic French heroine Sister Julie, who proudly wore the Legion of Honor medal, pinned there by the president of France himself. The Geographic Society circulated to the press the letters Adams sent them in which she praised the courage and resilience of Frenchwomen. These women became the subject of the lectures she gave on her return home. Her article about her war experience ran in the November–December 1917 issue of *National Geographic*.

The Pageant of Women in the War

When the liner *New Amsterdam* sailed from New York in October 1916, Mabel Potter Daggett stood on deck taking the full blast of the wind and scanning the ominous gray waters. Being a correspondent for the women's magazine *Pictorial Review* had never carried such peril. Earlier that month a German submarine sank several ships just outside the three-mile limit of U.S. territorial waters. The complete expanse of the North Atlantic had suddenly become a war zone. Daggett revealed her disquiet, noting, "I think, right here, some of the sparkle begins to fade from the great adventure on which I am embarked."

The *New Amsterdam* was a neutral ship of the Holland American Line. Giant, four-foot-high letters spelled the ship's name on the hull, indicating to any would-be attacker that it was a neutral vessel. That name would be brightly illuminated at night. However, being on a neutral ship and a citizen of neutral America did not guarantee one's safety. In her cabin Daggett found that the steward had thoughtfully laid out her life vest. Above the washstand, a neatly printed card announced: "The occupant of this room is assigned to Lifeboat 17 on the starboard side."

There had been no such travel concerns on Daggett's previous crossing of the Atlantic. She had traveled to Europe in mid-1914 to study the conditions of women's lives. In Germany she learned how thrifty German housewives practiced "daily economies." In several countries she studied the practices surrounding divorce and provisions for the maintenance of illegitimate children. But the outbreak of war cut short her investigations.

Throughout 1915, as she published articles about her European findings and they got wide distribution through newspapers, she gained a reputation as an expert on the evolving role of women. "The modern woman has few more determined and capable champions than Mabel Potter Daggett," declared the editor of *Good Housekeeping* magazine. But so much had changed in that short time. The greatest war in human history became the catalyst for a seismic shift of attitudes toward women. Daggett knew she had to return to Europe to catalog the revolution.

In the book she would later write about her 1916 European trip, *Women Wanted* (1918), Daggett overly dramatized the moment she pitched the idea to *Pictorial Review* editor Arthur Vance. She had a vision, she told him, that the promise of freedom for women was written in blood-red letters across the battlefields of Europe. "He brushed aside the magazine 'lay-out' before him and lifted his eyes to the horizon of the world. And he too saw."

Daggett was not averse to such hyperbolic language, but she and others clearly saw that the war was rewriting the book on women's rights. The fall of 1916 just happened to be the perfect time to capture that phenomenon, Daggett the perfect one to do so, and the *Pictorial Review* the perfect venue for her findings.

The 1916 presidential election had moved women's issues front and center. Republican candidate Charles Evans Hughes supported women's suffrage; Woodrow Wilson, seeking a second term, did not. Since women could already vote in twelve states, it was hoped that their combined influence might tip the scales for Hughes and for universal women's suffrage. If the women of war-torn Europe were redefining their role in society, their experience might prove instructive for America.

Of all the women's magazines leading the charge for reform on issues important to women, none had the impact of the *Pictorial Review*. What had once been a magazine of "practical fashions for dressmakers and the home" dramatically changed in 1907 with the appointment of a new editor, Arthur T. Vance. Vance brought a commitment to social change and an editorial voice for "women who want to think and act as well as be entertained." With a circulation of two hundred thousand in 1907, it had climbed past one million by the time Daggett sailed to warring Europe.

Passenger anxiety peaked, one day out from the English coast, when the *New Amsterdam* crew stripped the canvas off the life-boats and a crane began hauling life rafts from the hold. They were entering the danger zone, the crew explained, that area of coastal waters where U-boats most often found their prey. Down in her cabin, Daggett struggled with a different anxiety.

In anticipation of arriving in England, she spread out on her bed all her letters of introduction, all eighty-four of them, which she hoped would provide entrée to various areas of society and government. Having been forewarned of the stringency of British suspicions, she now reevaluated those letters.

Her passport already contained a bouquet of colorful rubber visa stamps from the nations where she hoped to travel. At the British consulate in New York, they asked if she was a suffragist. "They don't want any trouble over there," the consular officer warned. Now she worried if her letters held any unexpected traps. Would it be incriminating that one of the letters indicated she was familiar with the German women's movement? Would it make trouble for her that she planned to meet with a British pacifist? One letter of introduction was signed by a perfectly loyal American who had the misfortune of having inherited a German-sounding name. In the end she removed two letters from her packet, walked onto deck, and dropped them into the sea. "Like this a journalist goes to Europe these days editing oneself, to be acceptable to the rows of men in khaki."

"Now what have you come over here for?" the inspecting officer asked when she stepped off the ship. She stood in a private room, into which each passenger was taken individually for a personal grilling. She handed over her passport and her stack of letters, including the "To Whom It May Concern" letter from the editor of the *Pictorial Review*, which described her assignment to write about the new role of women due to the war. Daggett had to tell her complete life story but was eventually passed through.

Nearly every journalist arriving in Europe during the war took as a first topic the stifling restrictions that made their job so difficult. Daggett arrived in London during a blackout against a Zeppelin raid. Her hotel required an extensive personal history form and registration with the police department. Travel to certain parts of the country was forbidden without the consent of Scotland Yard. Her planned trip to France would require the permission of the British Foreign Office, plus French and U.S. officials. "The government is regulating everything," Daggett lamented, "the icing a housewife may not put on a cake, the number of courses one may have for dinner, even the conversation at table. Let an American with the habit of free speech beware! Notices conspicuously posted in public places advise, 'Silence.'" When Daggett asked the woman conductor on the tram how she liked her job, she scurried away "like a frightened rabbit."

The archives of the International Suffrage Headquarters in London offered the first clue to the extent of women's involvement in the war. Its collection of sociological studies and newspaper clippings gave an extraordinary portrait of women's achievements. Before the war most suffrage offices maintained files of newspaper clippings about women stepping outside their traditional roles in the home. Every time a woman earned a medical degree, mastered a difficult skill, or ran a thriving business on her own, that news story went into the file. Every time some woman proved society wrong about what women could not do or were not supposed to do, it went into the file.

In the past these files stood as mute rebuttal to the arguments advanced by men for barring woman from full equality. Now the studies and the bulging files showed how completely the war had changed everything. The war provided so many instances of women working in new fields, performing under fire, serving their country, and being honored for that service. It was nothing short of a revolutionary change in attitude toward women in the workplace and, by implication, in women's rights. "Ideas that once seemed progressive, even radical, are now a given," Daggett wrote.

Before the war women had to push their way into virtually every business, industry, and profession, but now they were actively invited in, to replace the men sent to fight. And they were giving exemplary service. More than four million women now

15. During her 1916 visit to England and France, Mabel Potter Daggett reported on how the war was causing a revolution in the advancement of women's equality. *Delineator*, June 1919.

worked in British industry. In the first year of the war, Germany had recruited a half million women to make munitions. France had four hundred thousand munitionettes.

Women were invited to work not only in virtually all industries but in the war zone as well. One of the most common uniforms seen on the streets was not that of the soldier but of the nurse. "From the day the great slaughter began, it was accepted as a matter of course that woman's place was going to be at the bedside of the wounded soldier," Daggett told her readers. Half a million German women took nurse training courses. In France and Italy women of the nobility turned their homes into hospitals. In London the Women's Reserve Ambulance Corps retrieved the wounded in the midst of Zeppelin bombing raids on the city. Some hospitals in the war zone were staffed entirely by women: ambulance drivers, orderlies, nurses, physicians, and surgeons. A veritable pageant of women's progress was unfolding in the warring countries.

But how would she get access to this pageant? You couldn't just show up at a munitions factory and start asking questions. Suspicion of espionage ran so high, you would likely be arrested, jailed, or deported. Even her attempt to question the female tram conductor met with failure. Britain's Defence of the Realm Act and Trading with the Enemy Act thwarted the most well-meaning inquiries.

After several frustrated attempts to see things firsthand, she once again resorted to her letters of introduction. One frigid winter day, in her room at the Ritz Hotel, Daggett wrapped herself in her bed quilt and spread out her letters of introduction on the bed. Her cheeks were rosy, her fingers nipping from the cold. "The tiny open grate holds six or maybe seven coals," Daggett shared with her readers, "and you put them on delicately with things like the sugar tongs. It isn't good form to be warm in England. The best families aren't. It's plebian and American even to want to be."

Meeting people with connections was the time-honored approach to cracking closed systems. Daggett reviewed her letters, addressed to people in government, society, and the suffrage movement. Finally, she selected the final letter of introduction, handed to her by her editor as she boarded her ship. It was to Sir Gilbert Parker. She had no idea who Sir Gilbert was. The following night, when Parker received her in his home, she discovered that his home served as headquarters for the War Office Press Bureau and he was in charge of American publicity. Winning his approval could unlock the door of secrecy, but it didn't happen overnight. She had to make repeated visits to his house and have extended conversations that demonstrated that she was legitimate and trustworthy before he finally granted her the coveted permit required for a journalist to work in Britain. Invitations from government offices began arriving immediately.

Daggett's Press Bureau permit allowed her to circulate among industry, government, academia, and private organizations to gather examples about how totally the war had shaped the role of women. One reviewer of Daggett's book *Women Wanted*, in which her articles were collected, referred to the overall picture that emerges from her observations as a pageant, a motion picture, of women's progress.

Daggett presented the pageant as a catalog of women's accomplishment and changed attitudes. Women had become heroines of the war. Lady Louise Paget founded and ran a military hospital in Serbia, arriving there in October 1914, when every large building overflowed with wounded and diseases flourished. The courageous French teenager Émilienne Moreau turned her home into a first aid station during the Battle of Loos and won the Crois de Guerre. Emmeline Pankhurst, leader of the British suffrage movement, now worked with the government to recruit women into industry.

Before the war many women were discouraged from pursuing higher education because it was thought that the female mind could not master science, Greek, and mathematics. But now women had moved into the top teaching positions at many schools and universities. Sheffield University began offering classes for women in metallurgy. Bedford University graduated its first women in physics and bacteriology. Industrial firms actively recruited women scientists and technicians. The Royal Astronomical Society, the Architectural Association, other professional organizations, and trade unions opened their membership to women for the first time. "The tasks of the world," Daggett wrote, "were one by one being handed over to women by men who were taking up arms instead":

Who is it that is feeding and clothing and nursing the greatest armies of history? See that soldier in the trenches? A woman raised the grain for the bread, a woman is tending the flocks that provided the meat for his rations to-day. A woman made the boots and the uniform in which he stands. A woman made the shells with which his gun is loaded. A woman will nurse him when he's wounded. A woman's ambulance may even pick him up on the battlefield. A woman surgeon may perform the operation to save his life. And somewhere back home a woman holds the job he had to leave behind. There is no task to which women have not turned to-day to carry civilization.

In short, war had forced a profound feminist revolution: "Nothing that anybody ever said about women before August, 1914 . . . goes to-day. All the discoveries the scientists thought they had made about her, all the reports the sociologists solemnly filed over her, all the limitation the educators laid on her and all the jokes the punsters wrote about her—everything has gone to the scrap heap as repudiated as the one-time theory that the earth was square instead of round. Everything they said she wasn't and she couldn't and she didn't, she now is and she can and she does."

When the U.S. ambassador in France, William Sharpe, welcomed Daggett graciously to Paris, he provided her eighty-fifth letter of introduction, this one to the prime minister of France, requesting that he grant Daggett permission to visit the front. The letter appeared to work magic. The French war press bureau immediately notified her that it would be pleased to take her to the front. However, day after day slipped by without progress. Daggett spent many hours waiting at the press bureau, where officers remained charmingly solicitous but cautioned that "for a lady journalist it is so different and so difficult. The trip must be specially arranged." There finally came a letter extending the regrets of the bureau that it would not be able to arrange a visit to the front prior to her planned departure date from France.

"I hasten to write you that I cannot, for the sake of France, accept your decision as final," Daggett wrote in an immediate reply to the bureau. "You see, gentlemen, in the country from which I come, we have a feminism that is neither an ideal nor a theory, but a working reality." She explained that various state legislatures in the United States had already given the vote to four million women, four million voters who must be consulted by the U.S. Congress when it crafts its war policy. Their opinions helped to determine the amount of war relief sent to France.

Furthermore, she explained, the magazine for which she worked, the *Pictorial Review*, was the leading magazine championing the feminist cause, read by the very women who vote: "Believe me, gentlemen, the opportunity for propaganda that I offer you is unparalleled. I beg you therefore to reconsider. I earnestly desire to go to the front this week. Can you, I ask, permit me to leave this land without granting me the privilege? For the sake of France, gentlemen! Awaiting your reply." She mailed the letter at 11:00 p.m., and at noon the next day she received a call from the press office saying that her tour of the front had been arranged for Thursday.

The day before departure she gathered in the press office with the other members of her tour, six other journalists and a munitions manufacturer from Bridgeport, Connecticut. A French officer explained that they would be traveling to the city of Reims, which was regularly bombarded by German guns. "It is going to be perhaps a dangerous undertaking," he cautioned, then looked directly at Daggett. "Do you still wish to go?" All nodded their assent and were then issued their travel permits.

The night before her trip, Daggett removed the pink rose from her hat, as the officer had suggested, so as not to attract the attention of German gunners. She packed a "safety bag" she would wear around her waist, with travel permits, passport, and a business card with information on who to contact in case of death. Their group set off in three limousines and shortly passed the Marne battlefield. As the road approached Reims, a cloth curtain suspended on wires shielded traffic from the prying eyes of

German artillery spotters. The distant sound of explosion told of the continuing bombardment of the city.

Once home to 120,000 residents, Reims was now a deserted wasteland of ruined buildings and houses, from which rose the stink of death. The shell-damaged Gothic cathedral served as the centerpiece of all visits to the city and of France's campaign of anti-German propaganda. Their officer guide led the journalists into the cathedral, their footsteps crunching on bits of glass that had once been the stained glass windows crafted by medieval artisans. The bombardment had blasted great jagged holes through the roof. Broken statues of saints littered the floor. Fire had blackened the interior. The sudden nearby rumble of artillery caused them all to catch their breath. They had been instructed to rush into a cellar if the shells fell too close.

"I know of no more impressive place to be in the closing days of the year 1916 than here at the front of the terrible world war," Daggett wrote, clearly in the thrall of her war zone experience.

The visit to Reims didn't fit neatly into Daggett's other reporting, except that every correspondent who visited Europe at this time felt obliged to get a taste of war. The Allies had fully embraced the propaganda value of packaging the war to shape public opinion, an area of the conflict in which they now enjoyed superiority over the Central Powers. Almost every war tour itinerary included a visit to the "desecrated" cathedral.

E. Alexander Powell, of the *New York World*, explained how it worked:

> When the French have been pestered for permission to visit the front by some foreigner—usually an American—until their patience has been exhausted, or when there comes to Paris a visitor to whom they wish to show attention, they send him to Rheims. Artists, architects, ex-ambassadors, ex-congressmen, lady journalists, manufacturers in quest of war orders, bankers engaged in floating loans, millionaires who have given or are likely to give money to war-charities, editors of obscure newspapers and monthly magazines, are

packed off weekly, in personally conducted parties of a dozen or more, on a day's excursion to the City of the Desecrated Cathedral.

They grow indignant over the cathedral's shattered beauties, they visit the famous wine-cellars, they hear the occasional crack of a rifle or the crash of a field-gun, and, upon their return, they write articles for the magazines, and give lectures, and to their friends at home send long letters—usually copied in the local papers—describing their experiences "on the firing-line."

Although Powell sounded a cynical note about the publicizing of Reims, the cathedral had become an effective symbol to rouse sympathies in America. In December 1916, when Daggett visited the French city, forces in the United States were pushing the country inexorably toward entry into the fighting. By now journalists had been getting to the front lines, providing plenty of horrors-of-war stories. But could a constant litany of horrors move a distant reader in America as much as a ruined cathedral where nearly every king of France had been crowned? Where little girls now wandered among the visitors selling as souvenirs pieces of the cathedral's irreplaceable, thirteenth-century stained glass windows? Where the famous equestrian statue of Joan of Arc, opposite the cathedral, remained untouched and now flew a tiny French flag?

When Daggett returned to Paris on December 25, she was surprised to realize it was Christmas. The holiday had passed without note in the war zone. All her attention now focused on consolidating her notes, gathering her documents, and getting them in the mail to America. Everything had to make it past the censor, but it was a guessing game as to what he would allow. Would colorful language about women's progress be rejected? Would an openly feminist document be seen as seditious? What about the information she had gathered on the rising value of a baby in the warring states? Would these things be seen as giving aid and comfort to the enemy by divulging critical information?

She presented her huge package of writings and research to the press office. There it was finally stamped, signed in red ink, done up in packages, and officially sealed in red wax with the seal of France. She could then deliver it to the post office, register it, and mail it off, "committing it with a sigh to the mercies of the great Atlantic."

6

As the War Dragged On

From the day of my arrival to the moment of my
departure, we have but one topic of conversation—
Germany's virtues and America's sins.

—MADELEINE ZABRISKIE DOTY, *Short Rations*, 1917

Just as the passenger liner ss *Noordam* eased from its berth in New York Harbor on April 15, 1915, a gust of wind lifted the white flag on its mast to display the single word inscribed on it in large blue letters: PEACE. Not that a wartime mission of peace protected the delegates of the Women's Peace Party from the perils of the voyage. Although a neutral vessel, the ship would be sailing into dangerous waters. In February, Germany had escalated its submarine warfare by declaring the waters surrounding Great Britain to be a war zone. All ships sailing under British, French, or Russian flags in those waters would be sunk on sight. If ships from neutral nations chose to enter those waters, they did so at their own risk. The previous month German submarines sank forty-two Allied and neutral ships in and around British waters. With German planes and Zeppelins bombing London and Paris and its U-boats prowling the seas, the active war zone continued to expand.

Journalists Mary Heaton Vorse (*Century Magazine*), Madeleine Zabriskie Doty (*New York Evening Post*), and Mary Chamberlain (*Survey*) were among the forty-four American women aboard the *Noordam*, traveling to The Hague for the International Congress

16. Members of the American delegation to the Women's Peace Congress in The Hague embark on their voyage in April 1915. American social worker and political activist Jane Addams chaired the congress. She is pictured above the letter *P* in the banner. Journalist Mary Heaton Vorse accompanied the delegation. She is pictured above the letter *C*. Several of the delegates-journalists reported on the congress and on their subsequent visits to Germany in the wake of the *Lusitania* sinking. George Grantham Bain Collection, Prints & Photographs Division, Library of Congress, LC-B2-3443-11.

of Women, which would become better known as the Women's Peace Congress. The gathering came in response to a building international movement of women and women's organizations intent on stopping this war and preventing future wars.

During the voyage the women kept busy with morning discussions about history and diplomacy and spent evenings sharing personal stories. To New York attorney Madeleine Doty, who had been recruited by the *Evening Post* to report on the congress, the passengers reminded her of the wildly diverse pilgrims sharing their stories in the *Canterbury Tales*. One woman had organized a women's telephone union. There were also a poet, a doctor, three lawyers, a Quaker preacher, social workers, and writers.

Mary Heaton Vorse, a champion of feminist issues such as voting rights, economic independence, education, and birth control, described the delegates as the "most forward-looking women of America" but acknowledged that the group also included "women with nostrums for ending war and women who had come for the ride . . . cranks with Christian Science smiles and blue ribbons in their hair, hard-working Hull House women, little half-baked enthusiasts, [and] elderly war horses of peace." Dr. Alice Hamilton, who would publish a post-conference article for the *Survey*, compared shipboard activities to a perpetual meeting of a women's civic club.

On the eighth day, when the *Noordam* sailed into the stalking ground of German submarines, the unsettling process began of removing deck railings, stripping the canvas from lifeboats, and keeping the name of the ship illuminated at night to alert potential predators of its neutral status. Doty and her cabin mate unpacked their life preservers. Her roommate, unnerved by their mortal danger, slept in her best underwear and silk stockings so that in death she would look presentable. Small boats went before them to sweep their path of mines. Several British ships stopped them at gunpoint and officers boarded. After a search they marched off the ship two German stowaways, who shouted "Hoch der Kaiser!" and "Vaterland über alles!"

British authorities held up the ship at Dover for three days, without explanation. Britain opposed the peace conference and prevented the British delegation from attending. The British press labeled the women "Pro-Hun Peacettes" on their way to a tea party. Even the American ambassador in England, Walter Hines Page, scornfully dubbed their ship "The Palace of Doves." Finally, on opening day for the conference, April 28, 1915, the *Noordam* was allowed to proceed.

The American women arrived at the great hall in The Hague to find it crowded with more than twelve hundred delegates from twelve countries, including twenty-eight from Germany. No representatives attended from France, Russia, or Serbia, but a few British women managed to make the trip. The American social worker and political activist Jane Addams chaired the congress. They had gathered for the radical purpose of discussing peace.

For Mary Chamberlain the most extraordinary thing about the congress was that it was happening at all. "Nearly every one of those women who sat there side by side so dignified and courteous, had brothers, husbands or friends facing each other in maddened fury or even now mown down by each other's bullets. It was a great test of courage for these women to risk the bitterness of their families, the ridicule of their friends and the censure of their governments to come to this international women's congress."

From the press table the journalists had a perfect vantage point to watch the drama unfold. Delegates avoided clashing along national lines or laying blame for the war. The first speakers took the podium to testify about their personal experiences and the circumstances in their home countries. High-minded resolutions had to wait, Doty noted, while individuals spoke about the war. "Day by day, as we sat side by side, we had learned of the suffering in war-ridden lands. Black-clad wives had made speeches. Sorrowing mothers had shown their agony. The battlefield became a reality, covered with dead and dying sons and husbands. These glimpses of tragedy wrung our hearts. We ceased to be enemies or friends. We were just women. All preconceived plans vanished. There grew an urgent need to do something."

Eventually, resolutions emerged: small nations should have their integrity ensured, democratic parliaments should be allowed, future disputes should be submitted to arbitration, foreign policies should be under democratic control, and women should gain political rights equal to men.

As the close of the congress approached, the delegates realized that resolutions alone were not enough. They wanted immediate action. One delegate rose to challenge the women to have the courage to call for an immediate end to the fighting—"courage to say not one more shall be killed. Courage to say we can't wait—we must have peace now. Courage to carry this demand personally from nation to nation."

The resolution unleashed the pent-up emotions of the delegates, Doty noted. "Sobs broke from grief-stricken mothers. Tears streamed down faces. Women were stirred past utterance. No vote was needed to carry this motion. The audience rose as one."

As its final action, the congress created two committees to carry their resolutions to leaders in each of the capitals of the warring and neutral nations. One committee set off for the Scandinavian countries and Russia. Jane Addams headed the committee sent to England, Germany, France, Italy, and the United States.

Jane Addams's mission of peace to the warring capitals became doubly daunting only six days after the close of the congress, when a German submarine sank the British passenger ship RMS *Lusitania*, taking eleven hundred passengers and crew to their deaths. Splashed on headlines around the world, the act raised an outcry against Germany and further sharpened the animosities of the conflict.

Following the tragedy, two women journalists found themselves unexpectedly part of the *Lusitania* story. On the day after the sinking, *Brooklyn Daily Eagle* reporter Jean Cabell O'Neill sailed from Liverpool for home, with heightened anxiety about the voyage. She had just finished a two-month stint reporting from France and had never felt so imperiled. In the first week of May alone, U-boats sank thirty-one British, Commonwealth, and neutral ships. Her fellow passengers calculated their chances of making it safely to America as one in one hundred.

A short way into their voyage, just as the ship entered a vast debris field from the *Lusitania*, a few passengers gathered on deck to offer prayers for those lost at sea. The wreckage of broken wood, oars, chairs, hatches, and casks attracted the excited attention of the passengers. Shouts went up when some noticed the body of a woman clinging to a raft and clutching to her breast the body of a child. Three other dead children in life belts floated nearby. They showed no signs of life, so the ship did not stop. O'Neill rushed to her cabin and through a porthole dropped flowers onto the water. Then she cabled the Associated Press office in London with the alarming news that some victims of the tragedy remained on the scene. Several days of news stories featured O'Neill and her shocking account of the drowned mother and child.

In America reporters noted the name of well-known journalist adventurer Harriet Chalmers Adams on the list of *Lusitania* victims. Her family was besieged by telephone and telegraph for details and reactions. Some reporters showed up at her parents' house and were greeted at the door by Adams herself. She explained that she had booked passage on the *Lusitania*, on assignment for *Harper's Magazine*. She had even picked up her ticket. But at the last minute she learned that her father was ill and canceled her passage. Apparently, there had not been time to remove her name from the passenger list. The headline in the San Francisco newspaper the *Bulletin* on May 13, 1915, read, "Noted Woman Changes Mind; Escapes Death."

The *Lusitania* tragedy also abruptly altered the plans of two of the journalists who had covered the Women's Peace Congress— Madeleine Zabriskie Doty and Mary Heaton Vorse. Doty still bathed in the idealistic afterglow of the congress when reaction to the *Lusitania* sinking reverberated around the world. Who knew what might happen next? America might be provoked into the war.

The mysterious, threatening world of wartime Germany beckoned just beyond the Dutch border. The American embassy in The Hague warned Doty not to go to Germany. The timing was not right. Americans were not wanted there. But the call to adventure proved too strong: "I pinned my little American flag and my Hague Peace Congress badge to the lapel of my coat." With a passport, a small handbag, and a beating heart, she set forth for Berlin.

Following the congress, Mary Heaton Vorse had been exploring the "armed neutrality" of Holland with Associated Press reporter Paxton Hibben. They visited a refugee camp, where they met a Belgian woman who had been made to watch as German soldiers shot her husband and sons and other men in her village. Their driver told of losing his family during the German bombardment of Antwerp. Such stories only fueled Hibben's bitter hatred of Germany and Vorse's curiosity.

Vorse had been planning to travel to France via England, to gather refugee stories for *Century Magazine*, when the *Lusitania* got torpedoed and the Channel closed down. Her assignment had been to write about the civilian population, but the civilian population that most interested her now lived just across the Dutch border in Germany. She wanted to know what they thought about the *Lusitania*. On May 8, the day after the *Lusitania* became front-page news, Vorse crossed into the German Empire.

"I suppose no stupider person than I existed at that time," Vorse wrote many years later in her memoir, *A Footnote to Folly: Reminiscences of Mary Heaton Vorse* (1935). She had letters of introduction to important Germans and to the American ambassador. She should have proceeded directly to Berlin, registered with the authorities, arranged interviews, and done things properly. But it was comparatively easy to pass over the border from Holland. After the usual careful screening of luggage and passport, she found herself in Germany. As a child, she had traveled with her family in Germany, and she spoke the language reasonably well. She planned to travel to Frankfurt, which she had visited several years earlier.

From the first moments on the train and throughout Vorse's entire trip, the *Lusitania* was a prime topic of conversation. "People repeated over and over again, 'Well, it serves them right! Traveling on a munitions ship.' As is usual among traveling foreigners I was included in the conversation. As soon as I said I was an American their accusing eyes were turned on me. 'Why . . . is your country selling munitions to the Allies?'" In repeated conversations America was seen not as a neutral nation but as an enemy.

When she visited friends in Frankfurt, whose husbands and sons were dead or at the front, they spoke with pride of their sacrifice. "I began to feel a sense of unreality as though everyone was hypnotized. I was for the first time in the presence of a nation at war where all the normal activities of life are suspended, where one thought obsesses a whole nation."

She had planned to stay two days in Frankfurt but felt so uneasy that she left after one and headed for neutral Switzerland. At the border crossing point to Basel, Vorse cut a conspicuous figure among the small group of peasants with market baskets. Multiple officials stopped her for interrogations and luggage searches. One officer flew into a rage on learning she was an American. Why did Americans not get rid of their president, who so sympathized with the Allies? Why did her country sell arms to the enemies of Germany? Hours ticked by as additional agents continued questioning her and reexamining her bags. One remarked that American correspondents had been hostile to Germany.

When she finally convinced them to let her cross into Switzerland, she asked why she had been treated this way. "A woman alone in wartime, you know, traveling over great distances under such difficulties, speaking several languages," the official explained. "Women selected for difficult errands are frequently those of the quietest appearance and whose presence would cause least remarks." There she had her answer. Because she was a quiet, middle-aged woman, going about her business, she had been suspected of being a spy.

She could not have been more warmly received in Switzerland. Even though she lacked the customary letters of introduction, the authorities eagerly told their stories and assisted her at every turn. Switzerland had become a vast, neutral transit point between warring countries. Through this tiny country passed the exchange of civilian internees and wounded prisoners. Its postal services processed all mail going between France and French prisoners of war in Germany. However, hundreds of those letters and postcards never reached their destination because they lacked a full address.

Swiss officials sat Vorse at a table and handed her stacks of undelivered postcards. The messages overflowed with anguish. "My son: How are you? Are you wounded? Do they treat you well? What do you need?" Most replies mentioned the lack of food. "My dear father and mother: Send me, if you can, some bread."

"My dear wife: It doesn't go so badly with me, but we are hungry, all of us are hungry."

First in Switzerland and then France, Vorse wrote articles that drew attention to victims of war: internees; prisoners of war; evacuees; and the *sinistrées*, as the survivors in the devastated territories of northern France were called. In an article for the *Century Magazine*, "The Sinistrées of France," Vorse described conditions for those in regions already destroyed by the fighting. She seemed most moved by the disruption of families. A bureau in Paris maintained a vast card catalog of information on lost family members and children found roaming on roads—or even walking into trenches—having lost all their family.

Madeleine Zabriskie Doty encountered in Germany "an atmosphere of depression and suppression." Since she didn't speak German, she found a temporary traveling companion in a Hungarian newspaperwoman who had attended the congress and spoke German and English. The woman helped Doty find lodging in the home of a middle-aged German professor and his American-born wife. From the start they set about to convert her to the German cause. "They are all hospitality, but their zealousness torments me," she wrote. "I am the heathen whose soul must be saved."

Her determination to find Germans who wanted peace forced her to act like a spy. Although required to report her every movement to her hosts, she arranged to meet in secret with some women of the Social Democratic Party. They had broken with the party when it chose to support the war. Now their heroine was Rosa Luxemburg, the social activist who had been arrested for shouting at a unit of soldiers: "Don't go to war! Don't shoot your brothers!"

A few months after Luxemburg's arrest, a group of women marched to the Reichstag, chanting against war. The police dispersed them, and not a word about the march appeared in the newspapers. Working for peace from inside Germany was virtually impossible, the women confided to Doty. One could not advocate for peace through the mail or in newspapers, as both were censored. They met in secret and exchanged news by word of mouth.

Doty took on a dual life, living with the respectable German couple and escaping to meet with the women rebels who had become criminals for peace. She discovered that she was followed, her phone messages intercepted, and an innocent letter she sent to the women never arrived. Although Doty concluded that each citizen of Germany was only a cog in the military machine, she admired the courage of this small band of women who kept alive the vision of peace. "Through them I learned to love Germany."

Visiting the Warring Capitals

Even as Doty went about her dual existence in Berlin, the official delegation from the Peace Congress, led by Jane Addams, arrived in Berlin to talk to German leaders about ending the war. The delegation had already presented the resolutions from the congress to leaders in Holland and Britain. From Berlin they would travel to Vienna, Budapest, Berne, Rome, the Vatican, Paris, and La Havre (temporary Belgian capital), and eventually they would visit President Wilson in Washington. It was an audacious and challenging undertaking that briefly captured world attention but earned more derision than praise. The *Survey* had recruited Alice Hamilton to report on the venture. Addams herself would write an article for the same magazine summarizing the results of the delegation visits.

The Hague congress had been an inspiring experience, as the attendees shared their suffering and courage and gained the faint hope that their determination might prevail against the deadly militarism that gripped the Continent. However, that hope quickly eroded in the face of the intransigent will to fight. The emotional impact of their message was immediately undercut by the *Lusitania* sinking and the continuing momentum of war. Although the pope was supportive of Addams's mission and even issued his own call for peace shortly after meeting with her, the delegation arrived in Rome the day after Italy entered

17. Alice Hamilton, MD, served as a delegate to the Women's Peace Congress in The Hague, in April 1915. She reported on the congress and on the committee from the congress that delivered the call for immediate peace to the leaders of the warring and neutral nations. George Grantham Bain Collection, Prints & Photographs Division, Library of Congress, LC-B2-5118-815.

the war, and the resulting swell of nationalism there drowned any thought of peace.

In each capital the highest government ministers and members of parliament received them graciously. They also sought out politicians thought to be receptive to peace and women's organizations previously committed to peace and suffrage. Hamilton's article "At the War Capitals" captured the meetings, the arguments, and the mounting disappointments. In Berlin they met a Socialist politician, a prewar friend and staunch pacifist, who now served in the army and attacked them on the subject of America's sale of munitions to the Allies. "An attack to which we became wearily accustomed," Hamilton noted. The delegation met with women's suffrage groups but found little sympathy there either. Although individual women within these organizations shared the pacifist philosophy, they now supported their government's war effort.

It was perhaps one of the sharpest disappointments for Addams and her committee: that the women's organizations, once so committed to peace, now supported war. The bond of the suffering, determined women at The Hague had been so strong. Their shared roles as mothers and wives gave them a unique platform for opposing war. But nationalism and militarism trumped that. "In every country there are many, many women," Addams conceded in her article, "who believe that the war is inevitable and righteous, and that the highest possible service is being performed by their sons who go into the army."

Alice Hamilton's article about the Addams delegation's trip cast a broad focus that included many observations about life in the European capitals—seeing the casualties lists posted in Berlin, the bread rationing cards issued by their hotels, convalescent soldiers on the streets in Vienna, the obsession with spies, severe press censorship, blackouts in London and Paris, the proliferation of recruitment posters in London. These glimpses of life on the home fronts provided a context for the peace effort and for the war in general. The war had completely transformed life in these nations into something both noble and grotesque.

Life on the Home Fronts

When the warring nations became more open to journalists from neutral countries, in mid-1915, the flow of correspondents and other visitors to Europe increased markedly. A greater number and variety of publications sent writers on freelance assignments.

Government press offices became more practiced at packaging the news and standardizing press tours. French tours routinely visited the Marne battlefield, scene of France's greatest victory early in the war, and Reims cathedral, the cultural landmark damaged by German shells. Tours to the front ventured into areas where fighting was quiet but which provided a chance to meet with officers, visit hospitals, and possibly even have the ultimate experience of entering a trench. The sound of distant cannonading would allow reporters to boast that they had been under fire at the front.

However, as the world plodded wearily into the second and third years of the war, the interest of newspapers and magazines in America expanded beyond the battle lines to focus more on life in the warring countries. Now that it was clear the war would not end quickly, as so many had predicted, governments and citizens had to adjust to the new reality. A long war changed calculations completely. It shifted the question from how military victory would be achieved to which country could hold out the longest. Would questions about manpower, raw materials, food, and morale play a greater role in determining victory than military prowess?

During this period women journalists such as Mary Boyle O'Reilly and Eleanor Franklin Egan maintained a permanent presence in the war zones, traveling to numerous countries, tackling topics grand and small to feed the American public's insatiable interest in the war. Reporters Madeleine Doty and Maude Radford Warren made multiple visits to Europe to monitor the evolving story line.

On visits in 1915 and 1916 Maude Warren saw the Allies adjusting to the continuing war. She wrote about how fully Britain embraced advertising to manage its population. Only a few years earlier, most British firms had considered it beneath their dignity to advertise; now government advertising appeared everywhere, to stir recruitment, sell war bonds, discourage the purchase of luxury goods, and generally tell civilians what they must and must not do to support soldiers and the nation.

Warren reported that France struggled through a mental adjustment to a long war with "an air of self-reliance and high resolve." Shortages of everything were common. Prices for everything rose. Everything was taxed. The government admonished citizens to dress simply, economize on heat and light, observe meatless days, and eschew all luxuries. Everything that did not work or was not available or could not be accomplished was met with the universal phrase of resignation, *C'est la guerre* (It's the war).

Ever since the opening days of the war, Mary Boyle O'Reilly had continued to work for the news syndication service Newspaper Enterprise Association out of her office in London. A relatively new syndicate, established in 1902, the NEA grew to several hundred subscribing newspapers by 1915, when it moved its headquarters from Cleveland to Chicago. The war and Mary Boyle O'Reilly contributed to that growth.

O'Reilly made occasional forays to the Continent, to France, Norway, Sweden, and Russia. But London offered plenty of opportunities for good reporting. "Straws from all the corners of the war zone come by the wind's ways into this city," she explained in one news story. To supply the NEA's constant need for news, she sent feature stories and news notes every few days by gathering stories from London papers, interviewing people who passed through the city, or reaping the rich harvest of events around her. She reported on a mad Frenchwoman at Soissons who stabbed German wounded, an informal truce to retrieve wounded as gleaned from a soldier's letter, and an interview with a traveler about the fate of Jews in Palestine. When she learned that among the British upper classes there were now twelve marriageable women for each eligible man, she wrote about the declining birth rate in all the warring nations and its implications for the war, the future, and the weakening of the human race. Indulging her penchant for marking dramatic conclusions with capital letters, O'Reilly noted that the war "MAKES A HUSBAND FAMINE INEVITABLE."

Nor did she shy away from thorny labor issues or antiwar attitudes, criticizing the low wages paid in English sweatshops and interviewing the famous outspoken critic of the war George Bernard Shaw. "The England that grabbed Ireland, India and Egypt cannot delude the Germany of Wilhelm II," Shaw noted. "Our national trick of sanctimonious indignation is simple hypocrisy." Such articles had to be mailed to the United States to avoid the censors.

With increasing regularity the fighting war came to her. While O'Reilly was staying at a hotel in York, the maid told her:

"It seems a story is brewing, ma'am. There's a queer thunder at sea."

"I listened. Faint and far borne drifted the unmistakable reverberation of naval guns."

"Good Lord!" the maid exclaimed; "it's them! The Huns are here!"

O'Reilly rushed to the train station and headed for the coast. She arrived in the town of Hartlepool shortly after it suffered a shelling by German cruisers. O'Reilly's interviews with distraught survivors ran under the headline "Last Shell Brings Death to 2 Babies, Running in Fright."

Soon she did not even have to stir from London to be on the front lines of the fighting war. In February 1915 Germany launched a Zeppelin raid on London. The monstrous, lighter-than-air craft were straight out of science fiction. Only eight years earlier, H. G. Wells had written *The War in the Air*, a novel about German airships attacking New York City. Now they appeared at night over London, drifting silently over the city, large enough to blot stars from the sky. Germany had fully embraced the concept of total war, which saw no distinction between combatants and noncombatants.

In one raid O'Reilly followed "London's pluckiest policewoman" into the poor neighborhoods of the East End, where they encountered a hysterical woman and looters. Zeppelin raids provided O'Reilly with a succession of dramatic front-page stories. In March she told of approaching London by train one night and seeing flashes of exploding bombs in the distance and the dramatic illumination of a giant airship by a spotlight. Her train stopped for an hour in a tunnel and arrived at the station as victims gathered there, including one crying little girl whose father had been killed.

Several of the women war correspondents experienced London Zeppelin raids, but none as dramatically as Maude Radford Warren. When whispered rumors swept the city that a raid was imminent, Warren joined a crowd gathered outside her hotel to watch giant searchlights sweep the night sky. Suddenly the lights illuminated the ominous form of a huge airship. Gunfire from the ground set the Zeppelin ablaze. "Long tongues of flame shot out from it" as it descended for miles to a fiery destruction. On another occasion, while awaiting a raid, Warren noticed someone signaling with a light from an open window. Regulations required that shades be drawn at night so as not to let Zeppelin crews know they were over London. Warren reported the incident to the police the next day, and the occupant of that room was arrested as a spy.

By June, "Zep" raids had become routine. For one midnight raid O'Reilly and a friend drove through London streets as though on a sightseeing excursion. The raids no longer alarmed Londoners. Thousands of special constables maintained order, gun crews waited expectantly at their weapons, first-aid volunteers clustered at strategic locations. Most Londoners stood on the streets awaiting the show. This phase of the war had lost its shock value. Newspapers moved O'Reilly's Zeppelin raid stories off the front page.

For the NEA and the hundreds of newspapers that ran its news stories, O'Reilly offered a unique view of the war. The sheer quantity and range of her coverage delivered everything from war trivia and eyewitness accounts of fighting to reasoned articles about evolving attitudes. War had become the new normal, and O'Reilly brought it to her readers in its many iterations.

The Problem of Food

Along with five hundred other ferry passengers, Eleanor Franklin Egan sat on a boat for three days, waiting for U-boats to leave the English Channel. Being stranded with a menagerie of travelers proved fodder enough for an article about traveling in wartime. While providing a full account of her efforts to sleep, bathe, eat, and stay warm, she gave readers cameos of her traveling companions: French sailors who had been rescued from the Channel when their boat got torpedoed, an American "negro vaudeville troupe" on its way to performances in Paris, British nurses heading to Egypt, an English officer learning to play the ukulele, and a lady marksman entertainer. On the third night her ship made a dash for the French shore.

Egan had joined the *Saturday Evening Post*'s stable of war correspondents with a September 25, 1915, article about Serbia. She filed a half-dozen reports from Turkey during Britain's ill-fated Gallipoli campaign. Then, in early 1916, she turned her attention to the western front, as the mammoth battles of attrition at Verdun and the Somme raged. Her interests were not in the fighting war, however, but in how countries endured.

It was quickly impressed upon a visitor to any of the warring countries that food had become a critical element of the war, visible in the strict rationing, scant meals in hotels, labor-starved farms, and substitute food products. In a time of war, with free trade blockaded and the male workforce in the army, how did a nation feed its fighting men and the civilian population? By way of example, Egan noted that "the French heroes of Verdun, around a million of them, consume approximately twenty-four million five hundred thousand pounds of food every week." It required the round-the-clock labors of some fifteen thousand men just to feed the defenders of Verdun. Soldiers could live in the squalor of the trenches, harassed by vermin, under continuous assault by the enemy, but they could not function without food. Certainly, a component so key to military success and national survival warranted its own story.

Egan went to the press bureau in Paris, typically the first point of contact for a journalist arriving in a warring country. One blunt Frenchman had already warned Egan about the bureau's curious attitude toward American women: "Any American woman who has so much as knitted a pair of socks for a French soldier thinks her service has entitled her to the privilege of seeing the armies at the Front." In 1916 "the front" these women wanted to see was the ongoing battle at Verdun. The fact that many of these American women returned home on missions to raise money for French charities meant that their requests, however difficult to fulfill, merited some consideration.

In fact, American women enjoyed a privileged status with the French. Frenchwomen were forbidden near the front. English-women could cross the Channel only on the most urgent of business. "But the foreign woman, the neutral, and especially the American, may go almost anywhere," Egan explained, "if she has the qualities necessary to meet the difficulties of obtaining permits. Two of these are unlimited patience and dogged persistence."

A long bookshelf lined the entrance to the press bureau, stacked high with pamphlets in many languages. Titles included "German Theory and Practice of War," "The Suppression of the Armenians—German Methods—Turkish Performance," and "The Violation by Germany of the Neutrality of Belgium and Luxembourg." Egan grabbed a few, then marched into the main office and announced her ambitious request to "see the national pantry and clothespress—to say nothing of the kitchens, refrigerators, storerooms, wine cellars and other incidentals of national housekeeping."

Egan had mastered the first-person opinionated style favored by the *Saturday Evening Post*. Her articles chronicled her personal adventures in pursuit of the news. She also had an irrepressible humor, sometimes self-deprecating, sometimes laced with ridicule or cynicism. "When I made my innocent demands upon the secrets of the military economic processes everybody laughed," she noted about her initial visit to the press bureau, "and I think somebody said '*Mon Dieu!*'" But after considerable patience and persistence, Egan eventually found herself in possession of a commissariat map of France. Red anchors marked the principal ports, from which railroads ran to the many red-dotted warehouses and mills in the center of France. Red dots with a circle denoted distribution centers. From there the rail lines extended to the front.

Egan began at a distribution center where they prepared and shipped three hundred thousand rations every day. An adjacent complex devoted itself exclusively to the baking of bread on a massive scale. That delicious aroma mixed with the smell of roasting coffee. The beans had made their way here from Brazil and the East Indies. Like clockwork, those items and many more were loaded onto trains and sent to the front.

To explore the entire chain of distribution, Egan rode one of those trains to Bar-le-Duc, the station for Verdun, where the presence of the war made itself felt immediately: "A long, rolling, sullen rumble of guns spread itself out across the northern horizon. Verdun! Let me tell you that when you are within sound of the guns you can think of nothing else; you can hear nothing else; you can feel nothing else—the guns are killing and you know it." Verdun had already cost France nearly an entire generation of its best young men. Egan saw them bleeding in the many corrugated iron sheds behind the train station that served as the evacuation hospital.

Everyone Egan met went about their business so calmly and methodically, but the prospect of traveling into the heart of the fighting tested Egan's own composure. "Never for one instant in my life had I wanted to go to Verdun or near any other battle," she admitted. "But I was following food supplies up to the point of ultimate consumption."

For the first two months of the fighting at Verdun, all supplies traveled by truck along a winding, muddy road, named "The Sacred Way" for its critical role in sustaining the army. Nine to ten thousand trucks rolled twenty-four hours a day, taking forward men, munitions, and food. That monumental effort had passed into legend, details of which Egan heard from one of the men who had driven that road nonstop. Now narrow-gage rails delivered supplies to different points along the ten-mile front in this zone. From there trucks continued them on their way to field kitchens and headquarters, on the "brink of the trenches." Seeing the loading and unloading of the trains and trucks gave Egan the final link in the supply chain that kept Verdun's million-man army in the fight.

Egan continued to report on food and war supplies in two additional articles in 1916. To travel the supply line to Verdun required a dangerous train ride into the heart of one of the largest battles of the war. To reach the active, functioning Belgian government in exile required only a leisurely 125-mile drive from Paris to La Havre. There in the charming seaside village of Sainte-Addresse, a bathing resort suburb of La Havre, the Belgian government conducted its business. She shared lunch one day with senators and the ministers of war, foreign affairs, finance, commerce, science and arts, virtually the entire Belgian government in exile. The government had created a vast military industrial enterprise that not only supplied its own army with every necessity "from boot laces to bombs" but also managed to contribute munitions and supplies to its allies.

Egan toured a huge complex of buildings constructed within a few months. Extensive warehouses overflowed with raw materials from America, and factories buzzed with continuous activity, every day sending twenty-five railroad freight cars of war materials toward the front.

While Belgian industriousness helped to sustain the Allied war effort, neutral Holland supported both sides in the conflict, which placed it in the center of tensions between England and Germany. In a 1916 article, "An Innocent Bystander," Egan detailed the precarious tightrope Holland walked regarding trade with the two warring nations. Aside from having to feed its own population, Holland hosted one million Belgian refugees and thirty-two thousand interned soldiers and Allied war prisoners. Germany, its bellicose neighbor, insisted that Holland sell it food and everything else it had to sell or it would cut off its vital supply of coal—or do something even worse. England insisted that Holland not sell food to Germany or it would cut its supply of grain and imported raw materials.

Until recently, Holland had been free to sell to Germany its surplus of fish, fruits, dairy products, and produce. However, the generous price Germany was willing to pay for this food proved such an incentive to Dutch producers that food exports increased dramatically. Given that the British war strategy of blockading German maritime trade had begun to dig deeply into German life, London protested the Dutch trade.

Egan traveled around Holland investigating conditions. In Holland's seaside resorts Egan found many "Germans running away from starvation and Belgians running away from Germans." Conversations often turned to the subject of food. Germans loudly denied shortages of anything in Germany, while at the same time they condemned the British naval blockade for making war against starving women and children.

Elaborate trading compromises had been devised for how much and what products Holland could sell to Germany and what meager price England would pay Holland for its goods. Ships arriving in Dutch ports could not unload until the British navy inspected their cargo. The slightest violation of British rules put companies, banks, shipping lines, or individuals on the English Statutory List, a blacklist that forbade dealings with those entities. Once one trade issue was resolved, another flared up to take its place. Britain countenanced nothing that relieved the pressure that the blockade was putting on German food supplies.

Hunger and Unrest in Germany

"Every day there are fresh indications that the internal situation in Germany is steadily growing worse," reported the *International Herald Tribune* on July 22, 1916, "and food troubles are becoming more and more acute throughout the empire."

Among the rumors most eagerly circulated by the Allies in 1916 were those dealing with deteriorating economic and social conditions inside Germany. Reasoning held that the German government had not made economic plans for a long war. In 1914 Germany had relied on imports for about a third of its food, fodder, and fertilizer. The stifling British naval blockade interrupted these imports. Germany now depended for food on its allies and its own farms, from which men and horses had been stripped for the war effort. In short Germans were starving, and reports had leaked out of bread riots in some cities.

Because food shortages and civil unrest might portend an end to the war, editors were keen to learn the truth about conditions inside Germany. But reporting on Germany had become progressively more difficult. Germany had tightened entrance requirements and made censorship more restrictive, while the Allies continued to interrupt mail and cable traffic.

In the summer of 1916 three American journalists ventured into Germany to get the facts: Marie Reuter Gallison, Madeleine Zabriskie Doty, and Herbert Bayard Swope. Their first-hand accounts, which painted conflicting pictures of conditions, saw print that fall and winter, as the United States moved inexorably toward entering the war.

Actually, German-born Marie Gallison was by no stretch a journalist. The widow of noted landscape artist Henry H. Gallison, she had founded the Choral Society at Radcliffe College in 1899 and continued to serve as its director. For most of the thirty years she lived in America, her native Germany had been held in high regard. But since the outbreak of war, it had been "hooted, slandered, and reviled." She could not sort out the truth from articles and books about the war, so on May 31, 1916, she set off to investigate for herself. Appearing under the byline "Mrs. H. H. Gallison," her account of what she learned appeared in three articles in the *Outlook* that November and December.

Travelers to Germany took the sea-lanes north of Britain to Norway and from there to Germany via Denmark. Gallison's voyage began like a holiday trip until the ship's wireless reported the naval battle of Jutland and the loss of Britain's war leader Lord Herbert Kitchener when his ship struck a mine. As was customary, once in British waters, the ship was directed into a British port, where passengers were taken off and questioned. Contrary to what she had heard, British officials treated her courteously and gave her no trouble.

In Norway and Denmark Gallison heard stories about starvation in Germany, although she wondered if that was just wishful thinking to bring courage into French and British hearts. Once in Germany, she asked everyone she met about food shortages. Germany had implemented rationing, but all agreed that there was sufficient food. When Gallison took her questions to the Imperial Food Commission, officials gave her permission to travel anywhere and investigate as freely as she wished. Hearing of shortages in East Prussia, she traveled there and found adequate food. Back in Berlin she visited poor neighborhoods where women operated "war kitchens" to feed the destitute.

In Frankfurt, Heidelberg, Leipzig, and other cities Gallison learned that distribution problems occasionally caused temporary food shortages but that they all had food. She explained how rationing worked and quoted the reasonable cost of food from a price list. In fact, during the ten weeks she spent in Germany, Gallison gained ten pounds because she ate so well.

Despite what Western newspapers reported about discord in Germany, all but a few malcontents strongly supported the war effort, Gallison noted. She explained how efficiently Germany cared for the wounded and reeducated soldiers who were maimed. Only once did she encounter any hatred toward America, and on that occasion she stood up to the speaker and explained how the speaker was wrong.

Throughout her articles Gallison portrayed a sympathy and affection for Germany and its struggling citizens rarely found in the American press. American war reporters generally lauded the appearance and character of French and British soldiers and praised the resolve of those nations. Gallison's final article included this tribute to the German soldier: "At every railway station soldiers were coming and going. Such strong, sunburned faces! I felt like thanking each one of them singly for fighting for the Fatherland; for keeping the enemy away from the fields rich with abundant harvest; for defending the land of German *Kultur*, the home of music and kindergarten, of universal old-age insurance and the Mutterschutz [legal protections for motherhood], of the municipal theaters and opera that offer to the poorest the richest gems and compositions of all nations, the land of the 'cities beautiful,' the state of the Greek ideal of 'one for all.'"

When the *Outlook* published the first of Gallison's articles, it felt obliged to justify itself. "Mrs. Gallison does not pretend to be giving a scientific report of economic and social conditions. What she is giving is the moving picture that was imprinted upon the sensitive film of her mind as she went about among the German people during the strain of war," *Outlook* editors explained to readers. "It is the most vivid, the most convincing, the most understandable picture of Germany during these days that we have happened to see."

By the time Gallison's second article ran, on December 6, *Outlook* editors pointed out additionally that her account of conditions in Germany differed considerably from that of another woman, Madeleine Zabriskie Doty, whose articles were then appearing in the *New York Tribune* and *Chicago Tribune*. Doty reported that Germany faced an acute food shortage and the life of its people was grim. Running for several weeks in these two major newspapers, often on the front page, Doty's account reached far more readers than did Gallison's.

As a journalist, attorney, peace activist, and social reformer, Madeleine Zabriskie Doty seemed a good choice to report objectively on conditions inside the German Empire. Plus, she had visited Germany the previous year, after the Women's Peace Congress. Although she carried credentials from both the *New York Tribune* and the *Chicago Tribune*, she destroyed her New York credentials on the voyage over when she learned that German authorities despised the New York paper but tolerated the *Chicago Tribune*. Doty also traveled on a charitable mission to deliver funds to support German war orphans. For that reason

18. Madeleine Zabriskie Doty in Russia, 1917–18. Madeleine Z. Doty Papers, Sophia Smith Collection, Smith College, Northampton, MA.

she expected to be given official cooperation and enjoy full access to agencies supporting women and children.

Doty found life in Germany bleak. War suffering and privations weighed heavily on the people. "There are but two topics of conversation—war and food shortages. That is the whole of life. . . . Life has become a mere existence, a prison existence," she wrote. People assembled at two locations—food shops and the posted war bulletins that announced battlefield casualties. Walking the streets of Berlin one night, she came upon a small crowd of people gathered around the war bulletin, sliding their fingers along the list, searching for a familiar name. Doty estimated that the list, covering only the dates August 17–21, included forty-four thousand names of the dead, wounded, and missing.

Doty's subsequent book about her German visit, published only days before America entered the war, used the title *Short Rations*, which indicates the focus of much of her reporting: meatless days, fatless days, artificial "ersatz" foods, meager portions, severe rationing. The obsession with food captured Doty as much as the people she wrote about. She reported a good deal on what she ate and what foods were available. She visited several tenements and described the travails of one typical family—a mother, nine children, and a grandmother, in two rooms and a kitchen. They could not afford to eat the subsidized meals at the public food kitchens. The mother had to run a gauntlet of shops and interrogations in government offices just to replace her worn-out socks. All in the family were listless and undernourished. The six-month-old baby could not raise its arms. Only babies under six months of age received a milk allowance of a pint a day. The family survived on tea and potatoes. Doty encountered difficulty putting to use the $500 she carried for war orphans; she could not feed or clothe children when there was no food or clothing to be had.

Because they provided glimpses of a despondent population, wasting away physically and emotionally, Madeleine Doty's articles and book put a human face on the German population and empathized with its suffering. She provided some of the first reporting of the war to touch America's sentimentality for Germans. The German people are not "barbarians," she assured her readers. "They are like ourselves, just folks, kindly and generous, deceived and browbeaten by a ruthless military group."

By 1916 the *New York World* had also concluded that the reporting coming out of Germany had lost objectivity. The *World* already had a correspondent in Germany, Karl von Wiegand, but it was felt that, through sympathy or censorship, his reporting had become too friendly to the German cause, whereas the reporting found elsewhere in the Allied press went to the opposite extreme of consistently demonizing Germany. The *World*'s energetic young city editor, Herbert Bayard Swope, known for his scrupulous accuracy and objectivity, was just the right person to bring a balanced perspective to the issue. A visit to Germany early in the war had left Swope with a deep appreciation for the German people and the country's military capabilities.

Unlike Gallison's or Doty's first-person narrators, buffeted by their German impressions, Swope adopted the detached tone of an objective observer. Although he reached the same superficial conclusion as Doty—"Life in Germany is not pleasant to-day"—he gave more weight to Germany's organizational ingenuity in sustaining its war effort. The somber mood that now gripped the country was in fact a measure of its strength.

Having been in Germany at the start of the war, Swope could compare the mood of 1914 to that of 1916. When he did, two major shifts in attitude became clear. The buoyant arrogance with which Germany went to war had disappeared. German thinking had shifted from confidence of certain victory to fear of defeat. The slogan on everyone's lips had gone from *siegen* (conquer or win) to *durchhalten* (stick it out or hold on), exposing an iron resolve that would certainly keep the country in the war. Not everyone in Germany had supported a war of conquest, but everyone, with all their fiber, supported a war for the continued existence of Germany. Swope left the country in September convinced that Germany could not conquer Europe but also that it could not be defeated.

Swope's articles ran on the front page of the *World* in October and November 1916, simultaneous with Doty's articles in the *New York Tribune*. When their articles appeared as books in March 1917, it caused at least one reviewer to scratch his head: "Here's a pretty state of affairs for the seeker after truth." The same publisher (Century Company) published both books, within weeks of each other. Both books collected the articles written about their author's visit to Germany in late 1916, and yet they formed different opinions: Swope concluded that Germany could hold on indefinitely and Doty that discontent and hunger could soon lead to revolution. Given that the United States stood on the precipice of entering the war, it was more than an academic dispute.

Because their news gathering followed such parallel trajectories, it also put on display contrasting styles of reporting. As reviewers noted, Swope's objective writing was distinguished by its thoroughness in assessing the military, social, and economic conditions without resorting to the sensationalism or sentimentalism common in much war reporting. On the other hand, one reviewer lauded Doty's anecdotal, impressionistic account as a "vivid story made up of day-to-day scenes, of street episodes, of personal dangers to be avoided by Miss Doty herself, and personal fears to be assuaged. . . . One is not able to read this story without a renewed aching sense of the awful wickedness, the monstrous futility of the thing."

Critical reaction to the two books straddled the date on which the United States entered the war—April 6, 1917. Final word on Swope's work came in the form of a Pulitzer Prize, awarded for the first time that year. Herbert Bayard Swope won in the category of Reporting, "for the best example of a reporter's work during the year, the test being strict accuracy, terseness, [and] the accomplishment of some public good commanding public attention and respect."

Final word on Doty's book came from a reviewer with a very pragmatic objection to her portrayal of suffering Germans. "If we are going to fight Germany, we've got to hate Germany. Hate as well as ammunition has to be manufactured in preparation for war. It doesn't do to let the supply of either run low. And if we are to hate Germany, Madeleine Doty's book, 'Short Rations,' ought to be suppressed. You cannot hate starving women and children. You can ignore them, but you cannot want to make war on them."

7

On Other Fronts

I do not know how much the world outside Turkey knows about the latest Armenian massacres, which make all past performances of this kind look like mere sketches of Turkey's desire and intentions.

—ELEANOR FRANKLIN EGAN, "Day by Day in Constantinople,"
Saturday Evening Post, November 6, 1915

In 1915, despite Jane Addams's peace initiative visits to the belligerent and neutral capitals, the war quickly metastasized to more countries, more fronts, and fresh campaigns. Italy and Bulgaria entered the war on opposing sides. Italy began fighting Austro-Hungarian forces on its mountainous northern border. Bulgaria occupied Serbia. Britain and its Commonwealth allies drew out their bloody stalemate on Turkey's Gallipoli peninsula. Russian and Turkish fighting intensified in the Caucasus region, and Turkey turned on its own Armenian population. In Mesopotamia the British march on Baghdad failed, and Britain surrendered forces to the Ottoman besiegers of Kut. Reporters looking for a new angle on the war had a wealth of options.

There were only so many ways to report on stalemated battles, devastated towns, desperate refugees, and the well-coordinated efforts on the home front. As the war approached its first anniversary, publications needed new story lines. Different, more exotic locales added a new dimension to war reporting. American readers were familiar with the places and culture of Western Europe but not that of Eastern Europe, Russia, Islamic Turkey, or the far reaches of the Ottoman Empire. As coverage of the war spread beyond the western front, women reporters found their way into these new war zones, confronting hardships and dangers and capturing front-page headlines along the way.

A Journalist and a Pacifist Report from Italy

Rome's United Press bureau chief, Alice Rohe, had monitored day-to-day developments since the opening months of the war, when Italy declared its neutrality, despite being a member of the Triple Alliance with Germany and Austria-Hungary. As a hardworking, professional newswoman, Rohe was an anomaly in deeply patriarchal Italy. She had to fight through the patronizing attitudes of Italian officials and journalist colleagues to do her job.

Throughout spring 1915 Rohe reported on the prevailing mood in the country as sentiment built for Italy to join the conflict. Every few days she cabled a short article with the latest developments: the departure of German tourists from the country, peace efforts from the Vatican, Romans celebrating the Austrian defeat at Przemyśl, and anti-Austrian demonstrations, along with the occasional interview with a politician, writer, or feminist (a rare breed in Italy.)

As the descent to war quickened in late May, Rohe fired off a flurry of flashes. Mobilization orders had been drafted; Italian and Austrian armies sat poised on the borders; civilians fled from frontier towns; strategic bridges were destroyed. On May 23 Italy entered the war on the side of the Allies.

Rohe could not get permission to visit the front lines along Italy's rugged alpine border with Austria, but she kept the United Press supplied with general news and war-related stories from the newest warring capital. In June, she was joined in Rome by another female journalist, who proved a more disruptive presence.

On May 23, 1915, the day Italy entered the war, the *New York Tribune* featured a large page 1 photo of the famous Italian scientist Guglielmo Marconi, inventor of wireless telegraphy and Nobel laureate in physics. The attractive traveling companion clinging to his arm was identified as Inez Milholland Boissevain, "lawyer, writer, and suffragist." They were shown boarding the liner *St. Paul* in New York for their voyage to England, the first leg of their journey to Rome. The Italian government had summoned home its native son to oversee its military radio service. The *Tribune* was sending Boissevain to be its war correspondent in Italy. Marconi was well suited for his assignment, Boissevain less so.

The Marconi-Boissevain connection came with a curious backstory. In 1903 Inez Milholland sailed to Europe with her mother and siblings on a ship on which Marconi was conducting wireless experiments. In mid-ocean Marconi managed the astounding feat of transmitting messages to both North America and Europe. Captivated by the new technology, the Milholland family made Marconi's acquaintance and avidly followed his experiments. One morning the family found a "Marconi-gram" message pinned to the ship's bulletin board from Mr. Milholland in New York. It was supposedly the first-ever wireless message sent to a passenger at sea.

Aside from pioneering wireless telegraphy, Marconi also had a predilection for attractive young women. Although only seventeen years old at that time, Inez Milholland was soon engaged to the twenty-nine-year-old scientist. Theirs appears to have been largely a platonic engagement that ended amicably two years later, when another woman caught Marconi's eye. Marconi went on to earn his Nobel Prize in 1909 and Milholland her law degree from New York University in 1912. Now the pair had reunited to travel to the war zone: a world-famous genius and a young woman famous in her own right as a flamboyant advocate for many progressive causes, such as suffrage, racial equality, labor reform, and pacifism.

Boissevain's first war article for the *New York Tribune* fell into her lap before she even left the ship. When the *St. Paul* reached Liverpool, the captain confided to Marconi and Boissevain that a German submarine had followed the ship on its approach to harbor, until driven off by British warships. This news gave substance to a pre-voyage warning Marconi had received from the

19. Inez Milholland Boissevain, who briefly covered the war in Italy for the *New York Tribune*. Italian authorities objected to her outspoken pacifism and asked her to leave the country. Arnold Genthe Collection, Prints & Photographs Division, Library of Congress, LC-G432-0661-B.

Italian consul that Germany might try to kidnap him before he reached Italy.

Boissevain styled the incident as an attempted kidnapping. Her article ran in the *Tribune* and through syndication in other newspapers. Some headlines mentioned the alleged kidnapping of Marconi, while others focused on the reporter: "'Most Beautiful Suffragette' Says American Liner St. Paul Chased by German Submarine." Coming only weeks after the *Lusitania* sinking, both headlines drew attention.

That story may have eased some of the reservations of *Tribune* editors for sending to the war zone someone without journalism experience. But as someone who was more comfortable receiving the attention of journalists than being one, it also foreshadowed Boissevain's tendency to become part of a news story. From her undergraduate days at Vassar College, Milholland was every bit a "New Woman" of the early twentieth century, passionate about progressive causes, a flaunter of social conventions, and one of the most visible personalities of the suffrage movement. The image of her dressed in white and riding a white horse at the front of the 1913 suffrage parade in Washington DC was one of the movement's iconic symbols. That year she married Dutch coffee importer Eugen Jan Boissevain but continued to be an ardent champion of her causes and to live life on her own terms.

Passing through England and France on her way to Italy, she wrote lengthy articles about those countries, filled with her impressions. "I had no time to verify any of the impressions I am here recording," she confessed in an article critical of England, "and I offer them for what they are—impressions." She concluded that "England has been half asleep—playing at war. . . . Something like terror is clutching at her soul."

France was a different story. Boissevain had traveled in Europe in her youth. Her father, John Milholland, had been a *Tribune* reporter before making his fortune in the pneumatic tube business. The family spent time in Europe, and Inez attended schools in London and Berlin. But to arrive on the Continent now was to step into a military camp. Her entry port of Boulogne pulsed with activity: warships, Red Cross trains, dispatch officers, motor ambulances, comings and goings of all sorts. "I loved the throb of it and I felt my blood mounting with excitement," she confessed.

In Boulogne she connected with the *Tribune*'s regular war correspondent, Will Irwin, who would travel with her and Marconi to Paris and then to Italy, the new front in the war. En route to Paris, through the devastated regions, Boissevain registered her first sobering impressions of war: "women struggling through the lifeless streets, dull eyes, weary, and waiting" and girls "cheated of throbbing life, left behind to a dreary driven existence in a deserted town"; through garrison towns; past fields being worked by women and boys; the sadness of Paris. "The dreariness of a country at war as much as anything else is why I hate this business of fighting," she wrote. Her articles continued to be collections of impressions and opinions. In Will Irwin's memoir, *The Making of a Reporter* (1942), he described Boissevain as a "brilliant-hued vikingess" who had "every kind of courage, a talent for making herself liked on sight and few inhibitions."

From the start Boissevain seemed intent on flouting convention in her behavior and attitudes. Italy had more restrictive views toward women than any country in Europe. Whenever she was informed about what a woman should not do or say, she did it anyway, almost as a point of honor. Likewise, her strong commitment to pacifism intruded into her reporting. One could not even discuss ideas about peace, she complained in one article. As for the sinking of the *Lusitania*, it seemed justified to her, "granted the abomination of war."

She spoke to a maid in her hotel, to the headwaiter, and to a friend who had lived in the country for many years. They all opposed the war. She suggested to the waiter that he should protest the war or refuse to serve, but he said he would be shot as a traitor. "Better to take your chances in battle," he told her. Soldiers marching through the streets looked gloomy. In another article she opined that Italy had taken on much more than it could manage by joining the war, and that the government only sustained war enthusiasm by deceiving the people with accounts of exaggerated victories and minimized losses. But "when the pinch of war is felt," Italians will feel "cheated and exploited" by their government.

Her reporting from Italy often dripped with an acid sarcasm. If men allowed themselves to be led to the slaughter like dumb sheep, "perhaps they deserve to be massacred like dumb sheep." And as for the *Lusitania*, still very much an open wound, she wrote that "to sink a shipload of non-combatants is no worse than to attempt to starve a nation—women and children included—into submission." This was a reference to Britain's naval blockade of Germany. Boissevain's biographer Linda J. Lumsden described her war articles as more essays than journalism, "short on fact and long on indignation."

The *Tribune* rejected some of her articles for that reason. In August a reader wrote a letter to the editor disputing Boissevain's claim that Italians did not support the war. All his experience and contacts gave him the opposite opinion. He suggested that Mrs. Boissevain "looked at life through spectacles deeply colored with feminism," ignoring reality and selectively seeking evidence that supported her views. "Her ears are microphonically attuned to catch the plaints of bereft mothers and mourning sweethearts, but they are closed to the proud exultation of a people united in a patriotic cause."

The Italian government denied her request to interview Queen Elena but—surprisingly—granted her permission to visit the front. When she had been informed that neutral correspondents could not visit the front, she hastily arranged for credentials from a Canadian newspaper. The move worked. Will Irwin pointed out the irony of this arrangement, coming "at a time when regular women correspondents like the capable Alice Rohe were eating their hearts out for the chance" to visit the front.

But before Boissevain could record her impressions of the fighting line, the government recalled her. In Rome she was summoned to the foreign ministry, where an official complained that the pacifist articles she had been mailing back to the *Tribune* had not been approved by the Italian government. He courteously

20. Photojournalist Helen Johns Kirtland inspecting an exploded naval mine on the Belgian coast. This is one of several dramatic photographs of Kirtland taken during the war, perhaps by her husband, Lucian, also a photojournalist. Kirtland Collection, Prints & Photographs Division, Library of Congress, PR 13 CN 1981:255.

asked her to leave the country. Boissevain thought the move came because she was a woman or because other American correspondents had complained about her being given access to the front. Will Irwin added a follow-up note: "After she left the country she published an article calling upon women of the world to go on strike and stop the war. If there was anything that any censor would not stand for it was pacifism; hence a year's taboo on neutral correspondents, of each and every sex, at the Italian front."

Three years would pass before another woman journalist visited the Italian front. Photojournalist Helen Johns Kirtland arrived in Europe in November 1917 and set about photographing the war for *Leslie's Illustrated Weekly*. She did photographic stories on women war workers and the air war and also visited several fronts. Because she occasionally traveled with her photojournalist husband, Lucian Kirtland, or with other photographers, Kirtland herself sometimes became the subject of photographs, some of which saw print and now reside in the Kirtland Collection at the Library of Congress.

Fighting between Italy and the Austrian and German armies concentrated along the Piave River, north of Venice. Italy suffered a major defeat there at the Battle of Caporetto in the fall of 1917. A year later the same adversaries confronted each other again. Although women were still prohibited from visiting the Italian front, Kirtland persuaded Italian prime minister Vittorio Orlando to grant her permission. When the Italian army assaulted the Austrians at Monte Grappa in October 1918, in their final offensive of the war, Kirtland reported on the fighting from the front lines.

The Serbian Front

The same week that Inez Boissevain returned to the United States with her story of eviction from Italy, an article about Serbia appeared in the *Saturday Evening Post* from Eleanor Franklin Egan, "The Difficult Truth about Serbia." There had been precious little news coverage of Serbia, in part because the country was largely inaccessible and underdeveloped. A correspondent had to be willing to face severe hardships.

Serbia, in league with the Allied powers, had been gamely holding off assaults from Austria-Hungary since the opening days of the war. Its misery doubled in October, when Bulgaria entered the war on the side of the Central Powers and invaded

21. Helen Johns Kirtland (right) with Italian soldiers near the Piave River, Italy, in October 1918. Kirtland Collection, Prints & Photographs Division, Library of Congress, PR 13 CN 1981:339.

its neighbor. Not that suffering was in short supply when Egan visited in mid-1915.

Although she was a seasoned journalist, her September 25 article represented her first appearance in the *Post*, which had continued to deliver some of the best reporting on the war from its regular stable of writers: Irvin Cobb, Samuel Blythe, and Mary Roberts Rinehart. That list would be supplemented throughout the conflict with additional names, but none proved more prolific than Egan. Because of her willingness to travel to any location no matter how difficult or dangerous, her ability to navigate any political situation, and an uncanny knack to land on the spot of extraordinary breaking news, she became one of the most frequent *Post* contributors, writing more than sixty-five articles throughout the war and in the immediate postwar years of European turmoil.

Egan traveled to Serbia not so much to glimpse its war with

Austria as to investigate its war with typhus. Americans fought in that war. Late in 1914, when a virulent strain of typhus erupted throughout Serbia's army and civilian population, a call went out for assistance. Medical units arrived from England, France, and Russia. Even beleaguered Belgium sent doctors and nurses. From America came several hospital units and a sanitary commission supported by the Red Cross and the Rockefeller Foundation.

According to the director of the U.S. Red Cross Sanitary Commission, conditions in the country "beggar description." In addition to the disruption of a great war, Serbia struggled with inadequate infrastructure, hospitals, supplies, and medicine. The country had only three hundred doctors for a population of four million, and more than a third of those doctors died from typhus within the first six months of the epidemic.

By the time Egan arrived, in the summer of 1915, sanitary efforts had begun to make headway. The number of reported new cases had declined to a mere five thousand a day. Egan traveled widely in the country, by truck and horseback, to watch U.S. doctors, nurses, and sanitary workers disinfect the Serbian army and provide care to villages. War was being waged against the ever-present lice that spread the disease.

Although Egan labeled the sanitation effort an "American Victory," she was coming to the conclusion that the desperately poor, backward, and battered country was a lost cause. The Grand Hotel, where she stayed in Belgrade, might have been fifth-rate in ordinary times, she thought, but it no longer rose to that level of comfort. "Its shell-torn inner walls were shored up with timbers and scaffolding, its dirt and its insects were the unmistakable accumulation of months, and its atmosphere was somber with a sadness indescribable." The entire staff consisted of a "pitiful, ragged, harassed little boy, who spoke not a word of any known language," and a proprietor, who seemed totally detached from reality. The only nourishment available was coffee and bread.

As she rode the train to the wartime capital of Nish (Niš), Egan seemed to be giving the country one last chance to redeem itself in her eyes. After all, Nish was the seat of government, home to

22. Map of the Balkans and Turkey. Serbia was a difficult and dangerous assignment for journalists in 1915, when Eleanor Egan covered the country's war with typhus. Egan reported widely from this region throughout the war. Abbot, *Nations at War.*

all the foreign representatives. It was one of the oldest towns in the world, on the route between Europe and the Orient. Crusaders had traveled through Nish on their way to the Holy Land. It would likely be attractive and thoroughly livable, she reasoned.

But Nish only reinforced the overall wretchedness of this suffering land. "Nish is the most awful place that Heaven's sun shines on," she concluded, "and if I could think of any stronger language I would use it without fear of having anyone who knows accuse me of exaggeration." Not that she lacked for sharp criticism. Nish was dilapidated, bedraggled, miserable, full of odors, weeds, and vermin. Its streets had not been cleaned "since the passing of the last Crusade."

In "The Difficult Truth about Serbia" Egan separated her sympathies for Serbia from its primitive conditions. She thought the country a lost cause and that any aid beyond that needed to meet the immediate humanitarian crisis was worse than wasted. It would merely be "wicked encouragement of the greed and helplessness in everyday things, which are so conspicuous in the Serbian character."

At least one member of the U.S. Sanitary Commission, Fortier Jones, found fault with her hasty characterization of Serbia. "With the easy grace characteristic of a certain type of feminine mind the author of that article leaps over the economic isolation of Serbia, the deadly trade wars with Austria, soars over the most significant factors in the growth of nations," he complained. "After the stay of a fortnight you cannot convincingly impugn the honor, the kindness, pride, and hospitality of a people."

Egan departed Serbia for Turkey before Bulgaria's invasion took Serbia out of the war and plunged it into even deeper misery.

When Bulgaria declared war against its neighbor Serbia in October 1915, the Balkans suddenly became more strategically important and newsworthy. Allied troops and supplies poured into the nearest neutral port of Salonika, Greece. Journalists came as well. Most parked themselves in the bustling Greek port and awaited developments. They speculated that gathering Allied forces might soon enter Serbia; Bulgarian or Austrian troops might invade neutral Greece, or Greece might join the war.

Once the rail line from Serbia to Greece closed, refugees and escaping soldiers fled the Bulgarian advance through the unforgiving, snow-choked mountain passes of Albania and Montenegro. Survivors brought stories of the tragedy of death in the mountains. When United Press correspondent William Shepherd traveled into the southern edge of Serbia, he ran out of superlatives to describe what he saw. "The world war has developed no scene of greater horror" than the tragedy unfolding in Serbia. Dead bodies lined the road from Nish to Monastir, the "highway of agony"—men, women, and children who had succumbed to starvation, exhaustion, and disease while fleeing the invasion. What was happening in Serbia was the "blackest page in human history!"

Some American aid workers who survived that harrowing escape in late November reported that they had lost track of the journalist Mildred Farwell, of the *Chicago Tribune*, who had been staying with them at the Red Cross facility in the city of Monastir. They feared for her safety. Farwell's whereabouts suddenly became a top news story. "Chicago Woman Lost in Serbia," read the headline in the *New York Tribune*. When U.S. secretary of state Robert Lansing issued an urgent appeal, Bulgaria, Germany, Greece, and the American consul in Salonika all sent out emissaries to locate Farwell. The first pieces of the story emerged in the press a month later, when it was learned that Farwell and others were being held as virtual prisoners by the Bulgarian army in a Red Cross hospital compound in Monastir, five miles from the Greek border.

Farwell's husband, Walter Farwell, arrived from America to rescue his wife but was turned back by the Bulgarian army. A Red Cross official who traveled to Serbia to rescue her and the others also failed but did learn the story of what had happened. William Shepherd again took up the dramatic story and put Farwell on the front page of hundreds of U.S. newspapers. When others had scrambled to leave Serbia during the Bulgarian advance, Farwell and a few workers at the Red Cross hospital chose to remain. The retreating Serbian army entrusted to the hospital two carloads of flour to feed local residents. When the Bulgarians showed up and demanded the flour, the hospital staff refused. This led to an altercation, during which the Bulgarians tore down the U.S. flag and roughly treated Farwell when she tried to take a photograph. The Bulgarians refused to allow Farwell and the others to leave the country.

The events surrounding Mildred Farwell had all the makings of a rousing news story: an American trapped in the war zone, being mistreated, and the desecration of the U.S. flag. Shepherd's article referred to Farwell as a "Chicago society woman war correspondent." An editor's note established that her husband was the millionaire son of a senator and that her mother's first husband had been Stephen A. Douglas, who defeated Abraham Lincoln for the United States Senate. The story stayed in the news until March 1916, when Farwell was finally released. In a long series of articles in the *Chicago Tribune* and widely syndicated, Farwell detailed her experiences in Serbia.

Eleanor Egan in Constantinople

A Turkish boatman ferried Eleanor Franklin Egan to "old Stamboul," on the tip of the peninsula that poked into the Bosporus and the Marmara Sea. She had just arrived in Constantinople, and a young man named Fritz, whom she had known since his boyhood in Chicago, was giving her a tour of the Turkish capital. A German American, he had been studying in Berlin when the war began and now proudly served as an officer in the German army.

In this old part of the city, Egan and Fritz had to squeeze past crowds lined up at bread shops, waiting to break their Ramadan fast at sunset, and had to brush off the "wretched little beggars" who rushed any stranger, appealing for handouts. Their climb to a lookout point took them past an ancient mosque, a Muslim cemetery, and a dervish monastery. On the crest of the hill, above the trees, there stretched before them the "most magnificent panorama in all the world. . . . The sun had gone down behind a hill, but its glow, shining up the Dardanelles and across the Sea of Marmara, had caught the domes and minarets of old Stamboul and painted each with a separate and different ray."

"'There you are!' said Fritz. 'That's the principal thing they are fighting for.'" The tranquil view of the city belied the fact that only one hundred miles away, Allied, Turkish, and German troops fought and died for the Gallipoli peninsula that guarded the strategic water connection to Constantinople and the Black Sea.

What had begun as a naval engagement changed to a land battle when Allied forces launched an amphibious landing in April. Now Australian and New Zealand Army Corps (ANZAC) reinforcements were being poured into the battle to bolster the Allied effort. Fritz offered to take Egan to Gallipoli so she could

23. Eleanor Franklin Egan was one of the most prolific journalists of the war. She never hesitated to travel to the most isolated and dangerous locales and had an uncanny ability to be on the spot of a breaking news story. Arnold Genthe Collection, Prints & Photographs Division, Library of Congress, LC-G432-2468-A.

see the fighting, but in a gesture very uncharacteristic for a war correspondent, she declined.

"I was not afraid," she explained to her readers, "simply because I could not get a full sense of such danger, but I did get a vision of the sights to be seen, and I did not want to see them." Her reservation seemed in part that she saw no practical value in suffering such a grisly sight. "If I could do anything to help anyone—but what's the use. Nobody out of mere curiosity should go near a fearful thing like that." Her reluctance also reflected a more personal apprehension. "No, I would not go; I did not have the nerve."

Egan's highly personalized war reports often offered that sort of private disclosure. Such raw reaction made her experiences seem more genuine and her interpretations more trustworthy. Egan scholar David Hudson has suggested that such reactions might be "dismissed as a particularly feminine response to unpleasantness" but that Egan largely avoided that by setting such passages within the context of "extensive documentary detail and hard-headed analysis."

One of Egan's *Saturday Evening Post* articles carried the title "Day by Day in Constantinople." That is an apt description of all six articles she wrote about her visit to Turkey. She was no war correspondent novice, like Inez Milholland Boissevain, to be awed by a country at war. And unlike Serbia, Turkey did not put its horrors on public display. Egan found a vague wartime normalcy in Constantinople: a proliferation of German soldiers, the sight of wounded on the city streets, an overworked U.S. embassy that had assumed the responsibilities for all the Allied nations that had closed their embassies, the city's anxiety about British submarines harassing shipping in the Sea of Marmara, and, as in all the warring countries, an obsession with spies.

Her eyewitness, fly-on-the-wall glimpses of life in the city brought ordinary events to life and distilled from them insights about war and human nature. Some scenes have an "imagine this" feel to them. Imagine celebrating the birthday of Austrian emperor Franz Joseph in Constantinople. Flags bedecked the city, Turkish ones of course, but also American, Austrian, and German. "It is a fine thing to be a great nation, with a thrillingly beautiful flag, and at peace with the world these days!" Egan noted.

They celebrated the emperor's birthday in a beer garden, she explained, with musicians wearing red fezzes and playing German music from "the good old days when hearts rose to German music and were glad": "There were mostly Germans in the garden—big mothers with broods of youngsters bringing packages of food, to be unwrapped on the little iron tables and disposed of with large quantities of beer; swaggering young men with bamboo canes, and strings attached to their straw hats; excited girls in last year's very tight skirts, having the time of their dear young lives; and sailors—sailors off the Emden and the submarines, in regular German caps, and sailors off the Goeben and the Breslau, in red fezzes. Splendid boys—all of them; mothers' boys, with straight young shoulders and narrow hips—and that terrible look in the eyes of most."

Egan was at her descriptive best when she found an occasion worthy of extended observation. Lavishing attention on this beer hall event allowed her to draw out the poignancy of young men charged with the war spirit. "Does not everybody notice that terrible look?" she asked her readers. That "indescribable, withdrawn-from-the-world look; a mild unquestioning finality; a look that sees nothing beyond the now."

What seemed like an indictment of the impact of war on warriors became an admirable male trait when wrapped in her personal observation: "Is it not wonderful that men should be so made?" She went on: "After what I have seen I do not want anybody ever to talk to me again about sex equality. Certain phases of sex equality, yes; but I believe in the overwhelming superiority of the male, a superiority which is and should be."

Nowhere else in Egan's record of extraordinary war reporting does she so blatantly voice her conservative views on gender roles. Most of the women who reported the war passionately supported women's rights and universal suffrage, Egan less so. She could serve as the poster child of the strong, independent woman, aggressively pursuing a dangerous profession. But scholars have called her views on the issue of gender roles "conflicted" and have deconstructed her war reporting for evidence.

They point out that Egan sometimes targeted her reporting to female readers or that she noted with appreciation when she was treated differently because she was a woman. She described the pleasure of shopping for fashions in Paris and Vienna and confessed a reluctance to view ghastly scenes. She mentioned being the only woman at some location or being given the most comfortable accommodations because she was a woman among warriors. She remarked on men who were solicitous to her well-being. She was pleased when a man rescued her from a travel predicament on a French train or shielded her from a grizzly sight in Armenia.

Egan put a curious endnote to the matter with a May 22, 1920, *Saturday Evening Post* article, "Women in Politics to the Aid of the Party," in which she examined the impact of women voting for the first time in a U.S. general election. The Nineteenth Amendment on women's suffrage was then working its way through Congress, before heading to the states for ratification. Egan confessed: "I happen to be one of the vast majority of women who had nothing to do with the long struggle which is to result in the Nineteenth Amendment. If I had any feeling at all with regard to suffrage for women it was a feeling of opposition." Her views had been clouded by "old-fashioned conservatism and prejudice," she claimed, and she was not proud of her record of indifference. "I feel like apologizing to the women of the combat battalions who have done all the fighting and who now bear all the scars."

One story line from Egan's Turkish visit required a more serious, objective tone. During the summer Eleanor Egan began to hear horrendous reports about atrocities committed by the Turkish government against its Armenian population. Reports trickled in by whispers, "by devious underground routes," through a spy-like network. "And so ever present and breathless was the fear of retaliatory massacres in the city itself that nobody would speak freely, nobody would tell all he knew, and written communications were concealed or destroyed as though the possession of them constituted the highest crime."

"One terrible account came through of eight hundred women and children who were separated from their husbands and fathers, and . . . started on a forty-five days' march from their home town to Aleppo," Egan reported. Women of refinement and pregnant women had to carry everything to sustain themselves on this journey of resettlement. Children were born along the way, with no provisions for mother or baby. "The roads to the south are strewn and stenched with rotting bodies, and the streams are clogged with them," one eyewitness reported. "Despairing mothers—insane, of course—throw their infants into the rivers or leave them in the camps to die. Women give up everything they possess—jewels, money, their very clothes and coverings—to buy immunity."

Egan knew something about how entrenched racial and religious hatred could drive killings. In 1903, working as a correspondent for *Leslie's Weekly*, she wrote about pogroms against Jews in Russia. But the Armenian situation seemed much more organized and official. In Constantinople they began gathering up the Armenians at a rate of about fifty a day, "and the first to go were many of the teachers and servants from the American schools."

Armenians had long been a hated minority in the empire, but the current persecution came with a backstory. At the start of the war some Armenians in the border areas with Russia took up arms against the Ottomans or joined the Russian army. Since that move amounted to open rebellion, Turkey responded harshly, as would have any other nation. But the suppression of that revolt became an excuse to move against the entire Armenian population in the Ottoman Empire. Under a policy of resettlement, two million Armenians were given five days to abandon their homes and all their possessions for long journeys through mountains and deserts to camps in the interior. No provisions were made for food, shelter, or safe conduct for the refugees. The new policy inflamed long-standing animosity toward Armenians, which led to widespread abuses, violence, and massacres. Already one and a half million had been driven from their homes, Egan claimed, with a loss of life among them estimated at eight hundred thousand. Through secrecy and censorship the Turks took great pains to conceal their relocation policy and the resulting atrocities.

Egan charged that it was not fear of an Armenian rebellion that prompted this policy but evidence of a Holy War, in which imams in mosques exhorted the faithful to spill Christian blood:

"It is necessary that the people should know from to-day that the Holy War has become a sacred duty, and that the blood of infidels in Islamic lands may be shed with impunity."

By the time Egan thought to leave Constantinople, in October, the city was beginning to scare her. An order had been issued that all aliens should be off the street at night. Bands of Arabs and Kurds, brought up from Asia Minor to be soldiers, roamed the streets after dark with "long, murderous knives." Hotels took to rolling down their iron shutters for protection. "People began to look their thoughts into one another's eyes instead of expressing them in words." It made one's thoughts turn to places of safety. Egan wanted to stay and see it out, but concern for her safety won out.

Egan's flight to safety would be none too safe. The exigencies of war threw dangers in her path, and some she placed there herself. The route she had planned to take from Turkey through Bulgaria and Serbia to Athens got cut when Bulgaria entered the war. She would now have to travel by train to a Bulgarian port that was currently blockaded by British warships. There she might be able to catch a steamer to Athens—if any still sailed—and thence to Italy and England.

But before she set out, she faced a monumental decision. She came into possession of a copy of the original order that had been posted in Armenian towns in June, announcing the harsh steps of the dispersal policy. It represented one piece of concrete proof of these atrocities. Egan made the extraordinary decision to sneak the text of the order out of the country. She had already been strongly warned not to take any written material out of the country, any articles she had written, any notes, and particularly nothing related to the Armenian atrocities. Fully aware of the consequences if she were caught, Egan copied the text of the dispersal order into the innermost margins of a book that she planned to take with her when she left the country.

Her ordeal of leaving Turkey earned its own article in the *Saturday Evening Post*. One dangerous event along the way required another article and propelled Egan into the headlines. Sometimes the best war stories happened when you weren't even looking for them. Sometimes the reporter *was* the war story.

Before leaving Constantinople, Egan took great care to eliminate all of her notes and tear pages from her journals. However, inspectors at a border train station found a journal page she had overlooked and two postcards she had written but forgotten to mail. They were completely innocent scribblings, but she was put under house arrest for five days while they were shipped back to Constantinople to be reviewed by a censor. She was allowed to keep the book with the Armenian dispersal notice.

Eventually allowed to proceed, she made it to the Bulgarian port to find that no ships were sailing to Athens, but a rail line remained open to Salonika, Greece. It carried her through a Bulgaria in the grip of war, through regions of Macedonia still in ruins from the Greco-Bulgarian war of 1913. The backward, sad-eyed peasants she saw seemed holdovers from biblical times. The whole oppressive atmosphere made her wonder why all of Europe had not emigrated long ago.

In more settled times a traveler would have sailed from Athens to Brindisi, Italy, and then on to England and home across the Atlantic. But the times were not settled. Egan had already fled war in Serbia, Turkey, and Bulgaria, and now Greece, too, was mobilizing against an anticipated incursion from Bulgarian or German troops. The sea threatened with its own dangers. Ships still sailed to Brindisi, but Austrian submarines were rumored to be heavy in that direction. Egan opted instead to sail to Egypt because frequent British convoys along that route suggested greater safety. From there she could sail to Malta, then on to Palermo and Naples.

She caught the only available ship passage aboard the small, derelict, and dirty Greek ship *Borulos*, headed to Alexandria, "packed to her rails with a motley throng of Greeks and Arabs, men, women, and children." Somewhere south of Crete, the ship picked up twenty-seven British sailors from lifeboats. Their ship had been sunk two hours earlier. "Who is to describe the sullen, murmurous quiver that went through the crowd the minute they understood the full significance of the Englishman's situation! A submarine! A ship sunk two hours before!"

Many hours later the same submarine found the *Borulos*. Egan was standing on deck admiring the sunset when she caught sight of the submarine: "Your mind at such a moment is like a film in a camera. It catches and fixes every minutest detail. I remember the white wash of the sea off the submarine's decks . . . I remember the instantaneousness of the flash of fire and the reverberating boom which caught up just in time to mingle with the crack of an exploding shell and the loud swish of the geyser it threw into the air. It was the exploding of that shell that settled our fate. If the submarine could have used some other kind of signal the panic would not have been so instantaneous and complete."

The surfaced submarine had fired a warning shot to stop the *Borulos*, but everyone on board assumed the ship had been struck by a torpedo. A panic of passengers and seamen erupted from below deck and rushed for the lifeboats. Caught in the scramble to launch a boat, Egan got knocked into the sea, then hauled into a lifeboat. Passengers jumped in panic into the water. Women threw their babies overboard, calling for someone to rescue them. Egan re-created the scene for her readers: "I would, if I could, make you see the pitiful ship drifting aimlessly and dejectedly under the guns; and I would if I could, make you see how the sunset bathed all the horrors in a marvelous light. I would, if I could, make you hear the feeble wails of the little Arab baby I picked up and tucked away under my wet coat, and feel the weight of the dead woman they dragged in and threw across my knees. I would, if I could, call up before you all the twenty-five drowned— fourteen of them children, and only three of them men—and have you listen to their stories."

When the submarine approached the ship, its crew busied itself dragging victims from the water and trying to revive them. The Austrian captain could speak English, so Egan became the liaison. He was aghast at the struggling, drowning passengers in the water. Egan thought he must have been new to the job because he actually wept. "For God sake, go back to your ship," he instructed. "We are not murderers." The submarine remained alongside for five hours, until all survivors were rescued, bodies recovered, and the wounded treated. Then it submerged, and the ship continued its voyage. When the *Borulos* reached Alexandria, news of the encounter, and Egan's role, grabbed headlines.

Eleanor Egan's Extraordinary Journey

By the time the United States took the plunge into war in April 1917, Egan had firmly established her reputation as one of the war's leading correspondents. With fifteen articles published in the largest-circulation magazine, she had chronicled the war on multiple fronts and reported her personal adventures navigating those difficult and dangerous landscapes, including the less-reported fronts in Bulgaria, Serbia, and Turkey.

In the summer of 1917, when other chroniclers of the war traveled across the Atlantic to report on the first contingent of American troops in France, Egan set off in the opposite direction. A map of her itinerary would have traced a line halfway around the world, from San Francisco to the Orient to the subcontinent to the biblical land of Mesopotamia, modern-day Iraq.

The British had taken to calling the region "Mespot," and even in a war that encompassed the globe, it held an exotic attraction. In a season of Allied reverses and a revolution in Russia that threatened to take it out of the war, British successes in Mespot shone like a ray of bright sunlight. That spring British forces under Lieutenant General Sir Frederick Stanley Maude captured the Ottoman-held city of Baghdad. It amounted to a wildly successful reversal of fortune in the area. A year earlier the British campaign had suffered a crushing defeat when some thirteen thousand troops surrendered at the besieged city of Kut, a loss that British historian Jan Morris has described as "the most abject capitulation in Britain's military history."

Mespot had been a closed front. General Maude rigidly opposed allowing anyone into Mesopotamia who was not attached to the military. But Egan went to extraordinary lengths with British authorities to surmount that obstacle. Her résumé supported her

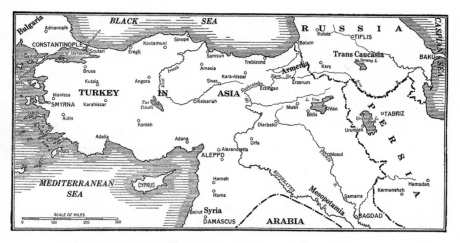

24. Eleanor Egan traveled throughout the vast Ottoman Empire to witness the Turkish extermination of its Armenian population and the British campaign in Mesopotamia. Abbot, *Nations at War.*

appeal. For over a decade her travels as a foreign correspondent had taken her throughout Europe and Asia, including a stint covering the Russo-Japanese War of 1904–5. While reporting that war, she met her husband, well-respected Associated Press correspondent Martin Egan. After their marriage, they jointly edited the *Manila Times* until 1914. The fact that she now wrote for the largest-circulation magazine in the United States leant weight to her request to bring some publicity to Britain's unqualified victory in the desert.

Egan won enthusiastic support for her Mesopotamia adventure from the British ambassador to the United States, Sir Cecil Spring-Rice. He provided her with a special British passport and sent "letters or cablegrams to most of his Majesty's ambassadors and colonial governors from Tokio to Bombay." Missing in that diplomatic red carpet, however, was any permission to actually enter the war zone in Mesopotamia.

Egan's assignment from *Saturday Evening Post* editor George Lorimer must have been fairly open-ended. Along her route she managed to dash off articles about the Philippines, Japan, Hong Kong, and India. When she reached Bombay, the staging area for

Mespot, she found herself sitting across from Freeman Freeman-Thomas, Lord Willingdon, governor of the city. He had been contacted to assist Egan, and so he asked what he might do for her. When she said she wanted to visit Baghdad, "he laughed, in a way that should have discouraged me utterly." It was impossible, he assured her. General Maude would never consent to it. He would not have a woman within a thousand miles of Baghdad. Egan had not traveled halfway around the globe to be so easily dissuaded. "'We might ask him,' I suggested."

Twenty-two days later permission came through. Egan caught a troop ship through the Persian Gulf to Basra, the entrance to Mespot. All the extensive preparation and the arduous travel had delivered for Egan a wartime exclusive. She found herself as the only journalist ever permitted to visit this obscure corner of the war, a guest of the British Army, on her way to meet the conqueror of Baghdad. In seven *Post* articles Egan would detail the political and military history of the British campaign in Mesopotamia.

The British military was solicitous to its guest, providing Major General Sir George MacMunn to escort her up the Tigris River for her rendezvous with General Maude. Notwithstanding summer temperatures that hit 130 degrees and the aggravating mosquitoes and sand flies, Egan enthused about the masterpiece of British planning and organization that had transformed the region: railroads along the river; steamboats; wharfs bustling with Arab workers; storage sheds stretching to the horizon; huge tent camps; endless supply trains of trucks, horses, donkeys, camels; electricity brought to the river towns; women freed from the veil—civilization, if you will, delivered to the cradle of civilization.

Despite his reputation for military secrecy, General Maude gave Egan free reign and assigned his own aides to be her guides: "He sent me everywhere I went in a big motor car, and I have memories now that are like nothing else in all my experience, of long rides at fifty miles an hour over great stretches of hard-packed desert as smooth as a billiard table; and I have memories, too, of hours spent in heavy laboring across other great stretches of loose sand and fine yellow dust which rose in choking clouds round me and made life for the time being a weariness and a test of endurance."

In the more moderate temperatures of a Mespot winter, British forces had renewed fighting in Tikrit and Ramadi. But Baghdad and General Maude represented the end of Egan's long journey. In one article exotic Baghdad served as backdrop for her recounting the British capture of the city, just as she had described the taking of Basra and the recapture of Kut in an earlier article. Since there had been no reporting from this zone, everything she wrote about it amounted to a scoop. Still, she never imagined the dramatic turn of events that would conclude her visit and put her on the scene when the conqueror of Baghdad died.

Egan began that story with the question that General Maude posed to her one day: "How would you like to see Hamlet played in Arabic by children of Israel who are direct descendants of the left-overs from the Babylonian captivity?"

As though tallying the clues in a good murder mystery, Egan meticulously laid out the details of that fateful evening. The theater performance was being held in a Jewish school. British sentries lined their route to the school, snapping to attention one after another as their car rolled by. At the school the audience of "Persians, Arabs, Kurds, Syrians, Chaldeans, and representatives of a dozen Eastern races," dressed in their finest clothes, rose to their feet and cheered Maude's arrival. A platform had been built for the general in the front row, with seats for him, Egan, and the chief rabbi of the city. There followed a half-hour of formal introductions.

Now the details of a simple ceremony became critically important. Egan explained, "They brought a small table and placed it before the army commander and me, on which were two cups, a pot of coffee, a bowl of sugar and a jug of milk." They partook of this refreshment and watched the play.

The next day Maude was too ill to keep his appointments. The following day, when his condition worsened, his doctors asked Egan what he had taken the night of the play. "He drank the coffee," she explained, "and he poured into it a large quantity of cold raw milk. I drank the coffee, too, but without milk." On day two, November 18, 1917, he died of cholera, apparently contracted from contaminated milk used in his coffee.

"One may speculate and wonder for all time," Egan reflected. "What can any one ever possibly know? As I write, General Maude lies dead in a desert grave, outside the old North Gate, and they are saying boldly and insistently in the bazaars to-night that he was murdered!"

The British lowered flags to mark the solemn occasion. "The only other flag that flies in Baghdad is the American; and our beautiful banner floating from its staff on the roof of our consulate . . . dropped its folds on a level with its friend, the Union Jack; and I felt that the two stood prophetically sentinel over the high destinies of humanity." Egan predicted that soon those flags "would lift themselves again; and together. Throughout the world, they would 'carry on'—lofty in purpose, clean in principle and resplendent with unconquerable power. That is the inevitable end for which this war is being waged."

Egan's articles about Mespot ran from April to July 1918 and were collected into her book, *The War in the Cradle of the World, Mesopotamia* (1918). They were the last articles she wrote during the war. The objectivity and critical reporting that she displayed in Turkey are missing from her coverage of Mesopotamia. She lionized Maude and British operations. Her language about the superiority of the English-speaking worldview might ring hollow with modern readers, but it did not with readers of the *Saturday Evening Post*—not when they were sending their own sons to war with the high-minded goal of making the world safe for democracy.

8

War and Revolution in Russia

They were dreaming big dreams in Russia that night;
scheming big schemes.
—BESSIE BEATTY, *The Red Heart of Russia*, 1918

Journalist Florence MacLeod Harper was operating on a hunch when she suggested to *Leslie's Illustrated Weekly Newspaper* in November 1916 that she do her war reporting from Russia. Russia's monumental battles with Germany and Austria-Hungary had received little coverage in the American press. But when Russia's initially successful Brusilov campaign of that summer sputtered to a halt, anxiety rose among the Allies. Had that been the last gasp of a depleted and demoralized Russian army? Would Germany press into Russia and take it out of the war? That nightmare scenario seemed too dreadful to contemplate.

Leslie's assigned Harper to travel to the Russian capital of Petrograd with its staff war photographer Donald C. Thompson, who had covered the war on many fronts, including Russia in 1915. Together the pair sailed from Vancouver on November 30 on a long, circuitous route via Japan, Philippines, and China, before reaching the eastern terminus of the Trans-Siberian Railway. The calendar had turned to February before they boarded the legendary train for the six-thousand-mile journey across the vast Russia Empire.

News and rumors assaulted them at every train station along the route: the army was planning a spring offensive; food shortages in Petrograd might cause problems if the government didn't do something. And the much-reviled Siberian monk Grigori Rasputin, favorite of the imperial court, had been murdered. But neither journalistic intuition nor the speculation of travelers foretold the wildly tumultuous year that lay ahead. Russia would end a three-hundred-year-old imperial dynasty, embrace democracy, renew its commitment to the Allies, see the collapse of its army, suffer a violent counterrevolution, and reach an armistice with the Central Powers that had a profound impact on the war. Russia was poised to be one of the biggest news stories of the war, and Harper would be there from the start.

Among the few journalists who shared Florence Harper's intuition about the newsworthiness of prerevolutionary Russia was Mildred Farwell (*Chicago Tribune*), who arrived in Petrograd in late 1916, in time to report on the murder of Rasputin. When 1917 brought revolution, a parade of other American journalists, including at least a half-dozen women, arrived to report on all that it promised and threatened.

Shortly after Harper and Thompson reached Petrograd on February 26, 1917, Thompson made a hasty visit to the front lines. Allied commanders lost sleep worrying about the Russian army. With the disastrous collapse of the Brusilov Offensive, many believed that Russia's army had lost the will to fight. If Russia could no longer occupy the attention of the million German troops along the eastern front, those troops would move quickly to the West and tip the tide of the war.

Thompson found things relatively quiet at the fighting line, but he saw supplies and artillery shells stockpiled everywhere, in preparation for a planned spring offensive. An officer promised Thompson lots of opportunities for good pictures in the spring. But opportunities for good pictures came sooner than that—and not at the front but on the streets of Petrograd.

An official at the American consulate warned Harper that the city was a tinderbox awaiting a match. Food shortages had stirred protests and strikes. People dressed in rags stood for hours in freezing temperatures to get the terrible war bread, but there was often not enough for everyone. Posters announced the prohibition against demonstrations and parades. Cossacks patrolled the streets to maintain order. Machine guns posted around the city waited for trouble. Harper had letters of introduction to ministers of government, but with conditions so unsettled, she decided to wait before presenting them.

An eruption of some sort seemed so imminent that Harper wandered around town, "watching and waiting for it as I would for a circus parade." That parade appeared one day in the form of fifty women gathered in the street. One of them made an angry speech about the lack of bread. Others spoke up with their stories, and their numbers grew. When they began to sing the wobbly notes of "La Marseillaise" and march down the street, Harper followed. The French national anthem, "La Marseillaise," and a Russian variation, the "Worker's Marseillaise," had been popular protest songs since Russia's 1905 revolution. To Harper it carried a portent of trouble.

The women's parade stopped several streetcars and scattered a unit of army recruits drilling on a parade ground. By the time they reached Nevsky Prospect, the city's main boulevard, their numbers had swelled to nearly five hundred. A line of policemen finally broke up the march. Harper noted it as the "first riot of the revolution."

City streets became venues for the unrest. Crowds came out every day, larger and uglier. Repeatedly, Thompson and Harper landed in the middle of churning marchers, jostled, knocked down, fleeing mounted police and Cossacks. Harper received two sharp jabs from the butt end of a Cossack lance for moving away too slowly from one march. Word came of rioting on the outskirts of the city. Streetcars had been overturned, phone and electric wires cut. The next day the crowds included a rougher element that smashed shop windows, stopped traffic, and scuffled with police. Harper and Thompson's translator had to repeatedly explain to protesters that the two were not police spies but *Americansky* reporters.

Given the flashpoint of tensions in the city, the crowd that gathered one sunny Sunday in March looked surprisingly peaceful. It reminded Harper of "Circus Day" in a small American town. Street marches had become spectacles for the curious, and on this day many children brought a lighthearted mood to the crowd. But when heading back to their hotel, Thompson and Harper encountered a large group of determined marchers singing "La Marseillaise." Something made the two reporters apprehensive. They hung back rather than following along. "Those poor devils are going to get it," Thompson said.

When the protesters reached the next cross street, there came an explosion of gunfire. Many fell dead or wounded, and the crowd wheeled around in panic. As the terrified men, women, and children ran screaming, a storm of gunfire greeted them from the opposite direction. Soldiers along the street fired, and rooftop snipers opened up. A well-dressed woman standing next to Harper groaned and sank to the pavement. A little girl ran past, clutching her throat where a bullet had struck.

Harper and Thompson hit the ground. "Pretend you are wounded," Thompson advised, "the ambulances will pick you up." Freezing and paralyzed with fear, Harper waited until an ambulance removed her to the hospital, from where she made it back to the Astoria Hotel. When she told them at the hotel what had happened and that hundreds had been killed, no one believed her.

Meanwhile, marches, demonstrations, and riots popped up around the city. Street corner orators exhorted passersby to protest food shortages. The whole city seemed captured by the unrest. All that night mobs paraded around the city, breaking windows and burning government buildings. Protesters and groups of soldiers sympathetic to the protesters clashed with the police.

The fury of the mobs made all attempts to monitor the situation perilous. At one point Thompson insisted that it was too dangerous for Harper to be with him in the streets. "No more dangerous for me than it is for you," she insisted. "I'm going." When he continued to argue the point, she parted ways with him and went off on her own. The American consul would later call her a brave woman for being on the streets during the fighting—but then he immediately changed his assessment to "No, you are not; you are a damn fool!"

Harper hung around on the edges of the fighting, dodging for shelter from one doorway to another. "I had seen policemen beaten and killed, had seen men topple off roofs of buildings, and had seen people blood-mad." On the way back to her hotel, she got caught up in a revolutionary mob and had to pretend to be a protester. "By shouting at the proper moments and cheering whenever necessary, and sometimes when it was not necessary, I managed to keep from being noticed."

That night a group of soldiers and civilians visited the Astoria Hotel, where Harper stayed, and met with the Allied officers living there. The officers assured them that no anti-revolutionary meetings were being held in the hotel and that they would observe a strict neutrality, after which the revolutionists pledged to leave the hotel alone. But the next morning a regiment crossing the square came under fire from a machine gun believed to be on the roof of the Astoria. An angry mob gathered in the street, and a few Russian officers staying at the hotel fired on them with their pistols. The mob answered with a fusillade of shots, killing some curious hotel guests standing at their windows. The crowd surged into the lobby and spread over the lower floors. A fire in the lobby sent smoke through the elevator shaft to the upper floors, further alarming the terrified guests.

Early in the melee, Harper slipped from the hotel and mingled with the crowd, which gave her the novel experience of assisting in the attack on her own hotel. "When it was over I found that I had rather enjoyed it." The women hotel guests were allowed to leave with whatever luggage they could carry. As the foreign officers left, the crowd cheered them, but most of the Russian officers were killed.

As the revolution reached its violent conclusion, Harper and Thompson repeatedly placed themselves in the thick of the action on the streets: dodging bullets, enduring nerve-wracking confrontations with revolutionists, and discovering numerous dead bodies. They had little understanding of what transpired behind the scenes, and the turmoil on the streets defied understanding. The only news gathering possible was to glimpse the carnage and survive long enough to report it.

Women Report the Revolution

Rheta Childe Dorr entered the newsroom of the *New York Evening Mail* on March 16, 1917, to find a bunch of men clustered excitedly around the news ticker tape. She assumed it was some important war news and hurried to look. Revolution had broken out in Russia; the czar had abdicated; Russia was a republic. She immediately grabbed the arm of the city editor and announced, "'I'm going to Russia.' I didn't ask to be sent, I just announced that I was going. Nobody else was so well fitted for the job."

It was a nod to the rising status of women in journalism and to Dorr's long career in the profession that she quickly won approval. In addition to being a champion of labor reform and women's suffrage, she had twice been to Russia, including a visit in 1906 in the aftermath of the revolution that created its first legislative body, the Duma. In addition, Dorr considered herself a student of the French Revolution, having read all the available histories, including her favorite, *Travels in France*, by English writer Arthur Young.

Young had wandered around France during its revolution and provided an impartial eyewitness account of events. "To be another Arthur Young, reporting another revolution, seemed to me to be the most wonderful opportunity, the most marvelous adventure I could hope for in my life," Dorr thought. "I never wanted a newspaper assignment more." The only advice from her editor: "For heaven's sake, Mrs. Dorr, don't send us any essays on the Russian soul. Everybody else has done that. Go to Russia and do a job of reporting."

The March Revolution that deposed the czar and promised social reform served as a clarion call for a new crop of American reporters who appeared in Petrograd in the spring and summer of 1917. (According to the Julian calendar then in use in Russia, the revolution occurred on February 23. All dates in this chapter refer to the Western, or Gregorian, calendar, by which the revolution occurred on March 8.) Those journalists who championed social causes such as labor reform and women's suffrage; who fought against poverty, political corruption, and social privilege; or who were members of the Socialist Party were inspired by the birth of democracy in Russia. Conspicuous among them was the largest group of female reporters ever assembled in the war. Most could not be labeled as war correspondents. They had cut their journalistic teeth by exposing corruption in government and the exploitation of women and workers. They felt in sympathy with the socialist values of the revolution and its Provisional Government.

Florence Harper had arrived to cover the war and ended up covering a revolution. But the other women who appeared in Petrograd throughout 1917 were drawn by the revolution itself. Journalist Rheta Childe Dorr arrived in May. Louise Bryant arrived in September, along with her famous socialist war correspondent husband, John Reed. The Bell Syndicate assigned Bryant to report on the war "from a woman's point of view." Translated from journalese, that meant to report on conditions on the home front. How was the civilian population—largely women and children—adapting to the privations of war? Reed's impeccable leftist credentials gave him and Bryant access to revolutionary leaders and placed them at locations where critical events unfolded.

Even before revolution stole headlines away from the war that spring, the *San Francisco Bulletin* sent its reporter Bessie Beatty globetrotting to write a series of articles called "Around the World in Wartime." *Good Housekeeping* magazine employed the same strategy for its correspondent, lawyer and social activist Madeleine Zabriskie Doty, when it sent her around the world that summer for a "bird's-eye view of a mixed up world."

Beatty swept westward over half the globe, reporting on social and cultural issues in Hawaii, Japan, and China. Like many reporters who traveled to Russia, she journeyed from the Pacific port of Vladivostok to Petrograd aboard the Trans-Siberian Railway. A fair proportion of any war correspondent's reporting involved travel writing. Good stories often emerged as they moved under difficult and dangerous conditions, thrown together with the wild mix of those forced to flitter along the edges of the conflict.

Riding the rails for twelve days through the vastness of Russia, Beatty glimpsed the warm afterglow of revolution. She traveled with soldiers heading to the front, political revolutionaries returning from exile in Siberia, the son of the famous novelist Leo Tolstoy returning to his homeland from America, and members of the Committee of Workmen's and Soldier's Deputies traveling to a meeting in the capital. A mood of optimism and great potential animated everyone. "The heavy heart of Russia lifted with a mighty shout of joy: 'Svoboda! (Freedom) We are free!'" Beatty reported. "For the moment this was enough. That single word, with its age-old power of placing man on the mountaintops, made Russia happy." When Beatty reached Petrograd, her round-the-world excursion ended. The rest of the world had nothing to match this.

The first thing that greeted Bessie Beatty when she arrived in the city was a "war demonstration" of legless, armless, and blind soldiers, exhorting their able-bodied brothers to fight the war to a victorious conclusion. Rheta Dorr saw the same cast-off victims all over Petrograd. Missing limbs, horribly disfigured, clad in tattered uniforms, they begged on street corners or on church steps. No soldiers' homes or pensions supported the forgotten wounded in Russia.

When Dorr checked into the Military Hotel, formerly the Astoria Hotel, she discovered that the revolution, too, had left physical scars. Pockmarks from revolutionary bullets still adorned its exterior, and two bullet holes marked the wall above her bed. On the floor beneath the window in her room lay a "pool of blood as big as a saucer." These were the harsh reminders that the two great forces of war and revolution were trying to find accommodation with each other. War had already pushed Russia beyond its limits, and now revolution challenged it for dominance.

Dorr began her coverage of the revolution by hiring a university student as a translator. Each day the translator read to her the local newspapers, and then they ventured out to take the pulse of the city. An amazing number of soapbox orators on the streets harangued passersby with strong opinions about the war and the government. Dorr listened attentively while her student companion spoke the translation into her ear. She spent most of her time roaming the city, talking to people on park benches, on trams and trains, and in public places. She met Russians from every walk of life and every political persuasion. In factories she spoke with workers and employers.

She interviewed the last member of the royal family still left in freedom, Grand Duchess Elisabeta Feodorovna, sister of the empress and widow of Grand Duke Serge, uncle of the emperor. The duchess had long ago withdrawn from courtly life and founded a convent, where she lived. "The Russian people are good and kind at heart," the duchess said, "but they are mostly children—big, ignorant, impulsive children. If they can find good leaders . . . they will emerge from this dreadful chaos and build up a strong, new Russia." Although neither the duchess nor Dorr seemed to believe it, they both expressed the hope that Alexander Kerensky, leader of the Provisional Government, might "succeed in getting his released giant back into its bottle."

Such optimism became harder to sustain with each passing day. Political factions had already emerged to tug at the fabric of the revolution and challenge the Provisional Government. Prisons had been emptied of old radicals, and exiles were welcomed back from Siberia and abroad. Socialist visionaries from the United States arrived to pursue their dream to refashion society. A profusion of councils, congresses, and committees gave voice to those who had never had a voice. Dorr watched young men march in the street with banners demanding "All Power to the Soviets."

The soviets were councils of workers, soldiers, and peasants that appeared everywhere in the wake of the revolution: in cities, factories, and the military. They arose along with the Provi-

25. Rheta Childe Dorr in 1913, when she served as editor of the magazine the *Suffragist*. Harris & Ewing Collection, Prints & Photographs Division, Library of Congress, LC-DIG-hec-03403.

sional Government as a parallel, competing political power. Dorr attended marathon sessions of the soviet that met in Petrograd's Tauride Palace, trying to follow the fiery speeches through her interpreter. The Petrograd Soviet launched the postrevolutionary period by issuing Order #1, which declared an end to military discipline. Soldiers' councils could now challenge orders of officers. As a way of preventing military units from being used against the revolution, it made perfect sense. As a policy for maintaining fighting order, it proved a disaster.

For reporters from the world's greatest democracy, the chaotic democracy of the workers' and soldiers' councils went beyond reason. Radicals controlled the council, Dorr concluded. The war did not matter to them. Some were well-meaning theorists and dreamers but generally reasonable. The others were a "noisy and troublesome" minority known as the Bolsheviks, who had their own vast dream of establishing a "new order of society not only for Russia but for the whole world." They demanded that dream immediately and would not compromise.

By May, Dorr concluded that "the crisis in Russia is not ended but has just begun." Petrograd was quiet for now, but many feared a period of anarchy. For Dorr, Russia was "gorged on something she has never known before—freedom: she is sick almost to die with excesses . . . she is not even morally responsible for what she is doing." A sharp tone of frustration emerged in Dorr's reporting, as she tried hard to explain developments that she did not fully understand.

Like some of the other correspondents, Dorr had been drawn to Russia by the March Revolution and its potential to reshape Russia, and she expected an upward trajectory: "The Russians want us to help them establish public schools; to show them how to build and operate great railroad systems; to farm scientifically; to do any number of things we have learned to do so well."

"We mustn't despise the Russians," Dorr wrote as she wrestled to put things in context. "We must learn to help them. And we can't do that unless we understand them." Help came in the form of an American commission that visited Russia that June, bringing a full complement of experts. But American assistance was contingent upon Russia remaining in the war, a prospect that diminished by the day.

That month the militant English suffragist Emmeline Pankhurst visited Petrograd "to help the women of Russia, to organize them, and to teach them how to use (that panacea for all ills) the vote." The revolution had given women the vote. Dorr noted that Pankhurst had succeeded in organizing a group of influential Russian women, but her project failed because Kerensky did not support it. In Dorr's opinion that was "one of Kerensky's many lost opportunities." According to Florence Harper, Pankhurst had failed for a different reason: "Her motive was good; she was sincere; but unfortunately the women of Russia were too busy revolutionizing to bother about being organized."

Surprisingly, the dramatic story about Russian women that captured world headlines that June had nothing to do with suffragists or revolution but with soldiers. In the seven-month period between Russia's two revolutions, the army became the center of attention for both those who wanted to protect the homeland and honor its commitment to the Allies by continuing to fight in the war (Provisional Government) and those who wanted to stop fighting because it only served the interests of capitalists and the bourgeoisie (Bolsheviks). While the Provisional Government tried to maintain discipline in the ranks and political support for the war, the Bolsheviks visited the trenches to promote disobedience and desertion.

The Women's "Battalion of Death"

War, revolution, and women's rights came together in one of the most publicized news stories of that momentous summer. It began when an illiterate peasant woman from Siberia named Maria Bochkareva knelt in the great square in front of Petrograd's Saint Isaac's Cathedral while priests sprinkled her with holy water. Along with thousands of other spectators, Florence Harper, Rheta Dorr, and Bessie Beatty watched with fascination as Bochkareva rose to her feet to have a sword buckled about her by three generals. This was a banner day for women's rights. Bochkareva had just become an officer in the Russian army. Two hundred and fifty female soldiers stood at rigid attention behind her, members of Bochkareva's newly formed "Battalion of Death." Each of them wore a red-and-black ribbon arrowhead on her right sleeve: red for blood and black for a death that was preferable to dishonor. Many news stories called Bochkareva "Russia's Joan of Arc."

The details surrounding this incredible story played out over the summer and attracted the interest of the world press. Drawing on threads of Russia's desperate military situation and the expectations for empowerment unleashed by the revolution, the story resonated with every segment of the confused and conflicted Russian society, except for those who opposed the war. Every foreign female reporter in Russia captured a piece of this story but none more fully than suffragist Rheta Dorr.

Dorr visited the women's battalion during training to learn the stories of these inspiring women who had taken center stage in Russia's war effort. A product of Russia's long-suffering peasant class and a widow of the war, Bochkareva had made up her mind to fight in the army. After many rebuffs and appeals that rose to the czar himself, she was allowed to join the army in November 1914. She served for two years, receiving three wounds and several medals for bravery. Although an ardent revolutionist, she was disgusted by the conduct of soldiers after the revolution. When the men of her army unit began to lose their discipline, riot, and desert, she asked permission to form a women's battalion. "We will go wherever men refuse to go," she insisted. "We will fight when they run. The women will lead the men back to the trenches."

Leaders of the Provisional Government saw the great symbolic value of a women's battalion. During this difficult time at the front, some battalions of male soldiers had formed "death battalions," composed of men committed to fight to the death to defend Russia. Bochkareva's innovation was to form a women's death battalion in the hopes of shaming men to return to the fighting, from which so many had fled.

At first Petrograd took the Women's Death Battalion as something of a joke. Thousands of men and women, civilians and soldiers on leave, traveled out from the city each day to see the "female soldiers" in training. The women recruits came from all ranks of society—peasants, factory workers, servants, also women with education and social prominence. The youngest was fourteen, the oldest a mother who, after losing four sons in the war, walked a hundred miles to Petrograd to join the battalion. Only the most physically fit were accepted. Only those who held up to Bochkareva's demanding standards and iron discipline survived the training. Dorr found them totally sincere in their conviction that they could rally a demoralized army. "Our men are suffering from a sickness of the soul," they told her. "It is our duty to lead them back to health."

While the battalion trained that June, Dorr applied to the War Ministry for permission to travel with the battalion to the front. She had still not received approval when the women got orders to ship out immediately. In a panic Dorr rushed between government offices seeking emergency permission, without success. Veteran correspondent Arno Dosch-Fleurot (*New York World*) told her not to worry. He suggested that she just get on the train and stay on until they threw her off or she got where she wanted to be. Either way, she would have a story.

So, without official permission, Dorr and Bessie Beatty joined the battalion on their train ride to the front. At every station along the route, crowds gathered to cheer them and to demand to see Bochkareva. Many were women—nurses, peasants, and working girls—fascinated by the battalion and all that it portended for women in Russia.

The farther the train traveled from Petrograd, however, the more apparent it became that "things were terribly wrong with the empire." The character of the station crowds began to reflect the widespread disruption in the army. Men in uniform crowded the stations, but they were soldiers in name only. "They slouched like convicts, they were dirty and unkempt, and their eyes were full of vacuous insolence," Dorr reported. "Absence of discipline and all restraint had robbed them of whatever manhood they had once possessed. The news of the women's battalion had drawn these men like a swarm of bees. They thrust their unshaven faces into the car windows. . . . 'Who fights for the damned capitalists?' they screamed. 'Who fights for the English bloodsuckers? We don't fight.'"

The women shot back scornfully, "That is the reason why we do. Go home, you cowards, and let women fight for Russia." The

men's heckling reminded Dorr of New Yorkers watching a suffrage parade in the early days, when suffragists were taunted
and ridiculed.

Dorr and Beatty spent a week with the battalion while it
underwent additional preparation. But they were back in Petrograd when word came that the women soldiers had seen their
first engagement. Dorr pieced together the story by interviewing wounded survivors in the hospital, including Bochkareva.
When the men in their unit wavered, the women stormed the
German trenches and took prisoners, the proud survivors
reported. But the men would not advance to support them,
forcing them to withdraw. Of the two hundred who went into
action, twenty were killed, eight taken prisoner, and most of
the rest wounded.

Because it was such an inspiring story, news accounts of the
women's battalion made it past the censors and briefly painted
a positive face on Russia's war effort. But the battalion saw
action as part of what had been named the "Kerensky Offensive," after the leader of the Provisional Government, Alexander
Kerensky. Meant as a last-ditch effort to change the momentum of the fighting and rally the army with a victory, it experienced initial success that quickly turned to defeat and a virtual
collapse of the army. Tens of thousands of deserters flooded
Petrograd or commandeered trains to take them back home.
Kerensky published numerous deadlines for soldiers to rejoin
their units, called them traitors to the revolution, and threatened to deprive their families of a share in the distribution of
the land. Nothing worked. An unpopular war had now become
unthinkable. "Anarchy pure and simple reigned on all the fronts
and in the rear," Dorr noted. No one called louder for immediate peace than the Bolsheviks.

The July Uprising

The telephone rang in Florence Harper's hotel room. "Hurry up!"
came the excited voice of Donald Thompson. "They are shooting
up the town, and there's hell to pay!" Harper donned her hat and

a sturdy pair of walking shoes and made her way through hallways and lobby, which were suddenly alive with anxious women and officers. One lesson that Russia's foreign visitors learned from the revolution was that one never knew what kind of fighting was occurring, who manned the machine guns and armored cars, and for which faction they fought.

Thompson and Harper walked miles through the city that night, dodging armed soldiers and civilians and the isolated crack of sniper fire from rooftops. Rheta Dorr and Bessie Beatty arrived at the hotel in the middle of the excitement, still caked with mud from their visit to the frontline trenches. They paused long enough to change, then hurried onto the street. The Bolsheviks were making their move against the Provisional Government. Carloads of their supporters, the Red Guard, raced through the streets armed with rifles and machine guns. They fell into clashes with the Cossacks, who supported the government. That night Dorr counted seventeen dead Cossack horses.

The following morning Thompson picked up Harper with his hired car. His uniformed driver and orderly rode in the front seat, while he set up his motion picture camera tripod in the back seat with Harper. Looking very much like one of the threatening armored cars patrolling the city, they took up a position at a crowded street corner. They didn't have long to wait before Bolshevik and Cossack forces clashed there, sweeping the street with machine-gun fire. People in the crowd fell to the ground or ran for safety, but Thompson kept cranking his camera.

Fueled by adrenaline and fear, Thompson and Harper chased the fighting and fled from it for the rest of the day, as the Cossacks began to get the upper hand. Making it back to the hotel that night, Harper, Thompson, and the orderly flopped onto a couch, physically and emotionally drained. Harper was shaking from head to foot. Thompson too. His orderly was crying. The next day word came that their driver had been killed the previous night after dropping them off.

"'Tribune' Writer in Thick of the Riot at Petrograd," read the headline on Mildred Farwell's article in the *Chicago Tribune* on

July 20. She reported being at dinner with friends when fighting broke out. She hurried back to her hotel to change her shoes. Still in evening dress, she rushed out to investigate, accompanied by a bank manager who was also a guest at the hotel. She stood in a crowd on the city's main street, Nevsky Prospect, watching a regiment of soldiers march by, when machine guns began to chatter and the soldiers fired in response. In an instant the street emptied as people dashed into doorways and up side streets. Farwell pressed to the side of a building. "It sounded like a bad hailstorm, the pavement being peppered two feet away," she reported. The danger didn't seem to unnerve her as much as the chivalry of her companion: "I kept thinking what a fool I was making of myself, with a man trying to protect me with his own body."

As Bolshevik sympathies continued to spread in the population, correspondents wrote about the true state of affairs, but their articles about deteriorating conditions rarely made it past the Russian or British censors. Harper concluded that "not one newspaper man [or woman] who was in Russia during that summer had a single serious article published."

When the Provisional Government temporarily closed the borders in late July, Harper and Thompson decided that if they didn't get out of Russia soon, they might not get out for a long time. In mid-August, Thompson packed his precious cameras and his film record of the Russian Revolution onto a Trans-Siberian train and began the long journey home. He had made arrangements with the Provisional Government to avoid the censorship of his films. Harper stayed on into September, frustrated that she could not get out any truthful stories about the growing mood of extremism. A young man on a streetcar snarled at her that she and all the damned bourgeoisie would soon be killed. Foreigners in the city could see Kerensky getting weaker by the day and the power of the Bolsheviks growing. And yet foreign newspapers that arrived in Petrograd weeks late glowed about the Provisional Government and Kerensky as the one man who could restore order and keep Russia in the war.

Russia had one more curveball to throw at Harper before she

departed. On the day she was scheduled to leave, her train was suddenly canceled. The commander in chief of the army, Cossack general Lavr Kornilov, was marching on the city to take control of the government. Many had long ago concluded that only a strongman such as Kornilov at the head of government could save the revolution from falling to the Bolsheviks.

Soldiers burst into Harper's hotel that night. No one knew if they were soldiers from the Provisional Government, the Bolsheviks, or Kornilov's troops. They interrogated her and marched off all the Russian officers. She ran into Arno Dosh-Fleurot in the hotel lobby, from whom she learned that Kornilov had failed. They were both overcome with emotional frustration and used "not exactly polite" language. "We all knew it was the last chance," she wrote. "The Bolsheviks were armed; the Red Guard was formed. The split was definite; Kerensky was doomed."

The Bolshevik Revolution

"We were a strange lot we Americans," Bessie Beatty noted late that summer, when correspondents, embassy officials, businessmen, and other Americans in the city formed a tight community with strong opinions about Russia. "Some of us were uncompromising idealists, and some pragmatists, and more were the usual complex mixture of both."

People often showed up in Beatty's hotel room for rousing late-night discussions. Someone would make a thoughtful observation about the sincerity of the Bolsheviks or predict a date for the restoration of the monarchy, and they would be off in excited debate. Every shade of political opinion got expressed, Beatty noted. "Most often the talk turned to the necessity of making the people at home understand the complex and difficult situation as it really is."

On one occasion conversation turned to the Bolshevik movement, and one person made the familiar claim that Bolshevism was a German plot to take Russia out of the war. A newcomer to the group, Albert Rhys Williams of the *New York Post*, asked how many of those present knew any Bolsheviks. No one did. A socialist and advocate for social causes back in America, Williams had covered the war from its beginning. He had just traveled in other parts of Russia, he explained, meeting with workers and peasants, and thought it was shortsighted to dismiss the Bolsheviks without knowledge of them and their ideas.

The following night Williams brought to the gathering a genuine Bolshevik named Peters. He hailed from the Baltic States and spoke English with a British accent. The young man impressed Beatty. On that occasion and on other nights that followed, Peters and Williams "opened up many windows on the Revolution to me that would otherwise have been closed."

By late in the summer most of the American correspondents had taken sides on Bolshevism. Dorr, Harper, and Thompson, who supported the Provisional Government, witnessed the aborted Bolshevik uprising in July but departed Russia before the Bolsheviks came to power. They hurried home to share their views with the American public through books. Harper and Thompson created separate written and photographic records of the revolution. Harper's book, *Runaway Russia* (1918), detailed her experiences gathering the news in the chaotic early months of the revolution, including visits by an American Commission and the British suffragist Emmeline Pankhurst and a news-gathering stint at the front during which she had to serve as a nurse and been forced to swear allegiance to the revolution.

For two of the three books Thompson published in 1918, he chose titles that reflected his disapproval of the Bolsheviks: *From Czar to Kaiser: The Betrayal of Russia* and *Blood Stained Russia*. In *Inside the Russian Revolution* (1917) Rheta Childe Dorr noted that "the most striking parallel between the French and the Russian revolutions lies in the facility with which both were snatched away from the sane and intelligent men who began them and placed in the hands of fanatics."

When socialist and war correspondent John Reed and his wife, Louise Bryant, arrived in Petrograd in September, Bryant made a chart of the various political parties: the Mensheviks, the Men-

26. Louise Bryant's name is rarely mentioned without being associated with her more famous husband, the war correspondent John Reed. However, Bryant established her own journalistic reputation with her coverage of Russia's Bolshevik Revolution. Louise Bryant papers (MS 1840), Manuscripts and Archives, Yale University Library.

shevik Internationalists, the Right and Left Socialist Revolutionists, the Bolsheviks; and of the array of governing bodies: the Duma, Petrograd Soviet, Council of the Russian Republic, All-Russian Soviet, and so forth. It was the only way for a newcomer to get her bearings.

The wild, raw democracy of the process impressed Bryant. Everywhere she went, people engaged in spirited discussion over this or that political philosophy or strategy. A Democratic Congress in September drew sixteen hundred representatives from across Russia. Delegates filled the immense Alexandrinsky Theater. From their assigned seats in the orchestra pit, the foreign correspondents watched the drama of an endless succession of speakers. Often a peasant, who had never made a speech in his life, poured out his most heartfelt thoughts and kept the audience's rapt attention. Little got accomplished, but from sunset to dawn speakers vented grievances and proposed solutions.

The same wild democracy that stalled legislative bodies did the same in the army. When they visited the Latvian front in October, Albert Rhys Williams and Reed found military units virtually crippled. Units had lost up to 60 percent of their strength through casualties and desertions. Those who remained were poorly fed and equipped. Regular army command and soldiers' councils struggled with each other over military decisions, while an increasingly radical rank and file flexed its opposition to both.

The two reporters attended an extraordinary five-hour meeting conducted in the middle of a battle, at which thousands of soldiers voiced their grievances. While a German artillery barrage sounded an ominous backdrop, soldier after soldier stood up to denounce the war, the Provisional Government, and Russia's capitalist allies. Reed imagined that never before in history had a fighting army convened such a peace meeting during a battle. Certainly, it did not bode well for Russia remaining in the war.

A similar scenario played out back in Petrograd. Kerensky and the Provisional Government improvised cabinets and coalitions. Great conferences and councils convened to discuss and plan. Meanwhile, ordinary Russians, the peasants, workers, and soldiers were taking matters into their own hands. Peasants seized estates; soldiers deserted their units; and workers went on strike or took control of factories. In September, Bolsheviks won a majority in the Petrograd Soviet.

A sense of doom haunted the city in October. From her hotel

window Louise Bryant watched wagon caravans carrying art treasures from the Hermitage Museum, bound for safe storage in Moscow. Even factory machinery was carted away, and everyone assumed the city would soon be evacuated. Meanwhile, loud speeches in the Council of the Russian Republic called more insistently for peace. Bryant documented the fraught moment: "And through all the confusion moved Kerensky, far from serene, occasionally breaking down, crying out from the tribunal, to indifferent ears: 'I am a doomed man. I cannot last much longer!'"

Some scholars have since suggested that the female reporters covering the revolution often spoke from the margins of the action. They were less inclined to dwell on the causes of the revolution than on the impact of events on individuals. That theme played out in Bryant's reporting. Whether she was interviewing former Women's Death Battalion soldiers bitter because they were now derided by all sides or painting a picture of Katherine Breshkovsky, the "grandmother of the revolution" called back from exile in Siberia and now living in a modest room at the Winter Palace, Bryant gave the impression of pulling back a curtain to see characters behind the grand political drama.

Revolution provided on-the-job training in journalism for Bryant. Bryant had a degree in history from the University of Oregon and had worked a brief stint as society editor at the *Spectator* newspaper in Portland, Oregon. As her political interests developed, she published a few articles in the socialist magazine the *Masses*. Earlier in 1917, she had spent two months in France, taking her first stab at war reporting. Reed had arranged that job for her with the Bell Syndicate. He served as mentor and editor for some of her early articles, polishing them before they went to Bell. In Russia she matured into a confident journalist with her own point of view.

John Reed approached his assignment as a historian, collecting every document and recording every speech, to be reproduced verbatim in his classic book on the revolution, *Ten Days That Shook the World* (1919). Bryant, on the other hand, reported on the texture of daily life. She often explained the confusing context of the revolutionary government as it struggled with the chore of governing but always painted the scene with character sketches and dramatic tableaus.

Through Breshkovsky, Bryant arranged a much-coveted interview with Alexander Kerensky. When she showed up at Kerensky's headquarters in the Winter Palace, his secretary escorted her into his office. "Kerensky lay on a couch with his face buried in his arms, as if he had been suddenly taken ill, or was completely exhausted," she reported. "We stood there for a minute or two and then went out. He did not notice us."

"Something serious must be the matter with your Minister-President," Bryant remarked to the secretary. "I heard him speak at the Council of the Russian Republic a few days ago and in the middle of his speech he rushed from the platform and burst into tears."

"I know," she replied. "He really is hysterical. If he does not weep there he weeps here; and he is so dreadfully alone."

Kerensky had stomach trouble, the secretary explained, plus a bad lung and kidney. He only kept going with brandy and morphine. With sad resignation she confessed, "We are going to wake up here one morning and find that there is no Provisional Government." Within two weeks her prediction came true.

When day dawned on November 7, 1917, nothing portended well for Alexander Kerensky, the Provisional Government, or Russia's continuing involvement in the war. In that chilling way history has of aligning enough small events to make a large event seem suddenly inevitable, so the pieces fell in place for the Bolsheviks. The Russian fleet declared for the Bolsheviks; the Petrograd garrison likewise declared. Bolshevik supporters won majorities in the Soviet councils. All reports from the front indicated that more and more of the troops wanted immediate action on the Bolshevik call to end the war.

Even the old baron staying in Bessie Beatty's hotel seemed pleased with the prospect of a Bolshevik takeover. He was a monarchist through and through. His title and estates depended on the return of the monarchy. A week earlier Beatty had dined with him in the home of an Englishman, where they toasted the czar and sang the now-forbidden old national anthem. But he despised Kerensky and felt confident that a few weeks of Bolshevik incompetence would bring the Russian people around to his way of thinking.

As Kerensky and the Provisional Government bobbed like a cork on a stormy sea, assailed by forces from inside and outside the country, from the right and left, by the demands of fighting a war, and by a counterrevolutionary energy that grew stronger by the day, John Reed and Louise Bryant roamed the city in great excitement. Knowing that they were eyewitnesses to history, they took on the responsibility to capture it.

In *Ten Days That Shook the World* Reed gave dramatic structure to the swirl of events by setting them in two rival locations, the Winter Palace and the Smolny Institute. The Winter Palace was the opulent residence of the former czar, which now housed the Provisional Government and the Duma, the one scrambling desperately to salvage its revolutionary vision and the other being rendered increasingly irrelevant by fast-moving events. The Smolny Institute, a former school for girls of the privileged class, was now the base for the Petrograd Soviet, controlled by the Bolsheviks, and the meeting place for the All-Russian Congress of Soviets, the massive, unruly gathering of representatives from across Russia.

Granted access denied to other reporters, Reed and Bryant, along with Bessie Beatty and Albert Rhys Williams, were the only eyewitnesses from the American press to be on hand when the final pieces fell into place for the Bolsheviks. Reed's book focuses on events from November 6 to 15, but the Bolshevik seizure of power came on November 7. A more momentous and dramatic day would be hard to imagine.

At nine that morning a servant at her hotel informed Beatty that Bolshevik soldiers, the Red Guard, had just taken possession of the hotel. Soon they knocked on her door, and the familiar ritual began of interrogations, room inspections, and the marching

27. Reporters Bessie Beatty (left) and Louise Bryant with a Russian naval officer in 1917. Occidental College and College Archives and the Beatty Family, Papers of Bessie Beatty.

away of Russian officers. The two local newspapers still being published gave spotty reports of events unfolding around the city. The Bolsheviks captured the Telephone Exchange, the Telegraph Agency, and the Baltic Train Station. Some government ministers had been arrested, the chief of the city militia shot, and skirmishes occurred between soldiers and the Red Guard.

Beatty found four armored cars lined up before the Winter Palace. It wasn't unusual in these chaotic times to have to ask soldiers which side they were on. But the car doors bore freshly painted

Bolshevik red flags, and the word *Proletariat* adorned one of them. Beatty talked her way into the palace and found the ministers of the Provisional Government inside, fifteen of them seated around a mahogany table waiting grimly for events to unfold. Already impotent relics of the first revolution, they were guarded by a handful of military school cadets and another of the women's battalions that had formed in the wake of Bochkareva's battalion. The women had enlisted to fight German invaders and been reluctantly thrust into the role of guardians of the old order. Kerensky had gone to the front to round up loyal troops, they told Beatty.

Beatty made her way through several street skirmishes to Smolny Institute, where the Second All-Russian Congress of Soviets was under way. There she met up with Bryant, Reed, and Williams. They pushed through a seething crowd of workers, peasants, soldiers, and professionals. Sixteen hundred delegates from throughout Russia overflowed the available chairs, filled the aisles, sat on windowsills, and perched everywhere. Even as they awaited the start of the congress, the repeated boom of cannon fire filled the hall. When delegates learned that the cruiser *Aurora*, anchored in the Neva River, was shelling the Winter Palace, where ministers of the government still sheltered, they exploded with anger.

Why were the Bolsheviks seizing power now, speakers asked, only weeks before a constitutional assembly was planned to decide the form of government? Speaker after speaker rose to protest or to challenge those who protested, each met with heckles or cheers. Finally, those delegates opposing the Bolsheviks declared that they would perish with their comrades at the Winter Palace and walked out of the meeting. Reed recorded the words of Leon Trotsky as the delegates marched out: "Let them go. They are just so much refuse which will be swept away into the garbage heap of history!"

The promise of a confrontation at the Winter Palace was too tantalizing to ignore. The reporters hurried out. They paused first at a room in Smolny to get passes from the Bolsheviks' Military Revolutionary Committee. The area outside Smolny was alive with cars and trucks arriving and departing on secret missions. Reed approached some soldiers loading bundles of papers into a truck. They were going "downtown—all over—everywhere," they told Reed. They would likely be shot at, but if the reporters wanted to go along, they could.

Off the truck raced at top speed, bumping and swaying from side to side, the four correspondents lying on the bed of the truck next to rifles and bundles of papers. Sentries and armed men challenged the truck with raised guns, but it sped past them. A soldier on the truck tore open one of the bundles and tossed papers into the air. The correspondents joined in, grabbing papers and throwing them from the truck. The papers snowed down in the dark streets, where passersby rushed to grab them up to learn of the latest bewildering turn in the revolution.

In the fleeting glow of passing streetlights, the reporters read one of the papers:

TO THE CITIZENS OF RUSSIA!

Citizens! The Provisional Government is deposed. State Power has passed into the hands of the Petrograd Soviet of Workers' and Soldiers' Deputies, the Military Revolutionary Committee, which stands at the head of the Petrograd proletariat and garrison.

The cause for which the people were fighting: immediate proposal of a democratic peace, abolition of landlord property-rights over the land, labour control over production, creation of a Soviet Government—that cause is securely achieved.

LONG LIVE THE REVOLUTION OF WORKMEN, SOLDIERS, AND PEASANTS!

Military Revolutionary Committee
Petrograd Soviet of Workers' and Soldiers' Deputies.

"How far they had soared, these Bolsheviki," John Reed would remark on that momentous occasion, "from a despised and hunted sect less than four months ago, to this supreme place, the helm of great Russia in full tide of insurrection!"

Madeleine Zabriskie Doty arrived in Petrograd at 6:00 a.m. on the day after the Bolshevik takeover to find the city shrouded in a "great stillness." Her hotel provided few comforts—no heat, no hot water, only one electric light—but it did offer a splendid view of the street. She perched on her windowsill, shivering and gazing out at the silent snow-covered square below, waiting for the new day.

> The city began to stir before dawn. "Great lines of people formed. Weary, ragged soldiers stood a block long before tobacco shops. Women with shawls about their heads and baskets on their arms appeared before provision stores. The trams began to move.
>
> When the sun came over the horizon, the city throbbed to life. Little processions of men and women passed arm in arm under red flags, singing. There was the beat of drums and some Kronstadt sailors swung into sight. Everywhere there was movement and action, but no violence. People stopped to argue. Voices rose high and arms waved wildly. It was a people intensely alive and intensely intelligent. Every one had an opinion. It was my first glimpse of Russia. My heart leaped up.

Like Bessie Beatty, Doty was also on a round-the-world tour, looking for the "spiritual drama" unfolding in different countries, in parallel with the great military struggle. "I tried to discover the dreams and plans of the women of the future, what the folks at home strove for, where the spiritual drama led. I made no attempt to acquire facts and figures . . . merely a bird's-eye view of a mixed up world."

Attorney, ardent pacifist, and social reformer Madeline Doty had already explained to the readers of *Good Housekeeping* magazine that women in Japan were submissive and voiceless. In China they lived in the past but were beginning to embrace the future. In Petrograd the most striking spiritual drama seemed to be the reversal of the social order: "The cooks and waiters had become the aristocrats; the lawyers, bankers, and professors, the riff-raff."

One night, while Doty dined with Louise Bryant and John Reed, the sound of shooting interrupted their conversation. "I confess I was a coward," Doty admitted. She begged Bryant and Reed to see her home. Along the way the sounds of fighting got louder, and wounded men and fleeing soldiers rushed past them. Reed and Bryant wanted to see what all the excitement was about, "but I wanted to get home and bury my head under the bedclothes," Doty wrote.

In the upside-down world of revolutionary Russia, Doty needed a new game plan. She destroyed all her letters of introduction to prominent people because they had all been arrested or were dead. "The journalist these days must be a quick change artist, prepared to meet king or Bolshevik," she told her readers. She abandoned her editor's request that she interview the czarina. The czarina was being held in Siberia, and besides, it would have been a likely death sentence to arrange such a meeting.

To get a close-up view of events, she moved from her hotel into the home of a working-class family, a move that won for her ready acceptance by workers and soldiers. Although this made life more bearable, "Petrograd was not a place to live if you wanted a peaceful and luxurious life. It was a continual fight to get the bare necessities." And the threat of violence always lurked alarmingly close at hand.

As Doty got her bearings and ventured onto the streets, she captured snapshots of a city in the throes of a sweeping social and economic transformation. She visited the Winter Palace and the fortress of Peter and Paul and had rousing discussions with the guards about politics in America and Russia. She interviewed some of the former ministers of state being held in the fortress. On a train she talked with an aristocrat dressed as a nurse to avoid being harassed. The woman had lost everything and feared being killed.

The Smolny Institute had become the impromptu seat of the

Bolshevik government. Chalked signs or scraps of paper identified various government offices. Long tables displayed radical
literature. "Unshaven and collarless men littered the floor with
papers and argued hotly."

The working-class government issued a dizzying string of
decrees. The right to the private ownership of land was abolished. Citizens could not own more than one coat, and the number of blankets was limited. "One day all titles were abolished,"
Doty wrote, "the next judges and lawyers were eliminated." Doty,
being a lawyer, confessed a "wicked delight" over this directive.

Through John Reed, Doty met the two men who held the fate
of Russia in their hands: Vladimir Lenin and Leon Trotsky. Lenin
wore conservative clothes and looked more like a banker than a
radical, Doty thought. He was too busy to talk. Trotsky, on the
other hand, looked like a revolutionary, with a mass of bushy
hair, beard and mustache, and an open-neck shirt and flowing
black tie. Theirs was a "rushing, turbulent world. Plots and coun-
terplots were unfolding daily, food was running out, transportation was breaking down. The city was in a state of upheaval."

Good Housekeeping had asked Doty to study the women's movement in the midst of revolution—a near impossible task in Russia, where no women's movement existed. "The Russian woman
is a man in petticoats," Doty explained, which she offered as
praise. Women were equal helpmates to the men. They had won
suffrage in the early days of the revolution, and a woman served
in a senior position in the Bolshevik government. Madame Alex-
andra Kollontai had been made minister of social welfare, "the
first woman minister the world has had." Women will "rise tri-
umphant" as the spiritual leaders. "And in no country will she
be more magnificent than in Russia," Doty concluded.

As the Bolsheviks equivocated about making peace and the
German army continued to capture Russian territory, the Bolsheviks finally ran out of options. The two sides met in the town of
Brest-Litovsk to discuss terms, while a German delegation arrived
in Petrograd in January 1918. Both Bryant and Doty reported on
the peculiar tensions of having German officials in revolution-

ary Russia. The chance of lucrative contracts with the German army drew out Russian businessmen-capitalists, the anathema of the revolution.

Everything was new in new Russia. Everything had to be explained and interpreted for the American reader. Thorough interpretations would have to wait for the books all these women would write about their experience in Russia. For now the artful cameo of events had to suffice.

Doty saw the German-Russian tensions on vivid display when she visited the town of Brest-Litovsk, where official armistice negotiations were about to begin. American reporters were not permitted to interview the Germans, but, as Bryant noted, "there was no law against 'looking' at one's enemy." Her description of the first meeting of the two delegations spoke volumes of the chasm between their two worldviews:

> The Russian delegates were scrubby unshaven tired workmen. They wore blouses, faded uniforms and dilapidated business suits. They were met in state by Leopold, Prince of Bavaria, General Hoffman and other dignitaries, clad in resplendent uniforms and leather boots and clinking spurs, and shining medals. This opposing array stood rigidly heel to heel and hand to cap. But the Russian worker, unabashed, stepped forward with outstretched hand and said "brother." It was like a clap of thunder. The earth shook. The Teutonic officials lost their dignity. Such freedom was scandalous. It must be kept from the people. Large automobiles hurried the Russians to a hotel. There they were carefully hidden away.

Doty found equal place in her impressions of Russia for disillusionment and hope. "This compromise with Germany, the suppression of the press, the arrest of moderate socialists, and like intolerant acts were causing dissension among the Bolsheviki. It was making a break that may prove fatal to revolutionary Russia." Russia needed time to sort out its brand of self-government, Doty concluded. "Little by little Russia will right itself. Given freedom and a chance to breathe and she will stabilize and grow strong."

In February 1918 Madeleine Doty, Louise Bryant, and Bessie Beatty resolved to leave Russia. Doty wrote about the harrowing adventure for *Good Housekeeping*. Opting for the Scandinavian route, the trio left Petrograd in a blizzard, with temperatures well below zero, on the last train to leave for Finland. Civil war had already broken out in Finland, as the country tried to free itself from Russian rule. They passed into Sweden from the most northern corner of Finland, taking a frigid sleigh ride across a frozen river, bundled in fur coats and huddled together to avoid freezing.

Behind them in Russia, the Bolshevik dream of a new economic and social order remained unrealized. Bryant had the most faith in the socialist dream: "Socialism is here, whether we like it or not—just as woman suffrage is here—and it spreads with the years." All of the women were prepared to overlook the excesses of the revolution and be patient with its progress. Beatty thought that as eyewitnesses they were too close to the events to give them their proper value: "Time will be able to overlook the pathetic, the tragic, the cruel, the silly forms of expression that revolt frequently takes, and see only the magnificent urge behind those expressions." But they had lived the adventure and could share their experience. "I who saw the dawn of a new world can only present my fragmentary and scattered evidence to you with a good deal of awe," Bryant offered in the book she wrote about her experience, *Six Red Months in Russia* (1918). "I feel as one who went forth to gather pebbles and found pearls." At the end of her book on the revolution, *The Red Heart of Russia* (1918), Bessie Beatty echoed a similar sentiment: "Mingled with my sorrow, the morning I left Petrograd, was a certain exultant, tragic joy. I had been alive at a great moment and knew that it was great."

9

Covering American Involvement

I sit up and take out of the handbag still on my arm a pocket-
mirror. Half a dozen small wounds on my left cheek. Unimportant.
But my eyes fall casually on my feet, extended before me. Blood!
Thick and purplish, oozing slowly out of jagged holes in my heavy
English shoes and gaiters. I seem to be wounded.
—ELIZABETH SHEPLEY SERGEANT, "The Wing of Death," *North
American Review*, January 1920

In February 1917 the waters of the North Atlantic suddenly
became more perilous for American travelers. In an attempt
to press its advantage in the naval war of attrition with Britain, Germany renewed its sink-on-sight submarine policy of
attacking any ship of any nation in war zone waters. Mary Boyle
O'Reilly, who had been covering the war for the Newspaper Enterprise Association since its opening days, received an urgent telegram from her editor. Would she consider running the German
submarine blockade and reporting on her adventure? Of course
she would.

She set off from Liverpool in the first week of February, "thru
the submarine zone of frightfulness on the American liner New
York, THE LAST SHIP FOR HOME." O'Reilly's penchant for using
capital letters to drive home the significance of an event seemed
appropriate on this occasion. On the first night passengers were
instructed to sleep fully dressed, with life belts at the ready as
the ship slipped through the fogbound sea-lane that shrouded

the grave of the *Lusitania*. It navigated the vast mine fields and sailed passed the ring of guardian trawlers on patrol.

Lifeboat drills and a relentless vigil by passengers for submarines kept tensions high throughout the voyage. But they escalated on February 3, when the ship received news off the wireless that the United States had taken a fateful step toward war by severing diplomatic relations with Germany. The gravity of the occasion prompted one elderly passenger to sit at the ship's piano to sing "The Battle Hymn of the Republic." Finally, on the eighth day, Fire Island, off the southern shore of Long Island, rose out of the sea mist, "gilded by the sun rays." The crowd of passengers on deck swarmed as one mass to the railing, relieved and grateful to have escaped the madness in Europe and the danger of the Atlantic.

Waiting in London, at the tail end of her long exploration of the role of women in warring countries, Mabel Potter Daggett kept postponing her return home. Posters in the lobby of her hotel announced the sinking of seven ships in one day, including the liners *Laconia* and *California*. "Do you see the deterring, dampening effect that this might have on one's enthusiasm for departure?" she wrote.

But she took her "courage in both hands," bought a ticket on the *Carmania*, and sailed in late March. No shipboard games, dancing, or bands brightened the days for the sixteen passengers. Life preservers became their constant companions. No one lounged on steamer chairs on deck. Daggett described the sense of danger: "Death is so near that it seems fitting the glad activities of life should cease, as when a corpse is laid out in the front room of a house."

Each morning the ship's wireless newspaper appeared beside their breakfast plates with the news of the day. On April 6 it carried the announcement that the United States had declared war. "That must be a great relief for you," the Englishman sitting next to Daggett remarked. "I cannot answer for the choking in my throat," she lamented. "My country, oh, my country, too, at the gates of hell."

America Enters the War

Among the many great challenges that faced the American Expeditionary Forces and its commander, General John J. Pershing, was what to do about the journalists who wished to cover American involvement in the war. Pershing would have been quite happy not to have any reporters at all with the AEF. In theory he accepted their usefulness to an army; in practice, however, they posed an obvious threat to military secrecy and were a damned nuisance to manage.

Following the lead of the British and French, he elected to control journalists by limiting their number. Initially, fifteen was thought sufficient. By selecting only those from the largest urban newspapers and the syndicated news organizations, such as the Associated Press and United Press, the greatest number of publications and readers would be served. These credentialed journalists would be attached to the army, wear a military uniform, and be subject to military rules and censorship.

To select these fifteen accredited reporters, the War Department created requirements so onerous that few could be expected to qualify. Applicants had to write an essay about their qualifications and integrity and their plans for covering the war. They had to pay $1,000 upfront for military travel and accommodations. To ensure their loyalty and compliance with restrictions, they had to post a $10,000 bond. Additionally, they were expected to have previous experience as a war correspondent, supported by a letter of recommendation from a military official. In time these requirements would be lessened or disregarded, but initially, they managed to exclude any women from earning AEF credentials.

Although the U.S. Army had no official policy against women war correspondents, a 1910 article in the *Army Navy Journal* reflected its unofficial views. The article addressed the likely consequences of having war described "in the emotional chronicles of a female war correspondent," which would likely include "pitiful tales of disoriented privates, who suddenly discover that field rations are not like what mother used to cook," and other such "inhumanities of war." The underlying presumption, held by the military and much of the journalistic profession when the United States entered the conflict, was that the serious business of war should only be reported by those who knew about military matters and not through the personal impressions of women. All of which might explain the shocked reaction of James Black, editor of the *El Paso Morning Times*, when reporter Peggy Hull (Henrietta Eleanor Goodnough Hull) asked him to send her to France. Hull, who built a career on overcoming limitations, took delight in recounting his response: "'Send you to France?' [His] feet came down from the top of his desk with such a thud that his nose glasses fell off and clattered to the floor."

On one level Hull's request made perfect sense. She was one of the few women journalists in the country who had actual war correspondent experience. She had been a young reporter for the *Cleveland Plain Dealer* in 1916, when the U.S. Army launched its Punitive Expedition into Mexico. When the Ohio National Guard got mobilized to patrol the United States–Mexico border, Hull joined the Guard's Women's Auxiliary. "I'm a soldier now!" she announced in her column. "I'm going to learn to shoot a rifle and to do Red Cross work." Within two weeks she announced grander ambitions: "I'm studying hard to be an officer—I think I'd like to be a Brigadier General, or something like that, and of course it will take a lot of work and self-sacrifice." That article appeared with a photo of her in an Ohio National Guard uniform. It's tempting to discount the naive, gushy innocence that colored much of Hull's reporting in 1916—many of her colleagues did— and yet she did it with such confidence and flair that she created a unique brand of war reporting.

When the Ohio Guard shipped out, Hull went along. "Yes, I'm really going," she assured her readers, "and I'm going to write you lots of letters all about your friends and relatives who have responded to the call to arms."

Hull settled in El Paso, Texas, and took a job with the *El Paso Morning Times* but continued to write letters home to the *Cleve-*

land Plain Dealer. Refused permission to cross the border to report on the activities of American troops led by General Pershing—permission granted to male correspondents—she became a fixture at all the military bases and activities on the Texas side of the border. The *Times* claimed that "wherever the army was there was Peggy. When reviews were held at Fort Bliss, Peggy was there on the friskiest mount in the corrals. When General [Francisco] Murguia entertained General [J. Franklin] Bell, in the hippodrome in Juarez toasts were drunk to Señorita Peggy, the pride of the Americans present. She was the friend of every soldier in the American army."

The Punitive Expedition gave Hull experience working with the military and the opportunity to build friendships with generals and other journalists covering the campaign. She honed a style of war reporting that dealt less with military affairs than with the "little stories" of war that focused on her personal interaction with soldiers.

War reporting experience aside, Hull realized that on the practical level "asking the managing editor of a Texas paper with about 25,000 circulation to send me to France as a war correspondent was as preposterous in his eyes and as presumptuous on my part as it would be for a munitions worker in England to have matrimonial designs on the Prince of Wales."

There is no record of what caused Black to finally agree to her proposal. The newspaper already received its war news off the Associated Press wire, as it had during the army's involvement in Mexico. Perhaps he thought that Hull could put her own highly personalized stamp on the war as she had on the Mexican scrap. Perhaps she could write about El Paso or Texas soldiers. Perhaps having its own correspondent in France would allow the *El Paso Morning Times* to distinguish its war coverage from that of its primary competition, the *El Paso Herald*.

Having her editor's blessing did not immediately clear Hull's path to France. The life of a war correspondent was defined by an endless series of official permissions and restrictions. For one, the U.S. State Department controlled the flow of individuals to warring Europe by restricting passports. If applicants were working journalists and the newspaper or magazine for which they wrote did not espouse an antiwar message or some disruptive social cause, they might convince the State Department to issue them a passport. They would then undergo a similar screening to win a visa from the British and French consuls. Hull spent time in Washington and New York, arguing her qualifications and countering reservations about women war correspondents, before winning approval. It was a scene repeated by other women eager to get to France in 1917.

Hull's well-timed arrival in Paris on July 3 coincided with the appearance in the city of the first contingent of U.S. troops. She reported their warm welcome as American and French battalions paraded side by side on July 4, cheered by jubilant crowds. Hull wasted no time in rewarding her editor's faith in her by landing an interview with the commander of the AEF, General Pershing. With the monumental tasks facing him, Pershing had no time for press interviews. Doubtless, knowing Hull from his days in Mexico made him receptive to her request. It delighted Hull to report to her readers how pleased the general was to see her. "Why, Peggy! How in the world did you get over here?" Pershing asked. "I'm glad you are here, and it was splendid of the Times to send you—I'm sure the men will appreciate it." It's safe to say that no other journalist in the course of the war ever elicited such a warm response from the commander of U.S. forces.

Hull had started her war reporting with a bang. Few other correspondents in France could boast an acquaintance with Pershing. No others got an interview at this point. Hull's arrival on the scene even got mentioned in the Paris edition of the *Chicago Tribune*, often referred to as the "Army Tribune," a small-edition newspaper recently launched to provide news and features to American soldiers in France. It noted that the correspondent from the *El Paso Morning Times* was "the latest addition to the ranks of American war correspondents in Paris . . . whose readers have learned to like and look for the chatty news letters . . .

[and] whose experiences with the United States army in recent operations have qualified her as an interpreter of army life in garrison and in the field."

The *Army Tribune* already had on staff one of the first journalists to reach France after U.S entry, Ruth Hale. Hale was one of several female reporters who traveled to France with their journalist husbands. Ruth Hale and Heywood Broun married in New York on June 6, 1917, and sailed for France the following day. Hale, an ardent feminist, had to be pressured into having a church wedding and having someone "give her away." She insisted on keeping her maiden name. She had been a working journalist for over a decade, writing for the Hearst syndicate, *Washington Post, Philadelphia Public Ledger*, and *New York Times*. In 1916 she left the *Times* for a better-paying job as a theatrical press agent, the same year she met *New York Tribune* sports writer Heywood Broun.

Broun got one of the few credentials available from the AEF, while Hale, without a current newspaper affiliation, took a job with the *Army Tribune*. Hale helped to launch the new publication. On the understaffed newspaper, her duties included both production and reporting. Few of her stories saw publication back in the United States, but in one that did, she lamented the patronizing attitude of French authorities toward women journalists. She told of being on a war tour arranged just for women reporters: "We were five newspaper women, and we were to be improved, instructed, given our fill of those first hand impressions of the trail of war . . . then we were to be returned to our parents, our husbands or our newspapers, according to where guardianship of us was vested. . . . And above all, we were to do the thing safely and calmly, as ladies should, and have no shocks and no alarms with which our hosts would have need to reproach themselves." Although the tour included what was believed to be a safe staging area behind the lines, a German airplane bombed the location during their visit. Late in 1917, pregnancy persuaded Hale to return home.

Like Hale, Helen Johns Kirtland and Ruth Kauffman also traveled to France with their journalist husbands. Helen Johns and Lucian Swift Kirtland married on November 11, 1917, and immediately set off for France. Lucian, a photojournalist, worked for *Leslie's Illustrated Weekly*, under the auspices of the YMCA and the United States Army and Navy. Although different from AEF accreditation, such affiliations gave reporters greater freedom of travel and access to news.

Helen also became a photojournalist for *Leslie's* but worked separately from her husband. She spent more than a year covering the war on many fronts, including Belgium, Italy, and Poland. She also did photo spreads on women war workers and American soldiers in training.

Ruth Kauffman traveled to France with her husband, Reginald Wright Kauffman. He reported for a newspaper syndicate and she for an organization called The Vigilantes. In their effort to inspire patriotism and encourage support for America's war effort, The Vigilantes published pamphlets and syndicated news articles. The editorial note introducing Kauffman's first article, on American nurses in France, explained that Kauffman was "making a study there of the work that women are doing, in order to show American women what they can do to help win the war." Kauffman remained in France and England for a year, writing about the supportive role of women.

The introduction of America into the war did not diminish interest in the role of women in the Allied countries; in fact, it provided a new lens for viewing it. Now that America was a belligerent, its women could benefit by learning how British and French women supported their country's war efforts.

One Strategy for Covering the War

Anyone who got to France could call oneself a war correspondent. With only a residency permit from the police, they could live in Paris, which offered an abundance of war stories. The long-suffering French made good copy. Hospitals overflowed with the wounded. American soldiers in their distinctive khaki uniforms could be interviewed on the streets of Paris. Bombs reg-

28. Helen Johns Kirtland with her husband, Lucian Swift Kirtland. Both worked as photojournalists for *Leslie's Illustrated Weekly* from November 1917 through the Versailles Peace Conference in June 1919. Kirtland Collection, Prints & Photographs Division, Library of Congress, LC-USZ62-115861.

ularly fell on the French capital, allowing anyone there to claim they had been under fire.

But American readers wanted most to know about their own soldiers. Throughout the one-year period between the U.S. declaration of war and its introduction into combat, those troops arrived at unnamed French ports, trained at distant camps, and built mammoth infrastructure projects across France. To reach those locations required special permits and infrequently offered guided tours by French or American officers—unless one had a strategy for evading those restrictions. Fortunately, America's women journalists did.

Elizabeth Frazer's story of how she got to France and reported the war began when she took a three-month first aid course in New York in spring 1916, so that she might become a nurse's aide in France. She then reported for duty at the American hospital in Paris, where she quickly learned that she was totally unprepared for her duties. For a year she worked sixty-hour weeks tending to French wounded from the Battle of Verdun.

She embarked on her nursing adventure with both journalistic intentions and a "fine white flame of enthusiasm for the Allied cause." She had previously published articles and short stories in such magazines as *Good Housekeeping* and the *Saturday Evening Post*. Her nursing experience provided a rich lode of material for a *Saturday Evening Post* article, "Ward Eighty-Three," in which she told of her struggle to learn her duties and drew vignettes of her soldier patients.

For her first year in France, Frazer did not venture far from that base. "As yet, I have been to no battlefields," she confessed in the article. "I have letters, to be sure, which if presented in the proper quarters, I am told, would result in personally conducted trips to lines not engaged in an actual offensive. But those letters still lie, unsent, in my trunk. I may use them some day. But at present there is within me a reluctance to visiting ruins and battlefields. Perhaps it is because I have seen so many ruins who have returned from those battlefields."

Frazer sailed for home in March 1917 but returned to France

for the *Saturday Evening Post* when America entered the war. Her Red Cross connections positioned her to be an immediate observer of the American buildup and allowed her to evade restrictions on travel and access to the front. "When America went into this war she went into it Red Cross end first," Frazer explained. Following American entry, the Red Cross experienced explosive growth, establishing hospitals, caring for refugees, aiding in reconstruction, and providing many services at U.S. training camps. Red Cross volunteers worked throughout France and deep in the war zone. When American troops entered combat in the spring of 1918, Frazer volunteered at frontline hospitals, closer to the action than most of the credentialed correspondents.

Frazer had not invented this approach to gathering news. It had been employed effectively in the opening months of the war by Mary Roberts Rinehart, who worked through the Belgian Red Cross to visit the front lines. But during the period of American involvement, affiliation with an aid organization became a much-used stratagem for women journalists to circumvent restrictions on their reporting.

After an arduous five-week writing marathon in November 1917 to produce her book on revolutionary Russia, Rheta Childe Dorr felt like an "emptied pitcher." One dramatic chapter in her life had closed, and the next had yet to open. "Of course I was impatient to go to France. I had not half enough war corresponding," she confessed in her autobiography, *A Woman of Fifty* (1924). "I swanked around the office in my war correspondent's uniform, riding breeches and coat, parrying the jibes the men threw at me."

Dorr did considerable lecturing at this time about her Russian Revolution experience, but she declined an invitation to debate the "Bolshevik question" with Louise Bryant and "other local Reds." Dorr was fond of telling one story from this period because it so well illustrated the prevailing attitude toward women and war. She was speaking to a large group of women from the National Arts Club, regaling them with stories about Russia's Women's Death Battalion, explaining how these women soldiers inspired a nation by stepping into the trenches when men deserted the army. The listeners were "thrilled to their very hearts."

Meanwhile, a group of men in the same building had been listening to a British officer's stories of the war. One of the men interrupted Dorr's lecture to say that the women really had to hear the officer's exciting stories. The women politely paused their program, and the officer came in to tell about the heroic deeds of British soldiers. He concluded his remarks by explaining that the war was not being fought entirely by men, that women also had an important role to play. "Your part, ladies, is to *smile*." When Dorr recounted this story in her autobiography, she remarked that her audience "certainly smiled after the door closed on that dear man."

If anything, that clueless officer demonstrated that the job of telling about women's role in the war was far from complete. In fact, with the United States' entry into the war, American women had taken on a new role, that of mothers and wives of serving soldiers. Nothing monopolized Dorr's own thoughts as much as concern about her son, Julian, then serving in France: "I discovered that try as I might to think of armies, strategies and diplomacies, the only thing that vitally concerned me in France was to find out how my son was faring, and in doing so I [would find] out the things that other mothers wanted to know about their boys."

When Dorr arrived in France in December 1917, on assignment for the *New York Evening Mail*, French authorities refused to recognize her as a qualified war correspondent or to give her a pass to travel outside Paris. "Why did your newspaper send you over?" one French officer inquired. "'Why didn't it send a man?' I answered that I was sent because I was the person on the staff best fitted for the job. I said a little about my Russian experience, but they were unimpressed."

For centuries women had faced such attitudes, Dorr noted, and it had taught them to achieve their ends by indirection. When one avenue closed, they found another. Dorr contacted a former colleague, Reginald Wright Kauffman, then in France, to ask how his wife, Ruth, had managed to gain military access. Ruth Kauffman had already written articles about women nurses and ambulance drivers. Kauffman explained that Ruth got passes to travel because she worked with the YMCA. That organization provided extensive support services for the American army in training camps and throughout the country. He mentioned that the YMCA was currently looking for entertainers and asked if Dorr could sing or dance. She couldn't, she confessed, but would they like her to lecture about the Russian Revolution? He thought they would.

Everything happened quickly from there. Kauffman recommended Dorr to the YMCA, which agreed to book her at various American camps. But regarding her journalism, they first wanted her to get approval from General Pershing at his headquarters at Chaumont. There Dorr pleaded her case for being a mother reporting for other mothers. Although Pershing couldn't allow a woman to go into real danger, he seemed amused by the prospect of a war mother traveling around France. "'Have you seen your boy yet?' he chuckled. 'I bet you do.'"

During her time in France, Dorr visited some twenty-five American camps. "I told them about the Russian Revolution and how they would have to fight in place of those men whose morale Germany had broken down." She thought the men liked the unsentimental way she spoke about wounds and death and especially one fatalistic notion from a combat-wounded Russian woman: "When you get killed, you never know what hit you." For some reason that line always brought laughter and applause. "They used to crowd around me after each talk, touch me, press bits of chocolate or maple sugar in my hands. . . . I used to go on sightseeing excursions with half a dozen at a time. Sometimes they asked me to visit their quarters, sit on their cots, and write a card home to their mothers from the very places they slept."

A strong tone of reassurance ran through much of Dorr's reportage. As a stand-in mother for all the mothers waiting anxiously back home, she assured them that months of "training, outdoor living, good food, regular habits, obedience to orders, devotion to an idea, have worked their physical magic" on their sons. The men are strong as a "Rooseveltian bull moose," inured to cold and mud, with nerves as steady as an old clock.

Reporting from Aix les Bains, where she got to meet with her son, who was on leave, Dorr aimed her words directly at the concerned wives and mothers back home. The YMCA had virtually turned Aix les Bains into an American city, filled with safe distractions, she reported. The red-light district had been closed. Theaters offered free movies. The food was wonderful. There were no intoxicants. There were "plenty of nice girls" with whom the men could dance, but there was "no chance of mischief." Every American had shown himself "a man, a soldier and a gentleman." She quoted a French officer, who gave credit where credit was due: "The behavior of the American soldier is a credit to the American mother."

The thirty articles Dorr wrote under the heading "A Soldier's Mother in France" got widely reprinted and excerpted. Shortly after the final installment appeared, in the summer of 1918, the owner of the newspaper for which she worked, the *New York Evening Mail*, was arrested for purchasing the newspaper with German money. After more than a year in Europe as a successful correspondent, Dorr suddenly found herself unemployed.

Dorr reflected on that turn of events in her autobiography: "If this were a man's story there would be a paragraph telling how easily another job came my way. All over Europe since, I have met men in the foreign service of newspapers [who were] doing no better work than I did, if as good. But the thing we are never allowed to forget is that the masculine clan sticks together. Women have broken into the human race, but it will be a long time before men admit it."

The Curious Experience of Peggy Hull

Peggy Hull's war reporting career in France followed a unique trajectory, built upon her experience reporting a previous conflict and her distinctive personality. Hull followed up her Pershing interview in France with a series of touristy articles for the *El Paso Morning Times* detailing how she was adjusting to life in Paris. She could not understand the bellboy at the Continental Hotel when he paged her as "Mamselle Pezhgy." The hairdresser where she got her hair done operated under regular hours, but the cafés closed at 9:30 p.m. She was surprised to hear American calliope music at a skating rink. An aerial bombing raid on the city seemed to shock her less than public displays of affection by Parisian couples and dirty conditions at a meat market. Readers back in El Paso enjoyed Hull's window on the wartime Paris.

In August, Hull's stories also began to appear in the *Army Tribune,* under the heading "How Peggy Got to Paris." The paper was being run by *Chicago Tribune* reporter Floyd Gibbons, an acquaintance from her time on the Mexican border. In announcing her articles, the newspaper introduced Hull as a "typical American woman," full of "grit and energy," and noted that her stories were written in the "frank and genial [style] of the Rio Grande which will come as a breath of fresh air to the American soldiers in France."

The fact that the *Tribune* asked Hull to write additional articles attested to her popularity. She followed up with a series of "letters" from an imaginary soldier to an imaginary friend back home, in which they exchanged news from home and the war zone. Hull then revived a "Reader Help" column that she had run the previous year in the *El Paso Evening Times* for U.S. troops in Mexico.

The concept of such a column had to be explained to *Tribune* readers: "I have just been told to be the godmother to all the American soldiers in France. I'm expecting you to stand by me. The soldiers down in Mexico last winter used to have me get all kinds of things for them in El Paso. I bought everything from French pastry to boots and overcoats—and it was lots of fun. So, if you need anything, all you have to do is to write the Army Edition, and we promise to find it for you, if it is in Paris."

Through such features the *Tribune* was taking on the feel of a hometown newspaper, and Peggy Hull was its heartwarming link between the soldiers and home. Although Hull had a low profile back in America and a poor reputation among most war correspondents, who thought her work frivolous, she was becoming one of the best-known American reporters in France.

Her exceptional capacity for making friends and seizing opportunities ranked among her best journalistic assets. She befriended Mrs. Robert McCormick, wife of one of the owners of the *Chicago Tribune*. Robert McCormick was then an army major stationed at the artillery camp at Le Valdahon. When Mrs. McCormick hit on the idea of driving around France to explore the possibility of developing war charities to support the U.S. training camps, she recruited Hull to join her. "What a wonderful opportunity for a lonesome girl from the Texas Border," Hull wrote to her readers in El Paso.

Because a recent French national defense law prohibited such pleasure excursions, French police refused to issue a travel permit. Undeterred, Hull persisted and finally received a letter of support from a U.S. general she knew from her coverage of the army's border campaign. Throughout the trip Hull wrote about the soldiers she met along the way. The articles proved so popular in the *Army Tribune* that Major McCormick suggested that she write stories about life at the training camps, from a woman's angle.

Although the army occasionally arranged visits to training camps for journalists, Hull appealed directly to General Pershing for permission to remain at one camp for an extended period. Pershing, who was susceptible to her charms, gave her the temporary status of a YMCA worker, which allowed her to live at the artillery camp at La Valdahon and to move around with considerable freedom.

To add to her integration into the army, Hull had taken to wearing a military uniform, which consisted of a regulation campaign hat, American tunic with the Sam Browne belt worn by officers, a mid-calf-length skirt, and leather boots. Credentialed correspondents, all men, wore officer's uniforms without designation of rank. Since no woman correspondent wore an official-looking army officer uniform, Hull's outfit led to considerable curiosity and confusion. Soldiers occasionally saluted her, and civilians didn't know what to make of the odd sight. Hull reported to the folks in El Paso what happened during one train trip: "Here I

29. Peggy Hull reported from France during the period of American involvement. She became the first woman to be officially credentialed by the U.S. Army, when she reported on the activities of the American Expeditionary Force in Siberia in 1918–19. She is wearing the uniform of a credentialed war correspondent, an officer's uniform without designation of rank, and an armband with the letter *C*, designating "Correspondent." Author's collection.

was in the middle of a long platform crowded with civilians and soldiers—the only woman in khaki—probably the first one they had ever seen. They crowded around me; they pushed each other out of the way to get up closer; they inspected my boots, my uniform, my hat, my face and hair, my bags; they talked about me and laughed at me. They called their friends to see, and they all stayed around to watch what I was going to do."

Thus uniformed, Hull began to publish stories in the *Tribune* and the *Evening Times* about adjusting to life in the camp: rising to reveille at 5:45 a.m., washing in a basin, army chow, living in a tent and then in a barracks, being wet and cold. "There is nothing I don't know about being a soldier in France," she claimed.

Once integrated into camp life, she could then report the training activities. She took long hikes into the field to watch the men practice with trench mortars and artillery. An obliging French aviator took her for a flight to the Swiss border. When her editor from the *Tribune*, Floyd Gibbons, occasionally stopped by the camp, he would find her "holding court at the head of a table of officers." These occasions must have reminded Hull of her times along the Mexican border, when she had been so involved with army life.

In practical terms she had installed herself as a de facto credentialed war correspondent. She had negotiated privileged access to the troops from none other than the commander of U.S. forces. Officially denied the uniform of an accredited reporter, she had simply appropriated it.

In their wonderful biography of Hull, *The Wars of Peggy Hull: The Life and Times of a War Correspondent* (1991), Wilda M. Smith and Eleanor A. Bogart suggest that Hull's strength as a journalist was that she made her own opportunities in France: "Denied the right to move with the freedom of the accredited men reporters, she took her 'little' stories where she found them." Her stories about the day-to-day experiences of the soldiers proved enormously popular with her readers in El Paso. The editors of other newspapers around the country also began to notice her articles in the *Army Tribune*, which they quoted and excerpted. Hull seemed to be finding an endless supply of enticing stories, while the credentialed correspondents sat on their hands, waiting for the "big" story, when American troops would enter the fighting.

The credentialed correspondents began to complain loudly to the Army Press Office about the unique privileges granted to Hull. They charged that the *Army Tribune* already had an accredited correspondent, Floyd Gibbons, to gather news and therefore didn't need Hull. Hull had reported in an article that she lunched with General Pershing and that he had invited her personally to be the guest of the army at a training camp, a privilege not accorded to the credentialed reporters. And further, they charged that "the work she is doing is undignified."

The army—and General Pershing—finally accepted that Hull's unique access was not justified and withdrew her permit to stay at the training camp. That disappointment corresponded with word from home that her mother had taken ill. In late November, after nearly five months in France, Peggy Hull returned home to a heroine's welcome in El Paso.

If America needed to be reminded how dramatically its relationship with Europe had changed since it entered the war, it had to look no further than the shipboard companions of the war correspondent for the *New Republic*, Elizabeth Shepley Sergeant. She traveled with "three hundred and fifty strenuous idealists." Among them were forty-five YMCA secretaries trying to learn French, seventeen lady Red Cross cantineers discussing soup recipes, fifty Quakers preparing for their role of building portable houses and running a plow through mud and barbed wire. And then there were the nurses' aides, the ambulance boys, the teachers of the blind, and the tuberculosis and child specialists.

America's entry into the war had spawned a great eastward migration, not just of fighting men but also volunteers, bringing their expertise and enthusiasm. To Sergeant they defined a new type of American in the war zone: "Up to the spring of 1917, we had been here in relatively small numbers, and, whether in the army, in the hospitals, or in relief work, we were volunteers and guests who generally possessed long pocketbooks, European outlooks and fluency in the French tongue. Now, on the contrary, we arrive as those having a right here, and a duty; yet we are generally ignorant of the language and daily habits of our ally and try instinctively and immediately to transform his ancient, hand-made delicately adjusted civilization." The analogy Sergeant used to explain it to readers in late 1917: "France and America are exactly in the position of two people who have become engaged by correspondence and are meeting for the first time in the flesh."

To facilitate her news gathering, Sergeant joined that flood of American idealists. Like Elizabeth Frazer, she gained access and ease of travel by attaching herself to the American Red Cross. Her frequent articles for the *New Republic* helped to define the enormous role played by such charitable organizations as the Red Cross and YMCA. When she visited an isolated AEF aviation camp, she saw Red Cross and YMCA activities everywhere: a new bathhouse that provided hot showers; a canteen serving coffee, hot chocolate, and sandwiches; an officers' club; and a mending shop. In short the camp had been transformed from "an ugly wooden island in a muddy foreign plain into a home-like piece of United States soil." Traveling the war zone with the Red Cross medical teams and refugee support services also put Sergeant in some of the hottest combat locations.

The German Spring Offensive

When Eunice Tietjens reported for duty at the Paris office of the *Chicago Daily News* in the spring of 1918, she found herself in an active war zone. German airplanes made a habit of bombing the city. Bureau chief Paul Scott Mowrer assigned her to write human interest stories, including such topics as relief work, the war's impact on women and children, and interviews with any Chicago-area soldiers she could find. However, one of her earliest stories told of the first American woman to die in the war. The young woman had sailed to France to be a YMCA canteen worker. On the voyage over, she contracted scarlet fever and was

30. Eunice Tietjens, of the *Chicago Daily News*, reported from Paris in 1918. She often sought stories with a Chicago connection. Although not credentialed by the army, she wore a makeshift uniform. Newberry Library, Chicago, Eunice Tietjens Collection.

confined to her Paris hotel room to recover. That's where a German bomb took her life.

Madeleine Doty got a similar reception when she arrived in early March 1918, on the tail end of her round-the-world excursion. On her first night in Paris, she huddled in a dark cellar with other guests from her hotel while muffled explosions and fire engine sirens hinted at the destruction outside. But before the raid concluded, curiosity got the best of her. She climbed to the lobby and joined several American soldiers watching their first air raid: "We pushed open the great door. A bomb crashed to earth. There was a flash of light." French airplanes skimmed the rooftops. It served as her exciting introduction to wartime Paris.

Like the French, Doty soon adjusted to the danger and took little notice of the raids. She had just traveled from Russia in revolution, through Sweden, Norway, and England, and in each location had written about women. Only now did she have a sense of being in a country at war. In England the focus had been on "how to live without freezing or starving." However, in France the battlefield was only a few miles away. Hospital trains continually brought the wounded into the city. Newspapers blared ominous war headlines. Women in the black of mourning were everywhere. And yet the civilian population seemed to function quite well, thanks largely to its women. "They have poured themselves into the business of war," she explained. "They have done the drudgery, tilled the fields, preserved the food, mended the clothes, and through it all kept charm and grace alive."

Most of Madeleine Doty's articles about women in the warring countries appeared in *Good Housekeeping* magazine. Her article "The Women of France" ran in that magazine and was also included in her war memoir, *Behind the Battle Line: Around the World in 1918* (1918). Memoirs allowed for fuller and more candid accounts of experiences than did wartime reporting, which had to pass censors and accommodate the sensibilities of readers. What Doty neglected to tell the female readership of *Good Housekeeping* but did mention in her book was that the American soldiers she encountered in Paris were undergoing their own adjustment.

American doughboys, in their distinctive khaki uniforms, could be seen all over Paris. Doty continually ran into "our boys" in restaurants, struggling with the menu. When she used her French to help them, they fell into conversation. Out came a picture of a sweetheart, wife, or mother. They gave her messages to deliver to folks back home.

But Paris exerted an irresistible charm on the men, Doty explained. After a few weeks the loneliness and homesickness vanished. She related a conversation with a lieutenant she met at dinner. In response to her questions about how he was doing, he answered: "Great! Say, this is the life. You know we fellows will never be the same after this war. The little Western town I come from looks pretty dull. No grinding ten hours a day for me. I want to travel. And say, these French women are corkers. I have a girl at home but—well—I wonder what she'll seem like when I get back." No need to share that observation with the mothers and wives who read *Good Housekeeping*. No need to report that there were ten Frenchwomen for every American soldier.

The issue of *Good Housekeeping* that ran Doty's article announced that the magazine had received a one-word telegram from its associate editor Clara Savage—"Arrived." She was now in France to represent the magazine and ready to begin her assignment to tell readers "the things we all want to know about our boys." Now that American soldiers were pouring into France at a rate of 250,000 a month and their active role in combat seemed imminent, the magazine felt the need for its own perspective on the war.

Savage, who had previously worked for the *New York Evening Post* before joining the staff of *Good Housekeeping*, arrived in France in July 1918. She began her reporting with a typical first-impressions article about her ocean voyage and settling into wartime Paris. "The French love us," she assured her readers, and they loved the American soldiers who are so visible around the city. She touched on the delicate topic of Paris's "irresistible charm" a bit more directly than had Doty.

At lunch one day a woman entered the café. "There was no mistaking her," Savage wrote. A clinging silk dress set off the curves of her figure. Her eyes were "ferret-like." She undulated slowly through the middle of the café, hunting, and stopped to "curve her lips at three American boys." When they gave no reaction, she moved on. Savage noted that "disgust was written all over their faces. She was repulsive to them. They were just three typical American boys, young and clean and decent, and instinctively they loathed the horrible, commercial vulgarity of this street-woman of France."

Most of the women correspondents in Paris that spring and summer followed the strategy of connecting themselves in some way to either the Red Cross or the YMCA. They worked with these organizations in order to have greater freedom to travel, to glimpse one piece of the Great War effort, and to get close to the action at the front. Elizabeth Frazer worked as a volunteer nurse's aide with the Red Cross. Clara Savage and Madeleine Doty traveled with YMCA entertainment units. Maude Radford Warren's canteen work of delivering food and hot drinks to soldiers took her close to the front. Elizabeth Sergeant worked with the Red Cross division of "Civilian Affairs" that cared for refugees fleeing German advances in the spring of 1918.

As the German offensive pushed farther into France and the arrival of American troops changed from a trickle to a flood, the need for these services increased dramatically. Personnel from the Red Cross, YMCA, YWCA, Salvation Army, and other charitable organizations began to appear all over the war zone. Many volunteers got their baptism under fire during these months, and women correspondents had opportunities for dramatic war reporting.

Elizabeth Sergeant, living at a Red Cross facility that sheltered children from the occupied areas of France and from the dangerous regions near the front lines, gave eyewitness reports on that frantic and desperate spring. Every battle, every German advance, put more civilians at risk and pushed out a wave of refugees. Red Cross trucks raced from Paris to pick up civilians, and its volunteers were pressed into service in desperate situations. "Chauffeurs who all day evacuated civilians and hospitals and transported couriers under fire were at night called upon to become doctors' aides—even grave-diggers," Sergeant reported. "A mere publicity man was straightway transformed into an ambulance driver, a canteener, a herder of goats and cows, an evacuator of Old Ladies' Homes."

Working with aid organizations often thrust women reporters into the confusing turmoil behind the lines. Elizabeth Sergeant rode with a caravan of Red Cross trucks racing to evacuate a village when it stalled in a military traffic jam. Troops, artillery, and supply trucks headed to meet the latest threat, while wounded soldiers flowed in the opposite direction, along with refugees transporting their worldly possessions in wheelbarrows, baby carriages, and farm carts. Clara Savage explained to her readers that correspondents often tried to see the war and found it too colossal and confusing to see.

Trapped in her own jam of military vehicles that spring, Maude Radford Warren (*Woman's Home Companion, Saturday Evening Post*) acknowledged that she didn't have the "kind of mind that can think of a company of soldiers as 'part of our forces' or 'a small percentage of those who fight.'" She stepped from her traffic-stalled truck and went vehicle to vehicle talking to the soldiers: "I always see them as individuals. And behind them I see the little home in Scarborough, or East Aurora, or Decatur, or Davenport, or North Yakima, or the little apartment in New York or Chicago that sent them forth, where anxious relatives are waiting for letters."

The Red Cross and YMCA offered these women correspondent volunteers telling snapshots of the tragedy: the poignant, heartbreaking, and inspiring story lines of individuals caught in the catastrophe. Military traffic jams proved to be one of the many fascinating, narrow-focus tableaus of the war.

Elizabeth Sergeant was well positioned to take the measure of American soldiers that summer, when the question on everyone's minds was "whether anything so innocent and unequipped as this transatlantic force of ours could ever become an army trained to the 1918 arena." She traveled close behind the lines during the fighting along the Marne River, when Americans proved their fighting mettle; interacted with them in hospitals; and saw them march proudly through Paris streets on July 4 to the wild cheers of Frenchmen.

"It was good to be here the week the big offensive began to turn things our way," Clara Savage noted. "If you are an American in Paris, you find yourself trying not to be too blatantly proud of America and American soldiers." Eunice Tietjens told readers of the *Chicago Daily News* that after their successes on the Marne, American soldiers were the most popular people in France.

The Allies Take the Offensive

In her second article for *Good Housekeeping*, "Helping Out in France," Clara Savage noted the exact moment when the winds of war shifted and forced her to adopt a new style of reporting. The article began with an explanation of how she gathered news: "If you keep a diary or, better still, a book in which you scribble the things funny and sad, picturesque and real, you have at the end of a few weeks a multicolored picture of every-day life in Paris." By way of example, she offered snippets about the maid in her boardinghouse, American soldiers in Paris, and her own experience shopping.

But then the war intruded. "As soon as the Franco-American offensive was in full swing, the call came from Neuilly, the largest American hospital [in Paris] for women helpers," Savage explained. The Neuilly hospital, staffed with American doctors, surgeons, and nurses, had been providing medical care and ambulance service for Allied soldiers throughout the war. Now it suddenly overflowed with wounded Americans as well and issued a call for volunteer nurses. Like Elizabeth Frazer before her, Savage donned a white nurse's apron and cap and reported for duty to Ward 83. By chronicling her succession of frantic twelve-hour days, she shifted from observer to participant in the great conflict.

Overflowing hospitals provided a dramatic way to tell the story of this new phase of the war. Eunice Tietjens found her Chicago-area soldiers in Paris hospitals, suffering from wounds and the effects of gas. She gave their names and hometowns. All of them were in "capital spirits and [were] overflowing with stories of how the Americans put the fear of God into Heinie."

Tietjens found another Chicago angle story one day while visiting a salvage depot, where items were collected that had been lost or abandoned on the battlefield. Inside a uniform she discovered the photo of a girl taken at a Chicago photo studio. The owner of that photo had almost surely perished in battle. Tietjens thought it would make a poignant story to find that girl and learn about the young man who had carried her photograph into battle and to his death, sustained by her love. She sent the photo to the *Chicago Daily News*, which managed to track down the girl. Unfortunately, the girl could not confirm the identity of the soldier in whose uniform her photo had been found because she had given her photo to several soldiers.

At an evacuation hospital near the front, Elizabeth Frazer gave a more thoughtful and realistic view of the wounded. Throughout the night ambulances delivered the wounded, "silent, immobile, blanket-swathed figures, whose white bandages showed deep crimson stains." Through the triage and admission process, the wounded kept up a continuous low drone of conversation. But Frazer noted that it was not of their wounds or their suffering that they spoke. "The battle, what had happened up there, still intoxicated them, still held their brain in thrall. They talked of horrible, grotesque and sanguinary things in low, level, dispassionate tones, as if they were discussing the weather: 'I saw my captain and my lieutenant blown straight to hell; it was a head-on collision with a high explosive.'"

"It's heartbreaking work, if one's got any heart to break," Frazer conceded after a numbing twenty-four-hour stretch of admissions, but the cases continued to appear: the German wounded, those suffering from the effects of gas, and a curious, new affliction. "We don't know what it is yet," said a major. "Nobody does. But we have a special American hospital for its treatment. Look here: You see those two chaps crouching down by the steps? They both have it—hard." As Frazer looked at those men, "petrified, rendered deaf and dumb—by fear," she was looking at her first sight of the disorder that would become known as "shell shock."

The vantage point of hospital work gave women journalists privileged access to the war. But so, too, did other Red Cross and YMCA assignments. The YMCA duties assigned to journalist Maude Radford Warren seemed innocent enough—travel with YMCA officials between Paris and the front, carrying lots of cigarettes and chocolate to distribute to any troops met along the way, and then serve food and drink to the men behind the lines. However, YMCA workers never knew from hour to hour what they would encounter and when they would be "informally commandeered by the army." Warren often rode in ambulances to pick up the wounded, cared for them, and fed them on the front lines—all within artillery range of German guns.

Warren took delight in the fact that she regularly got closer to the front than the male correspondents. "I have passed them in my car, being turned back by the M.P. nashing [sic] their teeth while I shot by with two big casks of lemonade that I was going to serve to the boys just to go to the front." On that occasion her car stalled out and came under artillery fire that crept closer and closer while the frantic driver cranked the engine. They finally escaped at top speed, followed by geysers of earth from exploding shells. Close behind the front at Belleau Wood, Warren helped to set up an impromptu field kitchen, working past midnight feeding the men heading into the fight.

"It was possible to exchange only a word or two with each man, but brief as the time was, a good many boys showed me the photographs of those dearest to them, or asked for the latest news from the Front, or gave me a letter to post." While tending to one soldier in a hospital ward, Warren confessed, "I felt almost as if that boy belonged to me." Such maternalistic impulses added a level of emotional engagement not seen in the work of male reporters.

The appearance of women so near the front always managed to delight or shock. A major at one frontline unit was nonplussed

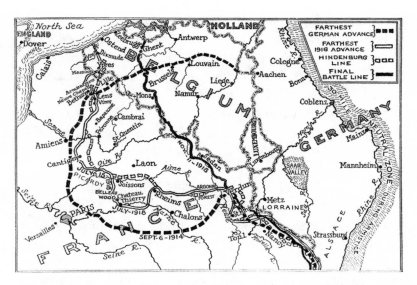

31. The western front, 1914–18. Working with aid organizations allowed women journalists to get close to the action when Americans entered the fight in the summer of 1918, at Chateau-Thierry, Belleau Wood, Saint-Mihiel, and the Meuse Argonne. Mackey, *Forward March*, 17.

when Clara Savage showed up one day. "May I enquire for what publication you are a correspondent?" he asked.

"*Good Housekeeping*," she said.

"'Good—God!' he said and dropped the coffee can. He could no longer keep up his attempt to look and act as though nothing unexpected were happening. He stared at me frankly. 'I have seen newspaper *men* up here,' he remarked, 'but you are the first woman.'"

On another occasion Savage gained access to the war zone while touring with a YMCA theater company, performing nightly shows, "creeping up night by night nearer and nearer the Front." One day her group came upon another of those great military traffic jams and guessed that it was a new phase of the American offensive. Her group had stumbled into the area in late September, at a time between the American victory at Saint-Mihiel and the start of the final campaign of the war, the Meuse-Argonne Offensive. War traffic forced them to pause for a few days in the small, liberated town of Saint-Mihiel. Savage captured the scene as "the tiny town went wild with joy. French soldiers embraced American soldiers, women kissed their hands, and children covered them with flowers. America had proved herself. Americans had set St. Mihiel free." When Savage entered a café, a French officer jumped to his feet and saluted her. "It will take some time," he told her, "but the end is in sight." When the headwaiter echoed the phrase, there followed "a moment of wordless silence very near to tears."

Even though larded with the nationalism that had crept into the work of all the correspondents after America joined the conflict, Savage's article represented a first-rate bit of war reporting. Like the best of the war correspondents, Savage proved adept at distilling poignancy from her experiences. While held up in Saint-Mihiel, she visited a local evacuation hospital, where she sketched for her readers touching cameos of three wounded soldiers. One soldier had a heavily bandaged face and an arm in a sling, so Savage took his dictation of a letter to his girl back home: "It was not a long letter, and yet it said all the things any woman wants the man she loves to say—that he thought of her always, that she meant so much to him that he wanted to be brave and good for her sake, that he loved her with all his heart and longed to come home and take her in his arms."

There he paused and asked Savage to help him find the words to tell his girl one more thing: that he had lost his right eye and his face was badly disfigured. "I couldn't say anything for a minute," Savage wrote.

"Do you think it will make a difference to her?" he asked. "Do you think a girl can love a man with a face that has been all smashed to pieces and a glass eye?" Savage assured him she would still love him because he was fine, good, and worth loving to begin with and now he was brave as well.

So, he found the words himself, and Savage added them to the letter. "As I wrote those words that some girl in America will read, I pitied her from the bottom of my heart, and yet I knew that if she is the kind of a girl that boy thinks she is, she will be brave and will love him even more now, because he so much needs her love."

When she set off for the war, Savage received a letter from a woman mentioning what she would be looking for in Savage's war reporting: "I hope you will help us women, away over here, to realize better the war. Tell us how French women find faith to bear its sacrifices and rise above its devastating horrors." Now that some of the horrors of war were being visited upon American women, that request took on urgency. Savage suggested that Frenchwomen seemed sustained by an "unconquerable faith in beauty and love and a Something outside themselves—and yet within themselves—that is stronger than agony and that will never forsake them."

Women's War Tour Casualty

On October 19 the French military arranged one of its women's war tours for three journalists, the wife of an American officer, and a French Red Cross official named Mademoiselle de la Vallette. The journalists included Cecil Dorrian (*Newark Daily News*), Elizabeth Shepley Sergeant (*New Republic*), and Eunice Tietjens (*Chicago Daily News*). They traveled on a one-day excursion out of Paris to visit one of the "safe" battlefields near to the city Reims. Although the French officer serving as their guide warned them not to pick up any objects from the ground, since the area had not yet been cleared, the urge to collect souvenirs proved too great. One of them found a German Bible, another a helmet. Vallette picked up what she thought was a German gas mask, but it was instead a hand grenade.

It exploded, instantly killing Vallette. It blew off an arm of the French officer and badly wounded Elizabeth Sergeant's legs. She later recalled her immediate stunned response of checking her face in a pocket mirror, before noticing the blood oozing from wounds in her legs.

Surprisingly few journalists got injured while covering the war. The most notable exception had occurred four months earlier, when reporter Floyd Gibbons (*Chicago Tribune*) took a bullet in the eye while charging into battle with U.S. Marines at Belleau Wood. Like Gibbons, Sergeant transformed from an observer of the war to a participant, wounded on a battlefield and a patient in a military hospital. Like Gibbons, Sergeant also wrote about that experience. She was delivered to a makeshift medical facility and triaged along with French soldiers wounded in battle. The attending surgeon was none too happy to waste his time on her "all because a foolish woman wanted a little souvenir of this great, great war." His first words to her: "We must cut off your clothes, Madame."

Sergeant's battlefield accident got widely reported in America. She spent seven months recuperating in the American hospital in Paris and from that experience wrote a war memoir, *Shadow-Shapes: The Journal of a Wounded Woman, October 1918–May 1919* (1920). Organized as a dated diary, the book followed the course of Sergeant's recovery, interrupted by reminiscences about her war experiences, and news reports of the armistice and peace negotiations that she received from hospital staff and visitors.

She did not get to experience Paris celebrating the end of the war, but a friend gave a dramatic rendering: "What a sense he gave me of the beloved city suddenly translated from its drab war-sadness; suddenly all brilliant with flags, white armistice streamers, embracing people, variegated soldiers and processions. . . . From every grey street and square, they emerged, spontaneously generated: French school-boys in long, singing columns, dragging enormous guns after them. American and British soldiers in huge motor trucks, workmen in blouses, employees of the 'Samartaine' or the 'Bon Marché,' with banners; housewives; refugee children in uniform guarded by Sisters of Charity."

The day of the armistice found Maude Radford Warren at a frontline wound-dressing station along the Meuse River. As a YMCA volunteer, she often found herself in the danger zone, feeding soldiers and the wounded or otherwise lending a hand. The wounded continued to arrive even after hostilities had officially ceased. Tags on the wounded noted the time of their wound, and

32. While on a French army war tour, Elizabeth Shepley Sergeant was injured by the accidental explosion of a hand grenade. She spent a long period of recovery in the American hospital in Paris. She is pictured here with nurses in the garden of the hospital. Elizabeth Shepley Sergeant Papers, American Literature Collection, Beinecke Rare Book and Manuscript Library, Yale University.

it grieved the station workers to see how narrowly these men had missed surviving the war unscathed.

The *Buffalo Morning Express* published a letter from ambulance driver Arthur F. Duncan, enthusing about Warren: "Have you read some of Maude Radford Warren's war stuff in the Post [*Saturday Evening Post*]? She was with our advanced dressing station during our offensive. How she obtained permission I do not know. But my, how she worked! She made and served hot chocolate to the wounded and helped with everything there was to be done for days. Wet, bedraggled, her hair in her eyes, her skirts mud to the knees, her shoes sodden, she worked on and on. Bursting shells. I don't believe she even knew when one went over. That woman's got guts."

On the day of the armistice, Warren's dressing station leap-frogged to a more forward location. Word of the cease-fire had not reached all units. From the front seat of an ambulance, Warren and the driver called out the news of peace to the soldiers they passed on the road. "We told it with hearts and faces alight; the boys received it, I feel sure, in the same way. Yet there was no cheering, no laughter; just wide smiles, and now and then a word about seeing the Statue of Liberty after all."

The armistice took Mary Roberts Rinehart by surprise. She reported standing on a Paris street marveling at the curious sight of a German airplane, rolling and looping in celebratory flight. The U.S. Army had just hurried her to France to record the end and aftermath of the war. There had been talk of an armistice, but she had not dared to believe it would come so soon. But then came the booming of the signal guns. "It was true, then. The war was over," she wrote. "Oh, thank God, thank God; the war was over."

With the backdrop of the wild celebration erupting throughout the city, Rinehart sounded a note of apprehension. She made her way through the crowds to join some women at the Crillon Hotel. Standing with them on a balcony, watching the throngs in the street below, Rinehart detected a profound uneasiness among the women. "They were known, most of them, all over America," she explained to her readers. "They stood for the dignity of position, the ease of great wealth. And now the war was over. They could go back to their enormous houses, to the dull and monotonous routine of their sheltered lives. They did not want to go back. They looked like women who had been engaged in some tremendous drama, and who now saw the curtain fall and were endeavoring to make their readjustments, to go out into the streets and face a commonplace world again."

That observation applied to the women journalists as well. They had been reporting on the high drama of life and death, the fate of nations, and the transformative role of women. They never had grander subjects on which to write, never had more eager readers, never felt more inspired. In their war coverage they often commented on the excitement of war and the great value of their role. The prospect, for some of them, of returning to their newspapers to edit the Women's Page must have lacked appeal. For all of them, the end of the war closed out a most dramatic chapter of their lives.

After the Fighting

Herr Muller and Herr Bell, plenipotentiaries, but nonentities,
pygmies in the midst of towering events, snatched out of obscurity
for this single encounter with fame; and there in the historic Hall of
Mirrors, under a thousand straining eyes, seated before a small table
they signed, one after the other, the death warrant of that haughty
powerful empire. . . . By my watch it took three-quarters of a minute.

—ELIZABETH FRAZER, "The Signature,"
Saturday Evening Post, August 30, 1919

P eggy Hull arrived in Washington DC in the summer of
1918 intent on returning to France and doing so as an
accredited correspondent. She came fully prepared to
fight whatever army bureaucracy stood in her way. To her surprise, however, she discovered that everyone was talking about
a completely new front in the war—Siberia. Preparation had
begun to send a force to that isolated region of Russia.

Exactly what they would be doing there, no one could say. The
Bolshevik seizure of government had removed Russia from the
war and precipitated a civil war. The Allies supported the anti-
Bolshevik forces, the Whites, in that conflict. Did the United States
intend to intervene in the fighting? Or would the "Siberian Expedition" merely safeguard the vast cache of armaments and supplies that had been stockpiled in the Siberian port of Vladivostok?

Regardless, it struck Hull as a golden opportunity to report
from a completely new war zone, one that would likely have very

few journalists, and to achieve her long-sought goal of becoming a credentialed war correspondent. Two big hurdles stood in her way: she had to find a newspaper willing to give her this assignment; and she had to break through the army's entrenched policy against credentialing women journalists.

Over the course of her career, Peggy Hull faced challenges of access so often that her battles had developed as a hallmark of determination, ingenuity, and persistence. In Ohio, when she wanted to accompany the National Guard to the Mexican border; in El Paso, when she sought to cover the army's incursion into Mexico; in France, where she fought to gain access more readily given to male correspondents, Hull pushed the envelope of acceptable procedure. A biographical sketch that appeared in *Ladies' Home Journal* detailed her strategy for getting to Siberia.

She began by visiting General Peyton C. March, who had recently returned from France to serve as army chief of staff. Another of her acquaintances from Mexico, March had proven instrumental in opening doors for her in France. Now she presented herself at his office and announced that she wanted to go to Siberia. March complimented her reporting in France and thought she'd also do well in Siberia. "Your stories are the sort that give people at home a real idea of what the American soldier is like and what he likes and dislikes," he said. "I'd like to see you go with the Siberian expedition. These men are likely to be lost sight of in view of the big things that are happening in France. If you can get an editor to send you, I'll accredit you."

March's tacit blessing launched Hull on a quest to find a newspaper to send her. She telegraphed and wrote to "all the editors I had ever known and to a lot I hadn't." Meanwhile, army units began to leave for Siberia in August, including the commander of the expedition, Major General William S. Graves. The total force would eventually number nearly eight thousand.

After six weeks of frustrated appeals to newspapers for this assignment, Hull finally convinced the syndicated news service Newspaper Enterprise Association to take her on. This position carried considerably more prestige than all her previous newspaper positions. No longer would she be writing only for readers in El Paso, Texas, or the American community in France, but for the hundreds of U.S. newspapers that subscribed to the NEA service. Her reports could potentially influence public opinion about this little-known appendix to the war.

Only one hurdle remained. When she applied to the Military Intelligence Office for her correspondent's pass and other credentials, an officer informed her, "I'm sorry to disappoint you, but there is a clear order to the effect that no woman shall be accredited." Many other women had already been denied credentials, he said. Within an hour Hull returned with a letter from General March: "If your only reason for refusing Miss Peggy Hull credentials is because she is a woman, issue them at once and facilitate her procedure to Vladivostok."

Peggy Hull got her credentials. In the final month of the war, she had become the first women correspondent to ever be officially credentialed by the U.S. Army. The approval date stamped on her Correspondent's Pass read, "Oct. 14, 1918." In addition to the practical advantages this pass offered, such as the right to military transportation and housing, accredited correspondents also wore the uniform of an officer, without an insignia of rank. That entitled them to military salutes. "Being human I liked that better than anything else in my military experience," Hull confessed.

By a curious irony America's first credentialed female war correspondent arrived in the Russian port of Vladivostok to cover this new front in the war on November 14, three days after the war ended. Hull's shock was immediate. The city was one of the most vile ports on the planet. The indigent castoffs of a dozen different nations swelled the population, as did criminals released from prison after the revolution. Even before the ship's gangway went down, Hull noted images of "human wrecks," "vermin-infested rags," "vacant eyes," "beings hardly a step removed from extreme savagery." Clearly, this assignment would not be like

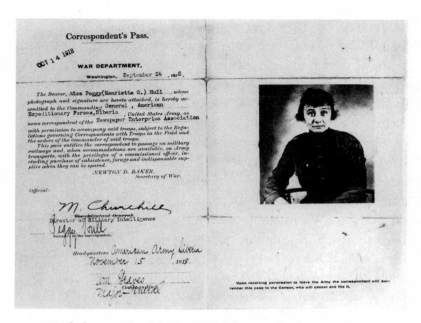

33. With these credentials, Peggy Hull became the first woman to be an officially accredited war correspondent with the U.S. Army. They were issued to her to cover the army's "Siberian Expedition," in the winter of 1918. Peggy Hull Deuell Collection, Kansas Collection, University of Kansas Libraries.

her pleasant sojourn in Paris or her congenial time at the American training base.

"Hold your breath," advised the officer sent to meet her as he led her through the customhouse. However, one accidental whiff sent her hurrying for the door. Their automobile raced through the pedestrian-clogged streets, along with cars carrying British, Russian, Czech, and Japanese flags. In response to her question about how the autos managed to avoid hitting anyone, an aide responded, "They get a drosky driver now and then, or a coolie."

Ahead of her first reports from Russia, the NEA introduced Hull to readers: "Daring the Bolsheviks, the perils of war and the rigors of a Siberian winter, War Correspondent Peggy Hull is adding one more achievement to her list, which is already a record-breaker for a girl reporter of 28." She was actually thirty years old.

Hull tried to gain an understanding of the U.S. mission and the political situation. "Our program, as far as I can learn, is to sit tight until it is determined which is the proper party to support in the regeneration of Russia." However, she quickly learned that her dark first impressions did not go nearly far enough in explaining the dire conditions, the chaos of warring factions, a near vacuum of civil authority, extreme overcrowding and disease, and the brutal Siberian winter. Bolsheviks controlled small pockets of territory; Cossack guerrilla bands harassed American troops and slaughtered civilians; and the huge Japanese force in the area seemed intent on territorial acquisition. "Further inland where the disorganization of the railroads has made it impossible to carry supplies they are starving to death, while roving bands of Bolsheviki and bandits terrorize the unprotected communities. Murder, pillage, starvation and bitter cold—what a desperate outlook!"

Whatever feel-good reporting the U.S. Army or the NEA had expected from Peggy Hull—something like the cheery reports from the Mexican border or France—they weren't getting it. Such stories were in short supply.

Hull accompanied British officers on a visit to the headquarters of Cossack general Grigory Mikhaylovich Seminoff and his "little army of Chinese bandits, Mongolian outlaws, and Cossacks." While the officers discussed Seminoff's falling out with another Cossack general, Hull interviewed the general's beautiful nineteen-year-old mistress. Interviews with other women gave glimpses into their ordeals. One woman showed Hull a Bolshevik edict asserting that all women must serve as sex slaves. On a more heartwarming occasion, she visited the home of a woman who had not seen her husband since he went into the army in 1914. While Hull was there, a knock came at the door—her husband had returned. He had been released from a German prisoner of war camp and spent months working his way back home, avoiding Red Army units and bandit gangs along the way.

Hull made clear that any such glimpse of human warmth gave a false impression: "New horrors pounce upon me from every direction. Atrocities fade the plunder and rape of Belgium into insignificance." One particularly Siberian permutation of horror was the "Death train." Civilians taken prisoner by one faction or the other were locked into train cars and sent on a journey into a Siberian winter without food or heat. One such train arrived in the Chinese border city of Harbin. When American engineers working there opened it, they found that most of the imprisoned had either frozen or died from disease. Housing was at such a premium in Vladivostok that aid workers reported finding rooms packed with local residents, half of them seriously ill, and with a few corpses, dead for no one knew how long. American Red Cross workers were forced to stay nine to a tiny room.

The weight of such darkness continually colored Hull's reporting. When she arrived in Vladivostok, she reported that U.S. forces were well fed, well housed, and well clothed, just like a vacation at a winter resort. After seven months she confessed that "there is no pleasure anywhere in Vladivostok." Restlessness and discontent had settled over the Allied forces, with an occasional suicide. "Americans have the feeling that they have been dumped on a garbage heap and left to exist as best they can." In France they felt as though they fought for humanity and civilization, Hull noted. In Russia they sit by while the worst atrocities go unchecked and in the process have earned the enmity of all sides. If they were not to fight, they wanted to go home.

Through the NEA Hull's stories received wide distribution in U.S. newspapers. But the public had little interest in happenings in faraway Siberia. The Great War had ended. The public's limited interest in further misery could be sated by news of starvation, disease, and fighting in the conquered countries of Europe. Public attention had shifted to the peace negotiations, domestic coal and steel strikes, and the threat of the Red Menace spreading to America.

Hull departed Siberia in early July 1919. She had gained considerable stature with her Russian reporting. She had tackled difficult topics in a challenging environment and reached a large audience. At a stop in Vancouver on her way home, the local paper noted that "Miss Peggy Hull is not only a lady war correspondent, she dresses the part and looks the part. She would not look more real if she were costumed to meet the exacting eye of the director of the great film play 'The Heroine of the Steppes or the Pursuits of Peggy.'"

Her employer, the NEA, announced that with her return home, Hull could now write uncensored stories about Siberia in which she "tears the veil off many mysterious happenings in the orient— happenings that previous cables have only vaguely hinted at." That lead introduced a rousing story of a U.S. Army major standing up to a Japanese force twenty times larger that demanded the life of a U.S. soldier who had struck a Japanese officer. "If you want war you can have it," the major asserted. It was an inspiring story to raise U.S. ire, but for all intents the ill-conceived Siberian Expedition had faded from public awareness. While America's Siberian fiasco muddled along out of the spotlight, a gloomier fate unfolded for another Allied incursion into Russia.

As she reported on the aftershock of war in the Balkans in the spring of 1919, Eleanor Franklin Egan heard rumors that the French intervention into Russia was doomed. French and Greek troops had entered Ukraine in December to aid White Russian forces fighting the Bolshevik Red Army in the Russian Civil War. But the Reds gained the upper hand and now surrounded Allied troops in the Black Sea port of Odessa. The end might be near. Some officials warned Egan that a visit there would be too dangerous, while others assured her that the French could hold out indefinitely. The first opinion reflected reality, but Egan chose to believe the second.

At the Romanian port of Constantza (Constanța), Egan boarded a French troop ship as it loaded a battalion of French colonial troops; a labor corps of prisoners of war, "the most villainous-looking, ragged and bedraggled Turks I had ever laid eyes on"; and vast quantities of war materials. It seemed the war had not ended, only been displaced to a new location.

An American military attaché gave Egan a tour of Odessa and

a sobering assessment of the situation. Hundreds of thousands of refugees crowded the city, fleeing from the steadily advancing Bolshevik forces, now only thirty miles away. The White Russian forces opposing the Red Army could not hold them off for long. Further confirmation of the desperateness of the situation came the following day, when French commander of Allied forces, General Phillippe d'Anselme, summoned Egan to his office. She found him pacing fretfully, while his aide-de-camp pored over maps. "Such was the atmosphere that my nerves jumped and I came close to exclaiming; 'What on earth has happened?'"

The general took her hand in his and said: "Madame, the situation is very grave." Red Army troops were close, he confided, but Bolsheviks already in the city as part of the bloated refugee population were of greater concern. "This is a difficult story to write," Egan told her readers, as she summarized how the crisis unfolded over the following days. The city population was hungry and increasingly desperate. "Every kind of rumor was afloat and the people were intensely nervous." Extra guards went up around the general's headquarters. The American consul sent frantic telegrams to Washington for instructions.

On the day she arranged to visit the front, her Russian officer guide informed her that the city would be evacuated. All Americans were to be on board a ship in the harbor that afternoon. "It was a helpful notification with which to begin the day," Egan noted with her typical nonchalance, "but we saw no reason why we should not go on with our program."

Her route to the front took her through the poorer parts of the city, teeming with refugees, living on the streets, barefoot, dirty, in rags. Outside Odessa her car bucked a continuous stream of refugees flowing into the city. Small detachments of Russian troops moved forward with artillery and ammunition wagons. Big guns boomed in the distance, and clouds of white smoke rose from the horizon.

In the hills they found field headquarters of the rear guard. "It consisted of a flag on a short staff stuck in the ground and five or six officers lying flat on their stomachs round a map, with telephone receivers clasped to their ears," Egan noted. About twelve hundred Russian volunteers manned this last line of defense for the city. They had eaten bread that day for the first time in forty-eight hours. "Both officers and men were so weary that their faces were white and drawn and their feet lagged as they walked."

"Hell had not broken loose when we got back to Odessa, but the city was in a fearful panic," Egan wrote. She again visited General d'Anselme to hear his plans for evacuation. But developments outpaced well-laid plans. The Bolsheviks forced their way into the city and took control. "Hour by hour the situation grew worse. Shootings and street robberies became so frequent that people ceased to notice them," Egan reported. "Everybody was hurrying about trying to arrange his own affairs." General d'Anselme communicated to the Bolsheviks that he was evacuating the city. If they maintained order and did not harass his troops, he would leave peacefully. Otherwise, he would bombard the city with his warships.

That night Egan slept on a French troop ship, while a cordon of soldiers guarded the wharf area. The crew of one ship in the harbor declared for the Bolsheviks, and French soldiers had to recapture the vessel. A crowd of desperate refugees gathered on the wharf, with massive piles of their possessions, hoping to be evacuated. Ships moved away from the piers into the harbor. Refugees hired small boats at exorbitant prices to row them to the ships, where they begged pitifully to come on board.

General d'Anselme finally arranged for a French torpedo boat to ferry Egan back to Romania. Her ship was three hours from Odessa when it received a wireless message that French battleships had begun to shell the city. "'Then the massacre must have begun in earnest!' I exclaimed, remembering the general's promise."

Few fears so consumed the postwar world as the spread of the Red Tide of Bolshevism, in Europe, Asia, even the United States. Egan had just witnessed one example of its relentless advance. Back in Bucharest, she summarized the fiasco for her *Saturday Evening Post* readers: "Odessa has been withdrawn behind the veil of Bolshevist Russia, and there is no news, except that a man who got away a day later than I says that when he left at least ten thousand had been murdered."

Covering the Postwar World

In one respect coverage of the postwar world began much like coverage of the war itself: the *Saturday Evening Post* deployed a team of women correspondents to capture it. That team now included Eleanor Egan, Elizabeth Frazer, and Maude Radford Warren. In the shattered lands that had experienced the fighting, in the conquered countries, amid the contentious nation building of eastern Europe, the dismantling of the U.S. war machine, the fight against Bolshevism, and the Paris Peace Conference, these *Post* writers detailed how Europe readjusted to life after the greatest war in history.

In the final months of the war, Warren, who wrote for the *Post* and other magazines, embraced her work as a YMCA canteen worker with unusual diligence and passion. Canteen work for her did not involve merely passing out doughnuts at some train station or training camp but service at frontline outposts, giving aid and comfort in whatever way possible. Traveling with some of the most advanced units, Warren moved directly from trench duty into liberated French towns and traveled with the first troops into Germany, still carrying out her YMCA duties. Along the way she became one of the first war correspondents to capture snapshots that defined the stunned moments immediately after the fighting ended.

In the hours following the armistice, the army unit with which Warren traveled halted at the Meuse River town of Laneauville. The unit had advanced quickly in the final weeks of the war, through many liberated towns, always with the Meuse as its imagined easternmost destination. Now they had arrived, and it seemed like a significant event.

Through binoculars Warren watched German troops departing from the French town of Stenay on the opposite banks of the Meuse. Warren and some officers decided to push across into Stenay. "The first woman in," her driver noted when they arrived. "If I cared about collecting unique sensations," Warren wrote, "I might roll under my tongue the pleasant morsel that I have been the first American woman in some ten war-ridden French towns and cities."

Other American troops came close on their heels and spread out through the town. French civilians began to peek cautiously from their windows, not yet certain they had been liberated. Slowly they emerged and thanked the soldiers. They told stories of "meager food, of enforced work, of men and women taken to Germany, of German insolence and ruthlessness. But always they ended, with a smile: 'It's finished—the war.'"

The next day Warren sat in a motorcycle sidecar, stalled by the side of the road near the German border, while her driver went looking for gasoline. Along the road walked an American soldier who appeared especially footsore and bedraggled. Warren reflexively reached for the cigarettes and chocolate she always carried.

"Gee, an American woman!" the surprised soldier said.

"You have not seen one lately, then?" Warren asked.

"They don't have 'em round German prisons," he replied. "Say, is this France yet?"

Warren and the former prisoner of war, who had just walked out of Germany, sat on a pile of rocks outside a liberated French town while he told his story about capture at Saint-Mihiel, his German prison, daily interrogations, conversations with his German guards about the war, the details of his release, and the several-day hike out. Like most of the soldiers Warren encountered, his thoughts had already turned to home: "We learned how to live up to war, and a darned dirty, silly, murderous performance it was too; but we did it and we did it well. Now when we get back we can't afford to settle down in the old ruts. Peace ought to mean chances for everybody to get a share of the good things of life."

There was something profoundly anticlimactic in that quiet roadside exchange, with German soldiers drifting home to the uncertain reality of their defeated homeland, French civilians facing the grim task of rebuilding their lives, and American soldiers quickly turning their thoughts to life back home. And yet the encounter captured that breath-catching pause between the slaughter and whatever came next.

Warren's articles about the end of the war and life in occupied Germany began to appear in February 1919 in the *Saturday Evening Post* and *Good Housekeeping*. At the same time newspaper stories circulated that Warren held the record for rapid promotion in the American Expeditionary Forces, having risen from sergeant to lieutenant to major within a few months. The fact that she was a journalist and these were merely honorary ranks distracted little from her accomplishments or the esteem with which she was held by the units with which she served. Her army citation read: "In appreciative recognition of her excellent work among our men and for the wounded at the front and during violent bombardment and her heroic and soldier-like conduct under fire, [we] do hereby nominate and appoint Maude Radford Warren honorary major of the 117th Field Signal Battalion."

Warren remained with her unit as it took up duties in Germany. The doughboys she watched crossing the Rhine River to join the occupation force looked less like conquerors than "tired boys not yet recovered from the fierce fighting of the Argonne and for the most part wearing the same clothes in which they had slept in the mud during those bitter, dragging autumn days." As her unit drove through German towns that day, they experienced their first encounters with the local population. As if "warned by some underground telepathy," the inhabitants in every town always awaited them, standing in stiff rows outside their houses to stare at the Americans.

In one town an army officer commandeered a room for Warren in the home of the mayor, despite his protests. She took up residence in the family's living room, which displayed a photograph of a son lost in the war. In her first article from Germany, "The First Invasion," Warren used the family's emotional struggle to deal with the American intruders in their home as a symbol for Germany adjusting to postwar reality: "We were to live

34. Maude Radford Warren stands with Lt. Col. Ruby D. Garrett and Maj. R.T. Smith of the 117th Field Signal Battalion, 42nd Division, in Bachem, Germany, on January 1, 1919, during the period of American occupation. George Grantham Bain Collection, Prints & Photographs Division, Library of Congress, LC-B2-4932-5.

side by side, we the conquerors, and the Germans fresh from the shock of defeat, knowing now the long list of their human losses, knowing, too, their commercial and financial disaster. No longer were we separated from our enemies by the reach of a shell, the range of a machine gun. We knew what their hatred of us had grown to be in a year and a half, and now we and they were to share the little commonplaces of daily life."

Her stay with the family was strained, but the mayor pointed out to her on a map where he had relatives living in the United States, and his wife told how she dreamed about her lost son when he was a youth and she would call out to him to put on his hat. "Then I wake up and remember—the war!" she confided to Warren. Through such painful and begrudgingly shared moments with the family, Warren began the process of humanizing the enemy for her readers.

During her travels through occupied Germany, Elizabeth Frazer also commented on the relationship between Allied troops and German civilians. In the early months of occupation, American troops got on well with the Germans: "Germans seemed like home folks." But as the months slipped by, "the pendulum swung slowly back in the other direction. Antagonism developed. The Germans turned out to be not genuinely friendly but inimical; not honest, but sly; underhanded, venomous . . . And worst of all—from the soldier's point of view—they would not admit they had been defeated. They declared they had just stopped. 'The durned squareheads don't believe they've been licked!' complained a sergeant to me." A strong desire grew in the troops to finish the job, "to sail in and give the boches the thrashing of their lives. This desire manifested itself in frequent street rows and brawls in cafes." So the Americans in Germany began a none-too-subtle preparation for continued fighting, to send a message to the Germans.

Despite traveling extensively throughout the devastated regions of France and Belgium and through the Belgian, British, French, and American zones of occupation in Germany, Frazer wrote very little about her experiences there. The toll of being a witness to so much suffering had begun to wear on her: "I visited hospitals, soup kitchens, bread lines, clinics and homes, saw starving, rickety, malnourished, tuberculous children; and I gathered up enough first-hand material, concrete instances of sheer human misery and hopeless woe, to fill a volume that would make the devil himself shed tears."

To finish her investigation, she wanted to push farther east, into Prussia and Poland. But Frazer had reached her emotional limit. She did not have it in her to chronicle any additional suffering. Having spent one year as a nurse and two years as a correspondent, she had seen enough. Recent bouts of influenza and pneumonia had weakened her, and lice infestations drained her resolve. Too much filth, poor food, and cold. A postwar weariness began to creep into her reporting. In calling off her visit to Poland, Frazer confessed: "My heart failed me. I was sick of the whole ghastly, oppressive, putrid business called war—and war's putrid aftermath. It stank in my nostrils. I wanted to go home."

In her subsequent *Post* articles "Good-By, France" and "Good Old America!" Frazer shifted attention away from the human tragedy unfolding in the warring countries and toward the happy prospect of returning home. The articles contrasted the squalor, starvation, corruption, and squabbling in Europe with the efficiency, energy, abundance, and generosity of America.

She watched doughboys board transports at the embarkation port of Brest, France, as America began the daunting task of shipping home its two-million-man army. Men had been arriving in France at a rate of 250,000 a month, while vast quantities of munitions and materials of war continuously flowed from America. On November 12, 1918, that inflow stopped, and orders went out to begin the process in the opposite direction.

Huge ships arrived at Brest, discharged cargo, loaded thousands of men, and sailed off within twelve hours. The movement was continuous. The camp at Brest, which held some seventy thousand men, was a small city that had been constructed from nothing. The United States would be leaving behind the vast infrastructure it had created to support its war effort: port facilities, freight yards, warehouses, hundreds of miles of railroad track, hospitals, aviation centers. Not to mention immense stockpiles of food, clothing, equipment, ordnance, and medical supplies. Given the state of world markets, these stockpiles could not be sold, but they were exactly what the devastated, starving countries of Europe so sorely needed. Frazer detailed how the newly created United States Liquidation Commission planned to distribute it all.

Eleanor Egan wrote her first post-armistice article from Vienna, surrounded by the trappings of a more glorious past. The desk in her hotel room where she sat to write her articles was a massive mahogany piece with rose velvet under glass on top. Sumptuously carpeted hallways led to winding marble staircases beneath great crystal chandeliers. The dining and lounging rooms displayed fine woods and rich draperies. "I would be in condition to appreciate it all a whole lot more," she admitted, "if in addition it were possible to satisfy even fifty per cent of my normal demand for light and heat and food."

Wartime privations continued in the city. Egan got hot water for a few hours once a week, but there was no soap. No butter, milk, or coffee. There was a coffee substitute made of burnt corn and inedible war bread. That was life in the best hotel in Vienna. The city was filthy. There was no civil authority, only soldier and citizen committees. At an orphanage she saw malnourished children, dramatically underdeveloped for their age, standing barefoot on the ground in frigid January temperatures. The hospital she visited ran afternoon death wagons, transporting dozens of corpses a day to the cemetery, without coffins, since the city had no wood, and no gasoline or horses to transport wood from elsewhere, and no men to fashion it into coffins. Ironically, Austria was better off than other countries from which Egan reported after the war.

By the time of the armistice, Eleanor Egan had earned a reputation as one of the leading international journalists of her day.

The fearlessness she demonstrated during the war in reporting from the most remote, restricted, and dangerous locations continued after the conflict. During 1919 Egan traveled from Paris to Italy, Austria, Yugoslavia, Hungary, Romania, Russia, Turkey, and the killing fields of Armenia.

In many of these countries the armistice had not even brought an end to fighting. With her characteristic dry humor, she noted that "the Jugoslavs and Czechoslovaks have lightened the tedium of the armistice with a number of interesting little skirmishes. . . . Hungary meanwhile is engaged in an effort to check the Jugoslavs and Czechoslovaks—to say nothing of the Romanians—on her own soil and to set limits if possible to their perhaps too generous interpretation of their right to self-determination."

The concept of self-determination came as an echo of Woodrow Wilson's principles for peace laid down in his Fourteen Points and now debated at the peace conference at Versailles. "Mr. Wilson's idea of self-determination is like the war and the Spanish grip," Egan quipped. "It has taken hold of the masses the world over and will have to run its course."

To calculate terms of the peace, officials at the Versailles conference dispatched an army of experts to assess conditions. "Europe was awash in Peace conference investigators," Egan remarked from Budapest, "representatives of the negotiators at Versailles who were trying to sort out the postwar world." Vienna, too, had its share of "allied experts in the city, scientific men, geographers, economists, ethnographers whose job it is to sort out the conditions in the regions and the competing claims of the countries and communicate their findings to the peace negotiators in Paris."

While experts and academics assessed the problems of the postwar world, Egan reported on the suffering countries of Austria, Hungary, Romania, and Turkey, which she placed before her American audience through vivid descriptions and dramatizations. She had never hesitated from challenging assignments. Now as an eyewitness, a stand-in American, she went cold and hungry, shopped for clothes at exorbitant prices in Vienna, dusted insect powder on her bed in Bucharest, and cried uncontrollably at the sight of starving women and children in Armenia.

Traveling in early 1919, she was often the first outside woman to appear in these locations and could testify to the beginning efforts of Americans and American organizations to provide food and orchestrate relief. But she could also report when American practice or vision fell short. In making her case for insufficient food in Vienna, she lambasted American and British investigators who swept into the city, had a few "satisfactory meals," and then returned to Versailles to report that "Vienna's cry of starvation is nothing but a characteristically German yip for sympathy." In the fighting among Armenian ethnic groups to establish their own autonomous regions, she saw the limitations of Woodrow Wilson's vision of self-determination and pointed out that self-determination "some times plays out as self-extermination."

Like Elizabeth Frazer, Egan also endured the continuous assault of tragic images. Nowhere else did she suffer the impact of that assault as much as on her nightmare visit to Armenia. Reports and rumors about Turkey's campaign to exterminate the Armenia population had circulated during the war. Egan had reported on them in 1916. And yet postwar rumors seemed so dire as to challenge belief, as if they might be inflated propaganda. She had already reached the point "when to look upon the things that had to be looked upon set my heart to quaking in a horror difficult to describe," and she had no desire to deepen that emotional wound by witnessing the suffering in Armenia.

She changed her mind when a U.S. aid official in Paris warned her that the worst of the Armenian rumors were true. "Merciful God!" he told her. "It's all true! Nobody has ever told the truth! Nobody could!" He issued both a warning and a challenge for her to witness it. "You will be sorry all your life that you did go. What you will see will make scars on you that you will never get rid of. But nevertheless you must go. It is a duty." Many of Egan's postwar articles already carried the burden of reporting the truth, no matter how uncomfortable or gut-wrenching. Despite confessing that she did not want to see Armenia, that she was prepared to take anyone's word for it that conditions were horrific, Egan once again accepted the responsibility to bear witness.

Traveling on the train of a British general and accompanied by two Americans, Egan passed into Armenia, "a land of hideous human suffering and degradation." Scenes of extreme starvation greeted her everywhere, people on their knees grazing on grass like cattle, starving crowds surrounding the train. She confessed to crying on several occasions. Her two traveling companions warned her against looking at some scenes: "Like protecting brothers they would get on either side of me and say, 'Don't look!'"

Egan served that role for her readers, shielding them from some sights, reluctant to be too graphic. Before she revealed the one incident that most haunted her, she begged her readers' permission with the line "And if you will consent to look with me upon a too awful thing."

When her train stopped at one station, Egan set about preparing a meal for her companions, while a ravenous crowd pressed against the train. Touched by a man who looked so "movingly awful in his too evident anguish," she opened the train window, pushed aside the "ravening others," and handed him a piece of bread. He wolfed it down. Moments later he let out a whining cry, staggered away a few steps, and crumpled dead in the mud. In the starkest emotional anguish of her trip, her act of compassion had killed the man because his famished body could not handle the sudden intake of solid food.

As Egan scholar David Hudson has noted, Egan's observations gained dramatic impact because she was a middle-aged American woman "enduring hardships and exploring territory traditionally the domain of only the most adventurous of men." As a stand-in eyewitness for the millions of readers of the *Saturday Evening Post*, Eleanor Egan forced herself to endure the emotional trauma of a devastated world to report the truth.

The *Delineator* Readers Do Their Part for France

George W. Wilder, director of Butterick Publications, which published the women's magazine the *Delineator*, called together the editorial staff in February 1919 to read a letter the magazine had received from a reader, a farm wife in Missouri. The woman had read in her newspaper how other women were doing things to help devastated France, and she wanted to do her part as well. With the letter she included $1.20 for the purchase of two trees she wished to be planted in France. "I wish the trees to be named Joy and Hope, as I trust they will bring a small measure of each to whoever possesses the trees. Sincerely I wish I were able to send a thousand trees. But I have to meet many calls from a slender purse."

Mabel Potter Daggett, on hand for the occasion, claimed that Wilder's hands trembled slightly as he read the letter and a mist clouded his eyes. In the silence that followed, Wilder drew a handkerchief from his pocket and violently blew his nose.

That letter's simple request set in motion a yearlong series in the magazine titled "The Tree of Joy." Daggett, the author of *Women Wanted*, packed her bags for a quick visit to the letter writer in Missouri and then headed for France as the magazine's "Commissioner." The magazine invited readers to join the Missouri farm wife in doing their part for France. "Send on the money to buy a chicken or a cow or a cook-stove or to build a house or to educate a child or to help a city in France." Daggett would ensure that the money was spent for the desired purpose and then report on the work and the beneficial results of readers' philanthropy.

Reader response was swift, generous, and heartfelt. A woman in Wyoming made layettes that Daggett took with her to France. A girl in Georgia sponsored a baby in France in memory of a man who had died at the front. She sent her first payment of $25. The citizens of Winston-Salem, North Carolina, sent $25,000 to purchase a mobile kitchen to serve lunches to schoolchildren in the devastated districts.

"Every country in Europe has sent up a despairing cry. Come over and help us!" Daggett explained that as the representative of *Delineator* readers, she had become part of the great wave of American generosity. "Literally by the boatload our countrymen in service uniform are arriving. On the steamship on which I crossed were food commissions taking bread to Belgium and Poland, health commissions to cure tuberculosis in France and Greece, housing commissions to help Italy and Greece, industrial commissions for Romania, and commercial commissions carrying capital to Russia. Add in the Quakers going over to build things and nuns to start schools."

Although Eleanor Egan clung to the notion that international aid efforts would eventually alleviate the suffering she witnessed, Daggett saw it happening. As fully as America had thrown itself into prosecuting the war, it now committed to reconstruction. "You can fairly feel the Yankees' driving force as they breeze by you over here in the streets of Paris or London or Rome," Daggett reported. "America is meeting the crisis with the greatest first-aid undertaking ever launched: millions of money, millions of men and women, and more to follow. Never before has history witnessed anything like it. It's a nation's pilgrimage of service to other peoples. And there is in it an ardor of devotion that amounts to a crusade."

It took Daggett several weeks to arrange all the necessary permits, then she struck out with a photographer and three others by auto into the Argonne region in search of the two French villages that had been adopted by the magazine. Their prewar maps proved of little use as they struggled over roads mangled by machines of war, through destroyed towns with no inhabitants. A group of American engineers near the front line gave them a tour of the battlefield where the Rainbow Division had fought. "All around us was that debris of the dead," Daggett wrote. "Garments lay on the ground fading in the wind and rain. Guns and swords rusted where they were dropped from hands that would never again hold them. Cartridge-belts crumpled in heaps." She found a diary that had belonged to a boy from Brooklyn. The last entry was dated "Sunday in Hell." Being in the Argonne, where Americans had fought and died, and seeing evidence of their presence in graffiti, battlefield wreckage, and graves seemed to sanctify her mission.

The *Delineator* planned to focus its philanthropy on the villages of Landres and St. Georges, which had been liberated by America's Rainbow Division and marines in October 1918. Daggett described what she found there: "Huddled heaps that used to be homes; sometimes swaying walls and falling rafters; scraps of bright china that were somebody's teacups and plates; a rag of lace from the parlor curtain flapping on a broken blind; a piece of a woman's dress caught on the rosebush past which she fled; on a pile of the chimney-brick a baby's worn shoe just as it was molded by some dear, tiny foot."

If shock and despair predominated Egan's postwar reporting, Daggett went heavy for progress and hope. "I have been all the way from the American Committee's supply headquarters in Thirty-Ninth Street, New York, to the warehouse in the Boulevard Lannes in Paris and right on into the devastated districts. Everything's going right through on a wonderful open line of communications. Dehydrated vegetables from Dakota, bedquilts and blankets from Brooklyn, ribbon-run lingerie from New York Metropolitan Life Insurance girl employees sent marked 'with our love' for France; they're all here. I've seen them. And they're given without money and without price, as you meant them to be."

Throughout 1919 Daggett wrote monthly articles that made a direct connection between readers and the individual victims of war who benefited from their generosity: homes were rebuilt, schools opened, people fed and clothed. To seal the bond with magazine readers, the two villages vowed to tend the American graves in a nearby military cemetery and to inscribe in a golden book the names of all readers who donated to their reconstruction.

The Peace Conference

Before Mabel Potter Daggett even began her work as the *Delineator*'s commissioner in France, she addressed a nagging issue of unfairness to women at the Versailles Peace Conference. The conference convened on January 18 with one glaring omission, she noted—no women sat at the peace table: "There was a place at the plow and the shell-machine. There was room in the ambulance corps at the firing-line. But the seats at the peace table were all taken."

For four years the Allied countries had promoted the slogan "Women Wanted." In industry, agriculture, commerce, the sciences and professions, women had proven themselves. But now only men gathered at Versailles. "In the strength of their victory and the splendor of their gold braid and the flashing of their medals, they said: 'Now we no longer have need of you. This we can do alone,'" Daggett reported.

Daggett felt confident that even though no women sat at the peace table, "the paramount concern of women will hover over the proceedings." Now that the killing had ended and the living could begin, women wanted assurance that war would never come again. The question for those shaping the future had to be: "What will you do with my children?"

The number of correspondents permitted to attend the signing of the peace treaty on June 28, 1919, was limited to one from each important publication. Elizabeth Frazer, representing the *Saturday Evening Post*, became the proud recipient of a red ticket bearing the seat number 212.

Frazer set the scene for her readers of the sumptuous venue in the Hall of Mirrors at the Palace of Versailles. "Conceive a long, narrow, lofty room, whose proportions, roughly, are twenty by a hundred feet." Mirrors, cloudy and yellow with age, set in gilded frames, lined the entire inner wall, reflecting back the assembled crowd. On the outside wall, seventeen long windows offered a view of a formal garden. At one end of the hall stood a sculptured archway through which the German delegates would pass. There, too, stood an arrangement of tables in an open rectangle, with a single desk in the center. That desk held the Treaty of Peace.

Far to the rear, long rows of benches filled the hall. It was there that Frazer found seat number 212, in an area reserved for the press. She could not see the front of the hall. As the reporters waited impatiently for three o'clock, the allotted hour for the signing, they fidgeted and grumbled. Some stood on their seats; others held cameras aloft and snapped them indiscriminately.

A polite French officer tried to manage the frustrated and unruly reporters. He ordered them, implored them, begged them, not to stand on their seats. Such behavior did not lend itself to the solemnness of the occasion or the grandeur of the palace. He was repeatedly ignored. Decorum be damned—the greatest event in world history was about to unfold, and they wanted a piece of it. Frazer confessed, "My own conduct at this juncture was neither better nor worse than that of the rest of the invited guests."

Frazer moved to another position closer to the front of the room and begged a woman for permission to stand on her seat. That perch offered a clearer view. Far in the distance she could now make out the figure of French prime minister Georges Clemenceau seated at the table, flanked by British prime minister Lloyd George and President Wilson, with other world leaders arranged behind them.

At a few minutes past 3:00, the two German delegates entered and took their seats. Clemenceau rose and gave brief remarks. Frazer made out the words *irrevocable, loyalty,* and *faith.* According to Frazer's watch, the Germans signed the treaty at 3:12 p.m. They then left the hall, and each world leader in turn affixed his signature. The entire ceremony took a mere forty-five minutes and left Frazer profoundly disappointed. Nothing grand and glorious had transpired, a mere bit of paperwork. The signing of a peace treaty brought no satisfying closure for Frazer. "What is a big moment for, anyway, if it can't be inspiring, dignified, noble?" she complained. "And this particular big moment, the biggest certainly in many a generation in its influence on events, was neither inspiring nor dignified nor noble."

As she stood benumbed in the Hall of Mirrors, a wave of vivid flashbacks drew from memory occasions that better defined those qualities: "Before my mind's eye flashed other moments— moments which had held a real spark, an electric thrill; moments when emotions took one like a strong hand at the throat and you did not have to shake yourself and exclaim: 'Come on. Rise to the occasion, can't you?' A correspondent's life in France during the war was not all together devoid of color, and one became practiced by sheer contact with big events in picking out the pinchbeck from the real, the fake situation from the genuine."

Three memories stood out for Frazer as more emotionally charged than the treaty signing. She had been profoundly moved when she caught sight of the American flag flying above the ancient German hilltop fortress of Ehrenbreitstein, opposite the Rhine River city of Coblenz. "The sudden sight of that flag, flying up there in the clean blue air," she recalled, "hit me like a strong jolt of electricity."

For sheer emotional impact, few occasions rivaled Frazer's entry into the French fortress at Verdun. That occasion came when the German spring offensive of 1918 had just broken the British line and then pushed hard from all directions. French and American troops rushed forward to stem the assault. At Verdun, Frazer entered a mess hall, forty feet below ground, where grizzled French soldiers bolted their meal while a phonograph played jazzy music in the corner. At the sight of American uniforms in Frazer's party, the French soldiers "leaped to their feet in a rush, roaring as with one voice, 'Vive l' Amérique!' 'Vivent les Américains!' Then tears of pure exaltation, pure joy, spring to the eyes."

The third memory flash Frazer experienced in the Hall of Mirrors came from June 1918, just after American troops had rushed into the line at Château-Thierry. Up near the front, at a newly organized hospital, she had walked passed a line of wounded soldiers lying in the grass: "As I passed through the yard, a boy, dying, not of his wound, which was slight, but of gas gangrene, with the gray death film already settling down over his young face, stretched out an arm as I passed, twitched my skirt, and looking up into my face said: 'Say, wait a minute, lady.' I waited. 'Say, a fellow don't die of a little wound like this? I ain't got much the matter with me—just a scratch.' . . . His bright dying eyes, straining up, implored assurance from mine. He gazed up. I gazed down. I would have given my right hand to help him."

Frazer was not tempted by the celebrations that followed the signing ceremony. Tired and depressed from the day, she returned to her hotel in Paris and ate dinner in her room. When the servants at the hotel pressed her for details of the great event, she invited them to dine with her. In short order they overflowed her room:

> There was François, tall, suave, distinguished, chef of the floor. There was Jean, the grouch, my valet de chambre, a peasant poilu who had fought at Verdun, on the Aisne and the Somme, and declared bitterly that peace was tougher than war. There was Henri, the best educated of all, a lieutenant in the army, who, wounded, had gone to America with the French Mission, and had been military instructor in one of our large Eastern universities. In Boston, in Washington, Henri had been feted, dined and wined, and had sat down at table with men whom he now served behind their chairs. There was Jacques, young, shy, countrified, just learning to stammer English, whom I had caught one morning reading my Shelley. All of these men were decorated. All had been wounded in the war. And it was as warriors, not as waiters, that they had collected to hear and discuss the news.

They discussed the war, the battles they fought, the British and American élan in fighting. They discussed France, the future, and their fears about the power of Germany and the ability of the League of Nations to protect them. Frazer concluded that she had never eaten a better meal, never heard better conversation.

That was how Elizabeth Frazer, correspondent for the largest-circulation magazine in the United States, who witnessed the signing of the peace treaty, ended the war: with a flash of vivid memories and a room full of demobilized French soldiers.

Like all the American women who reported the Great War, Frazer found the substance of her reporting less in the events of the conflict than in the impact of events on the lives of those involved—soldiers, civilians, and journalists. Numbed from war, they now had to face life in the aftermath.

Journalists Mentioned in *An Unladylike Profession*

Ellen Adair (May Christie) (1890–1946): *Philadelphia Evening Public Ledger*. Adair was editing a newspaper Women's Page in late 1914, when war news started to intrude. She traveled to Europe in 1915, 1916, and 1917 to report on the home fronts in England and France.

Harriet Chalmers Adams (1875–1937): *National Geographic*. Adams wrote about a French army war tour she took in 1916 to the Lorraine front. Before and after the war, she traveled with her husband, Franklin Pierce Adams, through South America, Asia, and the South Pacific. She chronicled her travels in numerous articles for *National Geographic* magazine.

Jane Addams (1860–1935): *Survey*. A pioneering social worker and feminist, Addams headed the American delegation to the Women's Peace Congress in The Hague in April 1915. The congress drafted resolutions calling for an end to the war. Addams delivered those resolutions to leaders in the belligerent and neutral countries and wrote about her efforts. She continued to champion the cause of peace and for her efforts won the Nobel Peace Prize in 1931.

Gertrude Atherton (1857–1948): *Delineator, New York Times*. A popular and prolific writer of novels, history, short stories, essays, and magazine articles, Atherton traveled to France in 1916 to write about the wartime work of women. Her articles were collected in the books *Life in the War Zone* (1916) and *The Living Present* (1917).

Bessie Beatty (1886–1947): *San Francisco Bulletin.* Beatty interrupted her round-the-world news-gathering trip in 1917 to cover revolutionary Russia. Following the war, she became editor of *McCall's Magazine* from 1918 to 1921. From 1940 until her death, she hosted a popular radio show on WOR in New York.

Nellie Bly (Elizabeth Jane Cochran Seaman) (1864–1922): *New York Evening Journal.* Bly gained fame for her "stunt" and exposé journalism at the *New York World* in the 1880s and 1890s. She had been out of journalism for nearly two decades when a chance visit to Vienna, Austria, in August 1914 coincided with the start of the Great War. She took advantage of the opportunity to become one of the first American journalists to report on fighting on the eastern front.

Inez Milholland Boissevain (1886–1916): *New York Tribune.* As a lawyer with a commitment to women's rights, she became one of the leading figures in the suffrage movement in the second decade of the twentieth century. In May 1915 the *New York Tribune* sent Boissevain to Italy to cover the war. Her ardent pacifism put her at odds with authorities, and she was asked to leave the country. She died in 1916 at the age of thirty of pernicious anemia while on a speaking tour for women's rights.

Mary Isabel Brush (1888–1944): *Saturday Evening Post.* Formerly a reporter for the *Chicago Tribune*, Brush went to Russia in the fall of 1914 to write about its adoption of prohibition upon entering the war.

Louise Bryant (1885–1936): Bell Syndicate. Along with her husband, John Reed, Bryant covered Russia's Bolshevik Revolution. She remained active in socialist and feminist causes and supported the Bolshevik Revolution through lectures and testimony before a congressional committee. After Reed died, in 1920, Bryant continued to write about European affairs. The 1981 movie *Reds* was about her time with Reed.

Mary Chamberlain (years not available): *Survey.* Chamberlain wrote about the Women's Peace Congress at The Hague in April 1915.

Mabel Potter Daggett (1870–1927): *Pictorial Review*. Formerly an editor at *Hampton's Magazine* and the *Delineator*, Daggett had studied the status of women in Europe in 1914. When wartime necessity dramatically altered the status of women, she returned to Europe, in 1916, to report on women's roles in the war.

Rheta Childe Dorr (1866–1948): *New York Evening Mail*. Dorr was a popular muckraking journalist and political activist, supporting the causes of women and the working class. She became the first editor of the influential newspaper the *Suffragist*. Dorr had several journalistic assignments in Europe prior to the war, including one to Russia after its 1905 revolution. She returned there to report on Russia between its two 1917 revolutions.

Cecil Dorrian (1882–1926): *Newark Daily News*. Dorrian made multiple trips to warring Europe, reporting from England, France, and Italy.

Madeleine Zabriskie Doty (1877–1963): *Chicago Tribune, Good Housekeeping, New York Evening Post*, and *New York Tribune*. A lawyer, social reformer, and peace activist, Doty made three trips to report on the war. She attended the Women's Peace Congress in The Hague in 1915 and then briefly reported from Germany. During her 1916 travels in Germany, she reported on the severe food shortage. Her final war excursion came as part of a round-the-world trip to assess the uneven social and economic development in different countries, particularly as they concerned women. She reported on revolutionary Russia in 1917.

Eleanor Pedigo Franklin Egan (1879–1925): *Saturday Evening Post*. No woman journalist had a better résumé as a reporter and war correspondent than Egan. She covered the Russo-Japanese War and the 1905 Russian Revolution for *Leslie's Weekly*. Her reporting during World War I is notable for the number of locations from which she reported, including difficult and dangerous locales such as Armenia, Mesopotamia, Serbia, and Turkey. She remained in Europe after the armistice to write about the turmoil in the immediate postwar period. For nearly a decade after the war, Egan continued to travel widely and write for the *Saturday Evening Post*.

Ernestine Evans (1889–1967): *New York Tribune.* In late 1914–early 1915 Evans reported from Bulgaria, Germany, and Russia, with a focus on women. She enjoyed a long career in journalism and publishing. During World War II Evans worked for the Office of War Information. From 1944 until the early 1950s she worked as a book reviewer for the *New York Herald Tribune*.

Mildred Farwell (1880–1941): *Chicago Tribune.* She reported from the Balkans, Belgium, France, Italy, and Russia. She made headlines in 1915 for being held captive by Bulgarian troops in Serbia.

Elizabeth Frazer (1877–1967): *Saturday Evening Post.* Frazer worked as a volunteer nurse in France in 1916. When she became a regular contributor to the *Saturday Evening Post*, in 1917, she wrote several articles about the extensive wartime role of the Red Cross. Through her Red Cross connections, Frazer gained access to frontline hospitals and proximity to American battles.

Marie Reuter Gallison (1860–1954): *Outlook.* Gallison took leave of her position as director of the Radcliffe College Choral Society to visit her native Germany in 1916 to write about wartime conditions. Her articles appeared under the name "Mrs. H. H. Gallison."

Ruth Hale (1887–1934): *Chicago Tribune* Paris edition. Before the war, Hale worked for the *New York Times*, *Philadelphia Public Ledger*, and *Washington Post*. She married journalist Heywood Broun in June 1917, and the pair immediately sailed for France. Until she returned home that September, she wrote for the Paris edition of the *Chicago Tribune*.

Alice Hamilton (1869–1970): *Survey.* A physician by profession, Hamilton was a delegate to the Women's Peace Congress in The Hague in 1915. She traveled with Jane Addams to the warring and neutral capitals to present the resolutions from the congress, calling for immediate peace. She reported on the congress and life in the warring capitals.

Florence MacLeod Harper (1886–1946): *Leslie's Illustrated Weekly.* Harper worked as a photojournalist in France before accepting an assignment in early 1917 to report from Russia. She was on hand in the Russian capital of Petrograd to witness the first revolution that deposed the czar. She remained in Petrograd until September of that year, reporting on the growing violence that led to the rise of the Bolsheviks.

Peggy Hull (Henrietta Eleanor Goodnough Deuell) (1890–1967): *El Paso Morning Times, Chicago Tribune* Paris edition, Newspaper Enterprise Association. Hull covered the U.S. Army's "Punitive Expedition" along the Texas-Mexico border in 1916. The connections she made there, including with General John J. Pershing, helped her to gain privileged access to an American training camp in France. In the closing days of the war, she became the first woman to be officially credentialed as a war correspondent with the U.S. Army. She accompanied the army on its expedition into Siberia, during the Russian Civil War. She lived abroad for some of the interwar years and took on freelance assignments, including reporting on the 1932 Japanese attack on Shanghai. In 1943 she took on her second world war, reporting from the Pacific theater for the *Cleveland Plain Dealer.*

Corra Harris (1869–1935): *Saturday Evening Post.* Harris rose to fame with the publication of her 1910 novel, *A Circuit Rider's Wife,* and continued to publish prolifically, both fiction and nonfiction. Reporting from England and France in September 1914, she drew attention to the considerable role being played by women in the war.

Fryniwyd Tennyson Jesse (1888–1958): *London Daily Mail, Collier's.* Jesse traveled to Belgium in August 1914 to report on the German invasion. In an article for *Collier's* magazine, she provided eyewitness glimpses from the war zone and the fall of Antwerp.

Ruth Wright Kauffman (1885–1952): *Outlook.* Kauffman traveled to Europe with her journalist husband, Reginald Wright Kauffman. Much of her wartime reporting focused on women.

Helen Johns Kirtland (1890–1979): *Leslie's Illustrated Weekly.* Both Helen and her husband, Lucian Swift Kirtland, worked as wartime photojournalists. She photographed action on the Italian front, in Belgium, France, and Poland. She and Lucian worked together to photograph the Versailles peace conference.

Jean Cabell O'Neill (1866–1950): *Brooklyn Daily Eagle.* O'Neill reported from Europe in 1915. She wrote an article about sailing through the waters where the liner RMS *Lusitania* had just been torpedoed by a German submarine and seeing wreckage and dead bodies in the water.

Mary Boyle O'Reilly (1873–1939): Newspaper Enterprise Association (NEA). When the war began. O'Reilly was serving as the London bureau chief for the NEA, a news syndication service. She hurried to Belgium and reported on the German invasion and occupation of that country. She remained in Europe, visiting many of the warring countries, until early 1917, when she returned to the United States and lectured about her war experience.

Jessica Lozier Payne (1870–1951): *Brooklyn Daily Eagle.* Payne's popular articles on conditions in the Allied countries in 1916 were reprinted in a booklet, *What I Saw in England and France.*

Mary Roberts Rinehart (1876–1958): *Saturday Evening Post.* Rinehart was already America's most popular mystery novelist when she traveled to Europe in 1915 to be a war correspondent. By winning the endorsement of the Belgian Red Cross, Rinehart gained unprecedented access to the front. Through that endorsement she also arranged to interview Belgian and British royalty and the commanders of British and French forces.

Alice Rohe (1876–1957): United Press. A veteran newspaperwoman, she worked for ten years for the *New York Evening World,* before becoming the Rome bureau chief for the United Press in 1914. She reported on developments in Italy during the war and remained in that country postwar. She wrote a 1922 article for the *New York Times* introducing Italy's new premier, Benito Mussolini.

Clara Savage (1891–1956): *Good Housekeeping.* As an associate editor for *Good Housekeeping*, Savage gave a woman's perspective on happenings in Washington DC. After the United States entered the war, the magazine sent Savage to France. By traveling with the YMCA, she got access to the war zone not typically given to reporters. Following the war, she became editor of *Parents' Magazine.*

Elizabeth Shepley Sergeant (1881–1965): *New Republic.* Sergeant reported during the period of American involvement and published two books about her war experiences. On October 19, 1918, she was severely wounded by the accidental discharge of a hand grenade while on an official French army press tour. In the book *Shadow-Shapes: The Journal of a Wounded Woman October 1918–May* 1919 she told about the long period of her recovery in a French hospital.

Eunice Tietjens (1884–1944): *Chicago Daily News.* She reported from France in 1918.

Sophie Treadwell (1885–1970): *San Francisco Bulletin, Harper's Weekly.* Treadwell reported from France in 1915. She would later work for the *New York American* and *New York Tribune.* In 1928 she wrote the popular feminist play *Machinal*, based on the life of a woman who murdered her husband.

Mary Heaton Vorse (1874–1966): *Century Magazine.* A noted pacifist, suffragist, and labor journalist, Vorse attended the Women's Peace Congress in The Hague in 1915. Following the conference, the day after a German submarine sank the British liner *Lusitania*, Vorse traveled into Germany to gauge reaction. After the war Vorse continued to report on and advocate for labor reform.

Maude Lavinia Radford Warren (1875–1934): *Woman's Home Companion, Delineator, Saturday Evening Post.* Born in Canada, Warren graduated from the University of Chicago and then worked in Chicago as a journalist. In 1914 she reported on Canada's mobilization for war and in 1918 reported from France. By traveling with a YMCA canteen unit, she gained access to the front lines. She accompanied the U.S. Army when it assumed occupation duties in Germany.

Edith Wharton (1862–1937): *Scribner's Magazine, Saturday Evening Post.* Wharton had been living in France before the war and continued to do so during the war. Through numerous charities and fund-raising projects, she supported the French war effort. In 1915 the French army took her on extensive tours of the western front to raise awareness in the United States about the French war effort and its need for charitable support. She described those tours in a series of articles for *Scribner's.*

A NOTE ON SOURCES

I imagine that a modern reader coming to this book will recognize only a few of the names. Edith Wharton's reputation has survived the passage of a century. Nellie Bly has embedded herself in popular culture. Mary Roberts Rinehart's mystery novels are still in print. Others linger as readings in women's studies courses because they also wrote about and campaigned for suffrage or various social causes. A few have attracted scholarly attention, an autobiography, an occasional journal article. Others are forgotten. But one hundred years ago the Great War animated all of them.

Alice Rohe (United Press) and Mary Boyle O'Reilly (Newspaper Enterprise Association) wrote for news syndication agencies. Their war articles appeared in the hundreds of newspapers that subscribed to these services, from major urban dailies to the smallest weekly papers. That explains why the bibliography contains citations from smaller newspapers, such as the *Bismarck Tribune*, the *Richmond Palladium*, the *Vicksburg Evening Post*, and the *Winnipeg Evening Tribune*. Other veteran newspaperwomen, such as Bessie Beatty (*San Francisco Bulletin*), Mildred Farwell (*Chicago Tribune*), and Peggy Hull (*El Paso Morning Times*), made one or more trips to warring Europe to give their papers fuller coverage of the war. Thanks to online archives, such as the Library of Congress's Chronicling America and Newspapers .com, their many articles are easy to locate.

The same can be said for the many magazines that thrived

during the war years. From the dusty shelves of university librar-ies, they have been brought to the computer screen by such ser-vices as Google Books, HathiTrust, Internet Archive, and Project Gutenberg. Many women who wrote about the war did so for mag-azines, for large circulation, general interest magazines such as *Collier's*, the *New Republic*, the *Saturday Evening Post*, and *Scrib-ner's Magazine*; for women's magazines; or for special interest publications devoted to social causes.

Especially during the period of American involvement, many women's magazines ran war articles that explored the role of women in the warring countries and the experiences of American soldiers. *Good Housekeeping* sent its associate editor Clara Sav-age to France in July 1918 to tell readers "the things we all want to know about our boys." The *Delineator* ran a yearlong series of articles detailing how donations from its readers were help-ing to rebuild a devastated France. *Ladies' Home Journal*, *Pic-torial Review*, and *Woman's Home Companion* sent well-known writers on assignment.

Writers who wrote numerous articles from the war zone often collected them into books. The series of articles written by Jes-sica Lozier Payne for the *Brooklyn Daily Eagle* proved so pop-ular that the *Eagle* reprinted them as a booklet, *What I Saw in England and France*. Elizabeth Frazer (*Saturday Evening Post*), Mabel Potter Daggett (*Delineator*), and others republished their articles as books. So, too, did well-known writers who covered the war, such as Gertrude Atherton (*Delineator*), Mary Roberts Rinehart (*Saturday Evening Post*), and Edith Wharton (*Scrib-ner's Magazine*).

The greatest amount of detail and immediacy appears in the memoirs some of the women wrote about their experiences reporting the war. They reveal behind-the-scene adventures and anecdotes and convey a better sense of how they did what they did. Such books as Bessie Beatty's *The Red Heart of Russia*, Lou-ise Bryant's *Six Red Months in Russia*, Mabel Potter Daggett's *Women Wanted*, Madeleine Zabriskie Doty's *Short Rations: An American Woman in Germany 1915 . . . 1916*, and Maude Radford

Warren's *The White Flame of France* were of great help in filling in the picture of these women war correspondents.

Lingering memories of their war experience showed up in autobiographies many years after the fact. Gertrude Atherton, *Adventures of a Novelist*, Rheta Childe Dorr's *A Woman of Fifty*, Corra Harris's *As a Woman Thinks*, Mary Roberts Rinehart, *My Story*, and others set their war adventures into the larger context of their lives. Sometimes reliving the experience added new insights; sometimes the accounts diverged from the original experience or from reality.

Collectively, these sources lift from the murky past a missing story element in the history of World War I.

BIBLIOGRAPHY

Abbot, Willis J. *The Nations at War.* New York: Leslie-Judge Co., 1918.

Adair, Ellen. "Women and the War." *Philadelphia Evening Public Ledger,* December 18, 1914, 10.

Adams, Harriet Chalmers. "In French Lorraine: That Part of France Where the First American Soldiers Have Fallen." *National Geographic,* November–December 1917, 499–518.

Addams, Jane. "The Revolt against War." *Survey,* July 17, 1915, 355–59.

Addams, Jane, Emily G. Balch, and Alice Hamilton. *Women at The Hague.* New York: Macmillan, 1916.

Agrafojo, Yolanda Morató. "More than a War Correspondent: Edith Wharton's Chronicles about French Civilians in the Great War and the Beginning of Citizen Journalism." *Oceánide,* no. 5 (2013): 1–7.

Anema, Durlynn. *Harriet Chalmer Adams, Adventurer and Explorer.* Greensboro NC: Morgan Reynolds, 1997.

Atherton, Gertrude. *Adventures of a Novelist.* New York: Liveright, 1932.

———. "Gertrude Atherton Sees Paris in War Time." *New York Times,* July 2, 1916, 54.

———. "Getting to the War Zone Is No Easy Matter." *New York Times,* September 10, 1916, 60.

———. *Life in the War Zone.* Published for the benefit of Le Bienêtre du Blessé, Société Franco-Américaine pour nos Combattants, by courtesy of the *New York Times,* 1916.

———. *The Living Present.* New York: Frederick A. Stokes, 1917.

———. "Mrs. Atherton Sees the War Ruins in France." *New York Times,* October 1, 1916, 70.

Beatty, Bessie. "Fall of the Winter Palace." *Century Magazine,* August 1918, 523–32.

———. *The Red Heart of Russia.* New York: Century, 1918.

———. "We Fight for Russia." *Woman's Home Companion,* March 1918, 10.

Bly, Nellie. "Nellie Bly at Front Writes about War." *Los Angeles Herald*, December 9, 1914, 1.

———. "Nellie Bly Describes Slavonian Town Demolished by Austrians in Invasion." *Richmond Palladium*, February 1, 1915, 1.

———. "Nellie Bly in War-Rent Przemysl." *Daytona Daily News*, January 29, 1915, 9.

———. "Nellie Bly Paints Horrors of War Seen in Eastern Field of Combat." *North Platte Semi-Weekly Tribune*, February 19, 1915, 3.

———. "Nellie Bly Sees Soldiers in Action on Battlefield." *San Francisco Examiner*, December 6, 1914, 3.

———. "Nellie Bly Tells Battle Horrors Pictures Cholera Victims' Den." *San Francisco Examiner*, December 8, 1914, 2.

———. "Poison Bullet of Servian Soldier in Hospital Wounds Nellie Bly." *Richmond Palladium*, January 28, 1915, 1.

———. "Russian Aim Is Deadly Says Woman at Front." *Los Angeles Herald*, December 15, 1914, 1.

Boissevain, Inez Milholland. (*See also* Milholland, Inez.) "Everything German, Even Names, Taboo in Rome." *New York Tribune*, July 31, 1915, 4.

———. "Gloom Darkens Italy's Homes as Her Men Go Forth to War." *Philadelphia Evening Ledger*, July 21, 1915, 8.

———. "Merrie England Hushed in Death Grip of War." *New York Tribune*, July 18, 1915, 1.

———. "Warlike France Bustles while England Blusters." *New York Tribune*, July 20, 1915, 1.

———. "Why 'Bellisimma Italia' Has Unsheathed Her Brave Sword." *Philadelphia Evening Ledger*, July 26, 1915.

Brush, Mary Isabel. "A Nation on the Water Wagon." *Saturday Evening Post*, February 13, 1915, 3–5, 29, and February 20, 1915, 10.

———. "Russia's Stake in the War." *Saturday Evening Post*, April 3, 1915, 13.

Bryant, Louise. *Six Red Months in Russia*. New York: George H. Doran, 1918.

Buitenhuis, Peter. "Edith Wharton and the First World War." *American Quarterly* 18, no. 3 (Fall 1966): 493–505.

Chamberlain, Mary. "The Women at the Hague." *Survey*, June 5, 1915, 219–22.

Chatterjee, Choi. "'Odds and Ends of the Russian Revolution,' 1917–1920: Gender and American Travel Narratives." *Journal of American Women's History* 20, no. 4 (Winter 2008): 10–33.

Cohn, Jan. *Creating America: George Horace Lorimer and the* Saturday Evening Post. Pittsburgh: University of Pittsburgh Press, 1989.

———. *Improbable Fiction: The Life of Mary Roberts Rinehart*. Pittsburgh: University of Pittsburgh Press, 1980.

Coffing, Karen. "Corra Harris and the *Saturday Evening Post*: Southern Domesticity Conveyed to the National Audience." *Georgia Historical Quarterly* 79 (Summer 1995): 367–93.

Colenbrander, Joanna. *A Portrait of Fryn: A Biography of F. Tennyson Jesse.* London: André Deutsch, 1984.

Crozier, Emmet. *American Reporters on the Western Front, 1914–1918.* New York: Oxford University Press, 1959.

Daggett, Mabel Potter. "The Girl with the Trench Look." *Delineator*, August 1919, 4.

———. "Glimpsing the Golden-Book Town." *Delineator*, December 1919, 19.

———. "A Lady with a Saucepan." *Delineator*, October 1919, 19.

———. "Nevertheless—The Woman Is There." *Delineator*, April 1919, 3.

———. "The Tree of Joy." *Delineator*, May 1919, 11.

———. *Women Wanted.* New York: George H. Doran, 1918.

Davis, Richard Harding. "Horrors of Louvain Told by Eyewitness." *New York Tribune*, August 31, 1914.

———. *With the Allies.* New York: Charles Scribner's Sons, 1919.

Dearborn, Mary V. *Queen of Bohemia: The Life of Louise Bryant.* Boston: Houghton Mifflin, 1996.

Desmond, Robert W. *Windows on the World: The Information Process in a Changing Society, 1900–1920.* Iowa City: University of Iowa Press, 1980.

Dickey, Jerry. "The Expressionist Moment: Sophie Treadwell." In *The Cambridge Companion to American Women Playwrights*, edited by Brenda Murphy, 66–81. New York: Cambridge University Press, 1999.

Dickey, Jerry, and Miriam Lopez-Rodriquez, eds. *Broadway's Bravest Woman: Selected Writings of Sophie Treadwell.* Carbondale: Southern Illinois University Press, 2006.

Dosch-Fleurot, Arno. *Through War to Revolution.* London: Bodley Head, 1931.

Dorr, Rheta Childe. *Inside the Russian Revolution.* New York: Macmillan, 1917.

———. *A Soldier's Mother in France.* Indianapolis: Bobbs-Merrill, 1918.

———. *A Woman of Fifty.* New York: Funk & Wagnalls, 1924.

Doty, Madeleine Zabriskie. *Behind the Battle Line: Around the World in 1918.* New York: Macmillan, 1918.

———. "How I Came to Petrograd." *Good Housekeeping*, June 1918, 42–43.

———. "Revolutionary Justice." *Atlantic*, July 1918, 129–39.

———. "Russia and Her Women." *Good Housekeeping*, July 1918, 44–45.

———. *Short Rations: An American Woman in Germany 1915 . . . 1916.* New York: Century, 1917.

———. "War Cripples." *New Republic*, November 13, 1915, 38–39.

———. "The Women of France." *Good Housekeeping*, September 1917, 36.

———. "Women Who Would Go A-Soldiering." *World Outlook*, September 1918, 7.

Edy, Carolyn M. "Conditions of Acceptance: The United States Military, the Press, and 'The Woman War Correspondent,' 1846–1945." Ph.D. diss., University of North Carolina, Chapel Hill, 2012. https://cdr.lib.unc.edu/indexablecontent/uuid:6e86594c-b200-4e08-8a09-b0e4c29d68c5.

Egan, Eleanor Franklin. "An Amazing River." *Saturday Evening Post*, July 13, 1918, 17.

———. "An American Victory in Serbia." *Saturday Evening Post*, October 16, 1915, 19.

———. "Armistice Days in Vienna." *Saturday Evening Post*, May 24, 1919, 8.

———. "Behind the Smoke of Battle." *Saturday Evening Post*, February 5, 1916, 12.

———. "Day by Day in Constantinople." *Saturday Evening Post*, November 6, 1915, 14.

———. "The Difficult Truth about Serbia." *Saturday Evening Post*, September 25, 1915, 14.

———. "Feeding a Million." *Saturday Evening Post*, February 10, 1917, 27.

———. "The Going Guest—How Turkey Speeds Her." *Saturday Evening Post*, November 27, 1915, 25.

———. "In the Danger Zone." *Saturday Evening Post*, April 28, 1917, 14.

———. "An Innocent Bystander." *Saturday Evening Post*, September 23, 1916, 12.

———. "Muffled Drums in Mesopotamia." *Saturday Evening Post*, April 13, 1918, 3.

———. "Nem! Nem! Soha!" *Saturday Evening Post*, August 3, 1919, 17.

———. "Our Sphere of Influence." *Saturday Evening Post*, September 20, 1919, 29.

———. "Roughing It from London to Paris." *Saturday Evening Post*, January 13, 1917, 23.

———. "Seven Million Hornets." *Saturday Evening Post*, December 2, 1916, 25.

———. "Starvation in Vienna." *Saturday Evening Post*, April 26, 1919, 12.

———. "This to Be Said for the Turk." *Saturday Evening Post*, December 20, 1919, 14.

———. "The Tragedy of Odessa." *Saturday Evening Post*, June 28, 1919, 13.

———. "Turkey with German Dressing." *Saturday Evening Post*, October 30, 1915, 23.

———. *The War in the Cradle of the World, Mesopotamia*. New York: Harper & Brothers, 1918.

———. "War Notes on the Golden Horn." *Saturday Evening Post*, October 23, 1915, 25.

———. "Women in Politics to the Aid of the Party." *Saturday Evening Post*, May 22, 1920.

Endres, Kathleen L., and Therese Lueck, eds. *Women's Periodicals in the United States: Consumer Magazines*. Santa Barbara CA: Greenwood, 1995.

"Ernestine Evans, Editor-Critic, 77." *New York Times*, July 4, 1967, 14.

Evans, Ernestine. "Bulgarian Queen Foresees Long Peace after War." *New York Tribune*, April 3, 1915, 9.

———. "Russia's Women Lovable in War Times." *New York Tribune*, January 31, 1915, 13.

———. "Woman Suffrage Waits on War in Germany." *New York Tribune*, March 5, 1916, 5.

Fahs, Alice. *Out on Assignment: Newspaper Women and the Making of Modern Public Space*. Chapel Hill: University of North Carolina Press, 2011.

Farkas, Laura Deanna. "The Influence of Sophie Treadwell's Journalism Career on Her Dramatic Works." Master's thesis, Ohio State University, 2001. http://rave.ohiolink.edu/etdc/view?acc_num=osu1163708150.

Farwell, Mildred. "Bulgars Seize Serb Food Left with Americans." *Chicago Tribune*, May 8, 1916, 10.

———. "Mrs. Farwell Tells Her War Experiences." *Chicago Tribune*, May 3, 1916, 1, 10.

Forrey, Carolyn. "Gertrude Atherton & the New Woman." *California Historical Quarterly* 55, no. 3 (Fall 1976): 194–209.

Frazer, Elizabeth. "Good-By, France!" *Saturday Evening Post*, August 9, 1919, 15.

———. "Good Old America!" *Saturday Evening Post*, December 20, 1919, 3.

———. *Old Glory and Verdun*. New York: Duffield & Co., 1918.

———. "Putting the Red Cross on a New War Basis." *Saturday Evening Post*, July 14, 1917, 3.

———. "The Signature." *Saturday Evening Post*, August 30, 1919, 16.

———. "When the Red Cross and the Army Meet." *Saturday Evening Post*, July 6, 1918, 10.

Gallison, Mrs. H. H. "German People and the War." *Outlook*, December 6, 1916, 775–78.

———. "Germany in War Time." *Outlook*, December 13, 1916, 828–34.

———. "Ten Weeks behind the Front in Germany." *Outlook*, November 29, 1916, 722–27.

"Germany as Miss Doty Saw it." *Outlook*, December 13, 1916, 780–81.

Hale, Ruth. "Newspaper Women under Fire on Visit to French Front." *New York Tribune*, August 5, 1917, 3.

Hamilton, Alice. "At the War Capitals." *Survey*, August 7, 1915, 417–36.

Harper, Florence MacLeod. *Runaway Russia*. New York: Century, 1918.

Harris, Corra. *As a Woman Thinks*. Boston: Houghton Mifflin, 1925.

———. *My Book and Heart*. Boston: Houghton Mifflin, 1924.

———. "The Bravest of the Brave." *Saturday Evening Post*, January 16, 1914, 6.

———. "A Communique." *Saturday Evening Post*, January 23, 1914, 14.

———. "The New Militants." *Saturday Evening Post*, November 21, 1914, 3.

———. "War and Hallucinations." *Saturday Evening Post*, February 13, 1914, 23.

———. "When the Germans Came." *Saturday Evening Post*, December 19, 1914, 16.

———. "The Women of France." *Saturday Evening Post*, December 12, 1914, 11.

"Hating Germany." *Northwest Worker*, April 26, 1917, 3.

Hollihan, Kerrie Logan. *Reporting under Fire: 16 Daring Women War Correspondents and Photojournalists*. Chicago: Chicago Review Press, 2014.

Hudson, David. "'Having Seen Enough': Eleanor Franklin Egan and the Journalism of Great War Displacement." In *Aftermaths of War: Women's Movements and Female Activists, 1918–1923*, edited by Ingrid Sharp and Matthew Stibbe, 375–94. The Netherlands: Brill. https://doi.org/10.1163/ej.9789004191723.i-432.110.

———. "Writing 'Mesopot': Eleanor Franklin Egan on the River to Baghdad, 1917." *West Virginia University Philological Papers* 51 (Fall 2004): 52–60.

Hughes, Sam T. "N.E.A. War Reports Gave Human Interest." *Editor and Publisher* 51, pt. 2, May 22, 1919, 132.

Hull, Peggy. "Allied Troops Unpopular Now in Vladivostok." *Tampa Daily Times*, January 17, 1919, 2.

———. "Lieut. Peggy Hull War Correspondent." *Vancouver Daily World*, July 16, 1919, 2.

———. "Our Girl Reporter's First News from the Land of Bolshevism." *Buffalo Times*, January 14, 1919, 4.

———. "Peggy Hull Tells of 'Death Train' of Russian Bolshevik." *Battle Creek Enquirer*, March 2, 1919, 5.

———. "Russ War Widow Is Loyal 4 Years." *Tampa Times*, June 17, 1919, 6.

———. "Says Siberian Gloom Drives Men to Suicide." *Winnipeg Evening Tribune*, July 21, 1919, 3.

———. "Soldiers Marooned in Filthy Siberia All Very Homesick." *Vicksburg Evening Post*, June 27, 1919, 1.

———. "Torture All Who Refuse to Give Aid." *Evansville Press*, June 13, 1919, 18.

———. "Woman Correspondent Tells of Bolshevism's Greatest Horror—Nationalization of Women." *Evansville (IN) Press*, June 6, 1919, 1.

———. "Women Rule in Siberia? 'Nyet' Shouts Zbaikoff, Who Knows." *Tampa Times*, March 11, 1919, 11.

———. "Yanks Outnumbered 20 to 1, Defy Japs to Battle in Siberia." *Bismarck Tribune*, August 4, 1919, 1.

"In the Name of Lafayette!" *Delineator*, March 1919, 1.

Irwin, Will. *The Making of a Reporter*. New York: G. P. Putnam's Sons, 1942.

———. *Men, Women and War*. London: Constable and Co., 1915.

Jesse, F. Tennyson. "A Woman in Battle." *Collier's*, November 14, 1914, 13.

Jones, Fortier. *With Serbia into Exile: An American's Adventures with the Army That Cannot Die*. New York: Century, 1916.

Kauffman, Ruth Wright. "The Woman Ambulance-Driver in France." *Outlook*, October 3, 1917, 170–72.

Kazin, Michael. *War against War: The American Fight for Peace, 1914–1918*. New York: Simon & Schuster, 2017.

Kirtland, Helen Johns. "A Woman on the Battle Front." *Leslie's Weekly Newspaper*, August 24, 1918, n.p.

Klekowski, Ed, and Libby Klekowski. *Eyewitnesses to the Great War*. Jefferson NC: McFarland & Co., 2012.

Knightley, Phillip. *The First Casualty: The War Correspondent as Hero, Propagandist, and Myth Maker*. New York: Harcourt Brace Jovanovich, 1976.

Kroeger, Brooke. *Nellie Bly*. New York: Random House, 1994.

Lehman, Daniel W. *John Reed and the Writing of Revolution*. Athens: Ohio University Press, 2002.

Leider, Emily Wortis. *California's Daughter: Gertrude Atherton and Her Times*. Stanford: Stanford University Press, 1991.

"Letters from Maude Radford Warren, '94." *University of Chicago Magazine*, November 1918, 84–87.

Lewis, R. W. B. *Edith Wharton: A Biography*. New York: Harper & Row, 1975.

Lubow, Arthur. *The Reporter Who Would Be King*. New York: Charles Scribner's Sons, 1992.

Lumsden, Linda J. *Inez: The Life and Times of Inez Milholland*. 2004. Reprint, Bloomington: Indiana University Press, 2016.

Lutes, Jean Marie. *Front Page Girls*. Ithaca: Cornell University Press, 2006.

———. "Into the Madhouse with Nellie Bly: Girl Stunt Reporting in Late Nineteenth Century America." *American Quarterly* 54, no. 2 (June 2002): 217–53.

Mackey, Frank J. *Forward March*. Chicago: Disabled American Veterans of the World War, Department of Rehabilitation, 1934.

MacLeod, Charlotte. *Had She But Known: A Biography of Mary Roberts Rinehart*. New York: Warner Books, 1994.

Marcellus, Jane. "'Dear D': Sophie Treadwell's 1915 Correspondence from the 'Big War Theatre.'" *American Journalism* 29, no. 4 (2012): 68–93.

Marzolf, Marion. *Up from the Footnote: A History of Women Journalists*. New York: Hastings House, 1977.

Milholland, Inez. (*See also* Boissevain, Inez Milholland.) "Submarine Chases U.S. Liner St. Paul to Kidnap Marconi." *Chicago Tribune*, June 2, 1915, 1.

Morató Agrafojo, Yolanda. "More than a War Correspondent: Edith Wharton's Chronicles about French Civilians in the Great War and the Beginning of Citizen Journalism." *Oceánide*, no. 5 (2013): 1–7.

Morris, Joe Alex. *Deadline Every Minute: The Story of the United Press*. New York: Doubleday, 1957.

"Mrs. Wharton and Kipling on the War." *New York Times*, December 5, 1915, R490.

"Nellie the War Correspondent." *Keokuk (IA) Daily Gate City*, March 8, 1915, 2.

Nevins, Allan, ed. *The Letters and Journal of Brand Whitlock*. New York: D. Appleton-Century, 1936.

O'Donnell, Jack. "Peggy Hull." *Ladies' Home Journal*, April 1920, 83.

O'Neill, Mrs. Jean Cabell. "Brooklyn Woman Drops Lilies on Lusitania's Dead." *Brooklyn Daily Eagle*, May 17, 1915, 3.

O'Reilly, Mary Boyle. "Call the War 'Unfair.'" *Chicago Day Book*, August 3, 1914, 12.

———. "Cleverest Man in All England Discusses War." *Seattle Star*, October 26, 1914, 2.

———. "The Death Song of Brussels—Pathetic Story of Bombardment of Capital." *Chicago Day Book*, September 11, 1914, 14.

———. "Eye-Witness Describes Ghastly Scenes on Liege Battlefield." *Chicago Day Book*, August 12, 1914, 26.

———. "Last Shell Brings Death to 2 Babies Running in Fright." *Tacoma Times*, January 4, 1915, 1.

———. "Mary Boyle O'Reilly, in Russia, Investigates 'Ritual' Murder." *Chicago Day Book*, October 6, 1913, 1.

———. "Mary Boyle O'Reilly Sees Town of Louvain Burned; People Taken Out of Homes and Slain, She Says!" *Seattle Star*, September 21, 1914, 1.

———. "Mary Boyle O'Reilly Tells How War Affected Women." *Seattle Star*, April 28, 1915, 3.

———. "Mary Boyle O'Reilly Tells of Thrilling Trip on Treasure Train in Belgium. *Chicago Day Book*, September 4, 1914, 24.

———. "Mary Boyle O'Reilly Travels a New War Route to Russia." *Seattle Star*, April 9, 1915, 8.

———. "No Milk for Babies; They Die Because They 'Are Enemies When Fatherland Is at War.'" *Seattle Star*, September 18, 1914, 1.

———. "Star Woman Runs Blockade." *Seattle Star*, February 17, 1917, 1, 8.

———. "Where Are the Lost Women of Louvain?" *Seattle Star*, September 19, 1914, 3.

———. "Woman Writer Sees Horrors of Battle." *Seattle Star*, September 23, 1914, 1.

———. "Woman Writer Visits German Prison Camp." *Seattle Star*, September 5, 1914, 3.

"Our Library Table." *Harrisburg (PA) Telegraph*, November 30, 1915, 2.

Payne, Jessica Lozier. *What I Saw in England and France*. New York: Brooklyn Daily Eagle, 1916.

Powell, E. Alexander. "In the Field with the Armies of France." *Scribner's Magazine*, September 1915, 261–79.

———. "On the British Battle Line." *Scribner's Magazine*, October 1915, 456–69.

———. *Slanting Lines of Steel*. New York: Macmillan, 1933.

Prenatt, Diane. "Negotiating Authority: Elizabeth Shepley Sergeant's World War I Memoir." *Studies in the Humanities* 41, nos. 1–2 (March 2015): 69–99.

Price, Alan. *The End of the Age of Innocence: Edith Wharton and the First World War*. New York: St. Martin's Griffon, 1998.

Prieto, Sara. "Traveling through Forbidden Zones: Comparing Edith Wharton's and Mary Roberts Rinehart's Experiences in the Great War." *Edith Wharton Review* 28, no. 2 (Fall 2002): 16–23.

Reed, John. *Ten Days That Shook the World*. New York: Boni & Liveright, 1919.

Rich, Paul, ed. *Iraq and Eleanor Egan's The War in the Cradle of the World*. New York: Lexington Books, 2009.

Rinehart, Alice Duffy, ed. *One Woman Determined to Make a Difference: The Life of Madeleine Zabriskie Doty*. Bethlehem PA: Lehigh University Press, 2001.

Rinehart, Mary Roberts. *Kings, Queens and Pawns: An American Woman at the Front*. New York: George H. Doran, 1915.

———. *My Story: A New Edition and Seventeen New Years*. New York: Rinehart & Co., 1948.

Rohe, Alice. "Once Gay Vienna Now City of Gloom." *Washington Times*, October 23, 1914, 12.

———. "Women of Italy Assert Selves." *Keokuk (IA) Daily Gate City*, April 18, 1915, 5.

Rosenstone, Robert A. *Romantic Revolutionary: A Biography of John Reed*. Cambridge: Harvard University Press, 1990.

Ross, Ishbel. *Ladies of the Press*. New York: Harper & Brothers, 1936.

Saltzman, Joe, "Sob Sisters: The Image of the Female Journalist in Popular Culture." Introductory essay to a research project published on the Image of the Journalist in Popular Culture website. 2003 http://www.ijpc.org/uploads/files/sobsessay.pdf.

Savage, Clara. "Behind the Scenes in France." *Good Housekeeping*, January 1919, 36.

———. "First Word from France." *Good Housekeeping*, October 1918, 38–39.

———. "Helping Out in France." *Good Housekeeping*, November 1918, 22.

Schneider, Dorothy, and Carl J. Schneider. *Into the Breach: American Women Overseas in World War I*. New York: Viking, 1991.

Sergeant, Elizabeth Shepley. "America Meets France." *New Republic*, December 29, 1917, 240–43.

———. *French Perspectives*. London: Constable & Co., 1917.

———. "Our Army and the Red Cross." *New Republic*, May 18, 1918, 73–75.

———. "Paris under Fire." *New Republic*, May 4, 1918, 10.

———. *Shadow-Shapes: The Journal of a Wounded Woman, October 1918–May 1919*. Boston: Houghton Mifflin, 1920.

———. "Temper of the AEF." *New Republic*, July 20, 1918, 336–38.

———. "Union behind the Lines." *New Republic*, May 11, 1918, 42–44.

———. "The Wing of Death." *North American Review*, January 1920, 94–107.

———. "With the Americans on the Marne." *New Republic*, August 3, 1918, 17–18.

Shepherd, William G. "Americans Are Attacked by Bulgers; Held as Prisoners." *Seattle Star*, December 20, 1915, 1.

————. "Austrian Retreat Soul Sickening." *Salem (OR) Capital Journal*, December 17, 1914, 3.

————. "Shepherd Sees Austrian Soldiers Dying of Cholera." *Seattle Star*, December 2, 1914, 7.

Simonton, Ann. "Four American Women Who Have Been to the War." *New York Tribune*, August 21, 1915, 13.

Smith, Wilda M., and Eleanor A. Bogart. *The Wars of Peggy Hull: The Life and Times of a War Correspondent*. El Paso: Texas Western Press, 1991.

Stevenson, Randall. *Literature and the Great War*. Oxford: Oxford University Press, 2013.

"Sweetheart to Many Yankees." *Wichita Daily Eagle*, September 8, 1918, 24.

Swope, Herbert Bayard. *Inside the German Empire*. New York: Century, 1917.

Talmadge, John E. "Corra Harris Goes to War." *Georgia Review* 18, no. 2 (Summer 1964): 150–56.

Tebbel, John. *George Horace Lorimer and the* Saturday Evening Post. Garden City NY: Doubleday & Co., 1948.

Thompson, Donald. *Donald Thompson in Russia*. New York: Harper & Brothers, 1918.

Tietjens, Eunice. "Fight at Juvigny Is 'Tough Scrap.'" *Washington (DC) Evening Star*, September 3, 1918, 5.

————. "Miss Martin, First U.S Woman Killed by Huns." *Washington (DC) Evening Star*, March 19, 1918, 5.

Treadwell, Sophie. "Women in Black." *Harper's Weekly*, July 31, 1915, 111–12.

"Visiting Women Imperiled by Exploding Grenade." *Reading (PA) Eagle*, October 22, 1918, 2.

Vorse, Mary Heaton. "Les Évacuées." *Outlook*, November 10, 1915, 622–26.

————. *A Footnote to Folly: Reminiscences of Mary Heaton Vorse*. New York: Farrar & Rinehart, 1935.

————. "Sinistrées of France." *Century Magazine*, January 1917, 445–50.

"War a Sorry Time for Correspondent." *New York Times*, August 16, 1914, 3.

Warren, Maude Radford. "American Rule in the Rhineland." *Saturday Evening Post*, May 3, 1919, 135.

————. "Backwash." *Everybody's Magazine*, September 1919, 9.

————. "Booked Through for the Empire." *Saturday Evening Post*, November 14, 1914, 22.

————. "The First Invasion." *Good Housekeeping*, June 1919, 56.

————. "Petticoat Professions: New Women in Old Professions." *Saturday Evening Post*, November 5, 1910, 20.

————. "We Took the Hill." *Saturday Evening Post*, November 2, 1918, 49.

————. "When It Dawned." *Saturday Evening Post*, February 1, 1919, 34.

————. *The White Flame of France*. Boston: Small, Maynard, 1918.

————. "Women over There." *Woman's Home Companion*, December 1917, 13.

Wharton, Edith. *A Backward Glance*. New York: Curtis Publishing Co., 1933.

———. *Fighting France, from Dunkerque to Belfort.* New York: Scribner's Sons, 1915.

———. "In Alsace." *Saturday Evening Post,* November 20, 1915, 9.

"What You Can Do for France." *Delineator,* June 1919, 25.

Whitlock, Brand. *Belgium: A Personal Narrative.* Vol. 1. New York: D. Appleton, 1918.

Winfield, Betty Houchin, ed. *Journalism 1908: Birth of a Profession.* Columbia: University of Missouri Press, 2008.

"Women Writers Tell Secret of Their Trade." *Philadelphia Evening Ledger,* February 9, 1917, 6.

"World of Society." *Buffalo Morning Express,* February 23, 1919, 48.

Zacher, Dale E. *The Scripps Newspapers Go to War.* Urbana: University of Illinois Press, 2008.

INDEX